EUROPEAN IMPERIALISM IN THE NINETEENTH AND TWENTIETH CENTURIES

Woodruff D. Smith

NELSON-HALL  CHICAGO

LIBRARY OF CONGRESS CATALOGING IN PUBLICATION DATA

Smith, Woodruff D.
  European imperialism in the nineteenth and
twentieth centuries.

  Bibliography: p.
  Includes index.
  1. Europe—Politics and government—1789-1900.
2. Europe—Politics and government—20th century.
3. Europe—Territorial expansion. 4. Europe—
Colonies. 5. Imperialism—History—19th century.
6. Imperialism—History—20th century. I. Title.
D359.S63   940.2′8   82-7859
ISBN 0-88229-706-6 (cloth)   AACR2
ISBN 0-88229-812-7 (paper)

Copyright © 1982 by Woodruff D. Smith

Manufactured in the United States of America.

10 9 8 7 6 5 4 3 2 1

The paper in this book is pH neutral (acid-free).

EUROPEAN
IMPERIALISM
IN THE
NINETEENTH AND
TWENTIETH
CENTURIES

CONTENTS

PREFACE

T HIS IS A SMALL BOOK ON A VERY large subject. It is written for the general reader and for students who want an overview of modern European imperialism and an indication of some of the major issues with which historians of imperialism are currently concerned. Obviously, such a book cannot go into detail on any aspect of the subject. I have attempted wherever possible to use particular cases of imperialism to represent larger phenomena that occurred in many different places and at different times. I have also included references to important works on the subjects discussed in each section of the book; preference has been given to recently published studies and to those in English which are most likely to be available to the reader. Although the book is not purely a narrative and is organized around a number of theses, the presentation of the theses is necessarily abbreviated and the support for them incomplete. They should be considered as means of structuring the material; fuller exposition must await future publications.

I should like to acknowledge the assistance of Ralph A. Austen and Sharon Turner, who read and commented on portions of the manuscript; Jane Helen Smith, who helped with the editing and proofreading; Elizabeth Perry, Marsha Josserand, Lyn Bonnell, Julie Ash, and Ada Chavez, who typed parts of the text; and my graduate students in the history of European expansion.

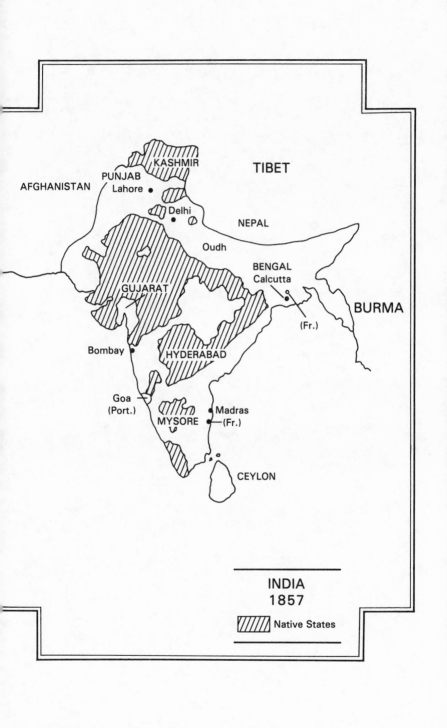

AFGHANISTAN

KASHMIR

PUNJAB
Lahore •

TIBET

Delhi

NEPAL

Oudh

GUJARAT

BENGAL
Calcutta

BURMA

(Fr.)

Bombay •

HYDERABAD

Goa
(Port.)

MYSORE

Madras
(Fr.)

CEYLON

INDIA
1857

///// Native States

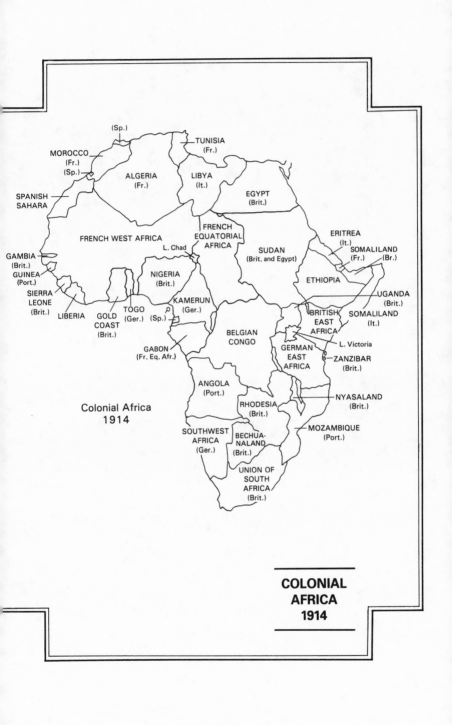

Colonial Africa
1914

**COLONIAL
AFRICA
1914**

ONE

Introduction

T HE "AGE OF IMPERIALISM" IS OVER. Most of the clichés associated with the huge European overseas empires of the past three centuries have by now been negated by twentieth-century realities. The sun definitely sets on the British Empire, every day. What is left of the British Empire is a handful of dependencies of little or no benefit to Britain, representing obligations acquired in more expansive, although not always more optimistic, times. On the other hand, "imperialism" itself, as a variety of human political and economic behavior, appears to be quite alive, judging from events in Vietnam and Afghanistan.

The book presents an overview of Europe's imperialist career from the end of the Napoleonic Wars in 1815 to the present; in other words, from the establishment of Britain's ascendancy as the major power in the world and the head of Europe's largest empire to the era of decolonization and the eclipse of Western Europe in world affairs. We shall examine the nature and extent of Europe's relations with the world overseas, the economic and political factors present in Europe during the era of industrialization that determined the direction of those relations, the effects of increased European penetration upon non-European

1

societies in the nineteenth century, and the explosion of European imperialism in the last quarter of the century. We shall also discuss the effects of modern European colonization in Africa, Asia, and the Middle East; the changes that occurred in Europe's economic relationships with the rest of the world in the twentieth century; and the process of decolonization in our own time. In the final chapter we shall try to assess the overall importance of European imperialism in world history.

A major difficulty arises almost immediately. What exactly is imperialism? Questions like this one at the beginnings of history books can be regarded as useful introductions to the material that follows or as exercises in pedantry, depending upon the reader's inclinations. Usually, historians are content to deal with subjects that possess hazy conventional meanings, since historians, perhaps more than most people, understand the inexactitude of social definitions and the frequent uselessness of attempts to clarify them. But in the case of imperialism, it is absolutely necessary to examine the meaning of the term. There is, in fact, no single accepted definition of imperialism that is useful for historical analysis. Rather, what we understand by *imperialism* is a set of social phenomena, sometimes only tangentially related to each other and grouped together by convention under the same heading.[1]

In modern times, the concept of imperialism has included the forcible establishment of political control by one state over others through such means as colonies and protectorates (*formal imperialism*), the exertion of influence by strong nations over weaker ones through real or potential exercise of force, the exploitation of economic advantages held by industrial countries over nonindustrial ones, and so forth. "Imperialism" also refers to attitudes evinced both by elite groups and by mass publics in Europe toward other peoples — attitudes of racial superiority that justified exploitation and, sometimes, ideas of the obligations of "civilized" to "uncivilized" peoples. Imperialism was also an issue of domestic politics in most Western countries in the nineteenth and early twentieth centuries. Fully developed imperialist ideologies, more directly related to the internal politics of European states than to the realities of the European presence overseas, existed almost everywhere. The term *imperialism* has thus referred to a great many different things. The kind of historical explanation one gives for it and the historical significance that is assigned to it depend largely on which definition one chooses.

A great many theories of modern imperialism exist, most of them developed in their original forms in the nineteenth century. There are many more explanations for particular events in the history of Europe's relations with the rest of the world which do not have the status of theories but which nevertheless have theoretical implications. To examine all but the best known of these would require the entire space of this book. Theories and explanations of imperialism are differentiated by many factors, and some are logically and evidentially superior to others. But one of the most important differences between them is that they fix upon different aspects of imperialism as the defining ones. The decision as to whether imperialism is basically a political, economic, intellectual, or psychological phenomenon is often made by theorists for reasons largely external to the facts with which they are dealing: ideological convictions, personal career experiences, beliefs about the normal direction of social causation, and so forth. The concept of imperialism possessed by a conservative retired colonial official, for example, is likely to be very different from that of a Marxist academic. The various faces of imperialism can be associated with each other in theories, but usually only by assuming that one aspect is more fundamental than the others, as for example Marxists do when they argue that economic events cause changes in other spheres of social life.

The answer that we give to the question, What is imperialism?, therefore, is a key to the answers to other questions with which a book of this sort must be concerned, such as: What caused modern imperialism? Is imperialism gone forever, at least in its nineteenth-century forms, or is it present today in international relations and domestic politics? What is the long-run historical significance of imperialism? We shall look briefly at some of the major explanatory approaches to nineteenth- and twentieth-century imperialism with these questions in mind.

Perhaps the greatest number of explanations of European imperialism see it either as an economic phenomenon or as a consequence of an economic phenomenon, and even approaches that concentrate on political or diplomatic aspects have an important place for economic factors. Europe, the first area in the world to experience full economic modernization and industrialization, became by the nineteenth century the "center" of a world economy, to which an increasing proportion of the non-European world became attached as an economic "periphery."[2] According to many historians, this "center periphery" arrangement constituted the basis of imperialism. European imperialism arose, therefore, from Europe's economic transformation in the early modern period, which gave it both a technological and an organizational superiority and a need for markets and sources of raw materials. These factors helped to create, even before the English Industrial Revolution of the late eighteenth century, a vast network of unequal economic relationships centering on Europe. The particular forms that elements of this network took varied from outright colonialism to trading relations in which the use of force was kept in the background, but Europe was almost always at the center. With the advent of industrialization, the network centering on Europe spread further to encompass practically the entire world, and tightened because of European needs for ever-larger markets. Great Britain became the preeminent imperial power because it was the first to industrialize. With industrialization, the variety of the connections between European and non-European societies increased. Even though in the political sphere the colonial form was temporarily devalued at the end of the eighteenth and the beginning of the nineteenth centuries, the degree of actual economic dependency increased almost everywhere. For many reasons, the direct colonial form of imperial rule was imposed during the last quarter of the nineteenth century on large areas of the world, especially Africa. The subsequent dissolution of the large colonial empires in our own time was simply the end of a phase in the history of imperialism. According to most exponents of the "center periphery" economic approach, imperialism still remains and will do so as long as the distinction between center and periphery is maintained and continues to imply inequality and dependency. The "center" has, of course, been extended to include the non-European industrialized countries, especially the United States and Japan. But the basic model still holds.

Among the theories that take the economic approach to imperialism, probably the best known are the Marxist ones. Marx himself, although he did not emphasize imperialism in his work, nevertheless employed the "center periphery" distinction and argued that the imposition of colonial rule by Europe on the rest of the world was both inevitable and, in a way, beneficial, because it started non-European societies on the necessary, unilineal path to capitalism and industrialization, to modern class conflict, and thus to revolution.[3] In the late nineteenth and early twentieth centuries other Marxists, faced with the necessity of explaining developments that Marx had not entirely anticipated, adapted general Marxist theory to arrive at more comprehensive treatments of imperialism. Lenin, following to some extent the work of the English Liberal J.A. Hobson and writing in the context of what he hoped was an incipient revolution in a country not yet fully industrialized, advanced the best-known of the Marxist theories of imperialism.[4] Lenin formulated his theory around the high rate of European external investment before 1914, a phenomenon particularly important for the industrialization of Russia. He argued that the declining profit margins of European businesses in the late nineteenth century, which were signs of the coming "crisis of capitalism" predicted by Marx, led business people to attempt to find new opportunities for profit. They therefore exported their capital to overseas areas where the process of industrialization was less advanced and where large profits could be made by exploiting labor. In order to guarantee their profits against the actions of non-European governments and against competition, business interests investing abroad pressured the governments of the European countries into adopting imperialist policies. These included both occasional military actions to ensure a "correct" business climate and full-scale colonial acquisition. The latter led to the partition of most of Africa among the imperialist powers in the 1880s and 1890s.

There are many other economic theories of imperialism, both Marxist and non-Marxist, to some of which we shall refer in the following chapters. These economic theories tend to suffer from certain conceptual and factual problems. They define imperialism so broadly that practically any economic relationship between countries that are in any sense unequal in power or degree of development could be included under it. Whether such a broad view of imperialism is meaningful is open to question. Also, while economic phenomena obviously played an important part in the history of European expansion, it is often difficult to argue on the basis of available evidence that economic factors were primary causes of particular events. As we shall see, Lenin's theory of imperialism does not, on the whole, work very well as an explanation for the partition of Africa, since the kinds of investment required by the theory were simply not present in most areas.

Some other approaches to imperialism have been deliberately formulated as counters to economic theories, most especially to Marxist ones. In a classic rejoinder to Lenin and Hobson, the economist Joseph Schumpeter argued in 1919 that late nineteenth-century imperialism was not a product of capitalism but rather of new conditions of modern social life.[5] Traditional European elite classes, increasingly finding their behavior constricted by new social conditions in industrial societies, reverted, according to Schumpeter, to "primitive" aggression in their dealings with non-European peoples as a kind of release of pent-up psychic energy. Schumpeter also pointed, as Hobson had done previously, to certain changes in European social structure as causes of colonial expansion, particularly the desire of aristocracies, threatened with loss of power and status, to find high-level positions for some of their members in governments of colonies being set up abroad. Whatever the merits of Schumpeter's theory, he undoubtedly put his finger on an important aspect of modern imperialism: the role of irrational, emotional aggressiveness. Whether such factors cause and define imperialism, however, or whether they are by-products of it, are questions that we shall consider in later chapters.

In recent years, a number of historians have attempted to give imperial studies a political focus. While not denying that Europe's growing economic penetration of the outside world in the nineteenth century created the context for imperial expansion, they tend to differentiate between "normal" economic relationships and specific policies that are peculiarly imperialist, and to focus on the genesis of political decisions that lead to the implementation of such policies. Not all of the interpretations that have come out of this approach agree, of course. John Gallagher and Ronald Robinson, in a series of now-classic studies, have argued that the "free-trade" policies of Britain in the mid-nineteenth century actually constituted a form of deliberate, politically conceived imperialism primarily intended to benefit British manufacturers by giving them access to new markets.[6] Others, especially D.C.M. Platt, have claimed that Gallagher and Robinson's "free-trade imperialism" did not exist at all and that the actions of, for example, the British navy in securing the trading rights of British merchants abroad were limited responses to short-term political problems.[7] Robinson and Gallagher have also argued that the British role in the partition of Africa resulted from the development of an "official mind," or idea-set, by the British political elite in coping with overseas policy in the mid-nineteenth century.[8] Complicated relationships that developed among British merchants, government agents, and African political elites created a series of essentially political problems, which tended to be perceived by policymakers in Britain in a uniform way in terms of the "official mind." These structured perceptions caused the British government to adopt imperialist responses to problems in Africa, which in turn set off a chain of territorial acquisitions by the European powers. This part of the Robinson-Gallagher thesis has also been much criticized, especially by historians who emphasize the purely economic aspects of imperialism.

Both Marxist ideas and suggestions by analysts such as Hobson have led some historians to propose that late Victorian imperialism was essentially the result of changes in the *social structures* of European countries in the late nineteenth century. Hans-Ulrich Wehler in his studies of Germany and Bernard Semmel in earlier work on England have focused on the use of imperialism by threatened elite groups as means of rallying support from the masses — or, at least, portions of the middle class — through the argument that domestic prosperity and an end to class conflict could be guaranteed by economic exploitation of overseas colonies.[9] Much useful research has been done by scholars using this "social imperialist" model. The major criticism of it has been that its proponents have unjustifiably expanded one aspect of late European imperialism into an explanation for all manifestations of expansion.

The largest body of recent work on imperialism has been aimed at seeing the colonial experiences of third-world peoples from their own perspectives. The guiding assumption of this type of research is that imperialism was a complex process in which European and non-European societies interacted. Recently, a number of leading imperial historians, including Ronald Robinson, D.K. Fieldhouse, and Anthony Hopkins, have argued that late nineteenth-century imperialism was primarily due to the "pull" of economic and political crises overseas, which drew European governments into expansion and which were caused by instabilities created by economic change. A large number of variations on this view are possible.[10]

A great many other approaches to imperialism are current in historical literature, and the ones we have just reviewed are, for the most part, only general types of approach within which there is considerable variation. In this book we shall attempt to consider most of the major definitions of imperialism as they have been applied in the last century and a half. It is necessary, however — if the book is not simply to become a recitation of dates and facts or, alternatively, an examination not of imperialism but of theories of imperialism — to have some central theme, focus, or approach. In the following pages, therefore, especially after the first three chapters, we shall concentrate on imperialism as a series of largely political responses to major economic and social changes that occurred in Europe in the nineteenth century — particularly industrialization and its social effects. While we shall not ignore the varieties of economic imperialism, it will be assumed that the exercise of political power in the relationship between unequal economic partners is one of the defining features of imperialism. Our emphasis will therefore be on the conscious use of power by European states to influence or control the policies of non-European countries ("informal" imperialism) and on the acquisition and direct governance of overseas territories ("formal" imperialism or "colonialism").

More importantly, primary attention will be focused on the Western European origins of imperialism and on factors that changed imperialism in the nineteenth and twentieth centuries. This is not, as we have just seen, the only way to look at the history of European imperialism. Also, it runs the danger of encouraging "Eurocentric" explanations, which are not only currently unfashionable but also a traditional source of historical misinterpretation. On the other hand, it is almost impossible to organize a general book on Europe's imperial relations with the rest of the world in any other way. If emphasis were placed on the non-European contexts of imperialism, the sheer variety of those contexts would destroy any central theme, unless everything were forced arbitrarily into a single model of imperialism. Since such an approach would probably distort much of the material, we shall avoid it. For better or worse, the European context provides whatever unity exists in the history of imperialism.

There is another reason for focusing on Western Europe. The attention that historians of imperialism have given in recent years to the non-European side of the imperial, and especially the colonial, relationship has added, quite literally, a new dimension to our understanding, but it has also tended to fragment our view of the European impingement on the rest of the world. Sometimes European expansion appears almost as if it were an accident, or the result entirely of blundering by European governments called in by one participant or another in local political disputes. There was a great deal more to imperialism than this. The non-European context will not be ignored in the following pages; a great number of them will be devoted to it. But the central concern around which the book is constructed is the European origin of changes in the pattern of imperial expansion.

Not all of the expansionary powers of the nineteenth and twentieth centuries were, of course, located in Europe. Not only did the United States and Japan join the ranks of the official colonial "empires" by the twentieth century, but also there existed in many areas so-called secondary imperial states, themselves increasingly dominated by European powers, which conducted local expansionary programs. Many of these, together with Russian continental imperialism, will be examined briefly where appropriate, but the major focus will be on the imperialism of the Western European countries. Our study begins, therefore, with Western Europe at the start of the nineteenth century.

TWO

The European Empires
Before 1815

I N 1815, WITH THE END OF THE NAPOLEONIC Wars and the Congress of Vienna, the structure of European international politics was fixed more or less firmly for the next half-century. Moreover, by 1815 Great Britain had become, after its setback during the American War of Independence, the undisputed leader of Europe in overseas expansion. It would continue to play this role for a century and a half. The year 1815 is therefore an appropriate point of reference for a survey of the colonial empires at the beginning of the modern era.

THE BRITISH OVERSEAS EMPIRE

The main reason for British predominance in imperial expansion was obvious to most observers in 1815: Britain possessed the world's leading national economy. Its overseas trade was by far the world's largest and the productivity of its mass-market industries the world's highest. Britain had replaced the Netherlands as Europe's and the world's financial center. British standards of living and rates of consumption, for at least the upper and middle classes, exceeded those of almost all the rest of Europe. To a great extent, these fortunate economic circumstances resulted from the

11

fact that Britain was the first (and in 1815 the only) country to experience an "industrial revolution." Even before industrialization, however, Britain had become the center of a huge network of international trade. The establishment of this network had helped to bring about British industrialization in the last third of the eighteenth century, and the destruction of French trade in the Napoleonic Wars had removed its only serious European rival. In the history of British imperialism, it is customary to distinguish between the "old imperial system" that had formed with the trade network and came crashing down with the American and Industrial revolutions, and the "new empire" that emerged in the nineteenth century. The "old imperial system" consisted of the colonies that England had acquired in the seventeenth and eighteenth centuries, the structure of governance through which they were controlled, the main British-based Atlantic trading network, and the ideology of empire that supposedly explained what the whole thing was all about. It is, in other words, an aggregate concept — political, economic, intellectual, and even psychological — and can be applied to other European empires as well.[1]

The old imperial system of Great Britain, parts of which still existed in 1815, had included a loosely linked system of colonies that British policymakers believed to be essentially conveniences for trade. The prevailing view of the functions of colonies had been concocted from different elements of the hodge-podge economic theory that we today refer to as "mercantilism."[2] Although mercantilism came in a multitude of ever-changing forms even in a single country such as Britain, its central precepts were more or less uniform. As far as most colonies were concerned, they were to serve as closed overseas marketing areas for the home country's products — usually manufactured products. The success of a government's economic policy was supposed to be measured by the existence of a favorable balance of trade and thus of a cash flow into the country. A colony (of the "plantation" type) was basically a foreign country that could be forced through political domination to import from the home country goods of greater value

than it exported. In addition, foreign competitors could be excluded from the colony's trade, thereby allowing the home
country's merchants to charge monopolists' prices and carrying
rates. Colonies could also supply products unavailable in the
home country, reducing dependence on sources controlled by
other European countries. Mercantilist theory also recognized
"factory" colonies, which were ports of trade abroad. While
some colonial products were employed in manufacturing processes, most were consumer goods like sugar, tobacco, coffee,
and so forth, not industrial raw materials. The carrying and
sale of these products brought profits to shippers and merchants, and governments' colonial policies aimed primarily at
protecting these profits. In practice, of course, the economic
realities of the British overseas empire differed considerably
from mercantilist theory. One factor leading to the American
Revolution was the fact that the mercantilist concepts
employed by British policymakers had little place for the kinds
of colonies that had evolved in North America: colonies with
large European populations and with commercial interests
directed primarily elsewhere than toward Great Britain.

The American Colonies

The geographical distribution of British overseas possessions in 1815 still reflected the economic structure of the old
empire. In the Atlantic area, the center of profitable colonial
enterprise had been the sugar producing islands of the West Indies, of which Jamaica had been the queen.[3] The economies
of the West Indian islands were based upon sugar plantations
owned and managed by whites and worked by masses of black
slave laborers. Up until the last third of the eighteenth century,
the growing of sugar, its transportation to England, and its
processing and re-export were by far the most profitable
segment of British overseas trade. The sugar trade, though
widely dispersed, was held tightly to England by several, mostly
economic, bonds. Plantations tended to be managed by
men who intended to return to England after making their

fortunes. Many plantations belonged to families in England who worked through agents. Even when plantations were owned by resident whites, a high degree of financial control was exercised by English merchants in Bristol and Liverpool who controlled transportation, the supply of slaves, and credit. Even the unusually high degree of legal autonomy that Jamaica and Barbados possessed (they had their own assemblies that were formally equal to Parliament with respect to internal legislation) did not lead to practical independence because of the economic centrality that Britain enjoyed. The white population of the West Indian colonies, only a few thousand in the eighteenth century, had no serious problems with the mercantile system of the old empire once free trade in slaves had been assured. The benefits of belonging to the "center" of the system extended to them as well. Not until the late eighteenth century — with the independence of the North American colonies, the beginnings of an active abolitionist movement, and the precipitous ejection of the West Indies from the center of British economic consciousness by the Industrial Revolution — did they lose these benefits.

The nature of sugar production in the West Indies helped to structure the old empire. Annually, thousands of black slaves planted and harvested the sugarcane in one of the most barbaric systems of labor exploitation ever devised. Until the second half of the eighteenth century, slave labor was so cheap that owners had little incentive to encourage the establishment of slave families in the West Indies or to create conditions in which slaves' lives would be prolonged beyond their working years. It was more economical to buy slaves at adolescence, thus saving the costs of upbringing, and then exploit their labor so thoroughly that few survived beyond the peak working years. A high-volume West African slave trade supplying replacement labor was essential to the profitable production of sugar and made the long-standing economic relationships between European merchants and West African societies another basic element in the old imperial system.

The English had first entered the West African slave trade in the sixteenth century as small-time competitors to the Portuguese in supplying the Spanish New World colonies with slaves. As English commercial prosperity and power had increased in the seventeenth century, however, English slaving ventures multiplied. With the establishment of English colonies in the West Indies and North America, especially Jamaica in 1655 with its huge demand for labor, the English slave trade became permanent and regularized, following the pattern previously established by the Portuguese.[4] The Royal African Company, in various guises, attempted in the second half of the century to monopolize the English slave trade, but failed. By the eighteenth century, the British slave trade operated largely on free-trade principles, except that the merchants trading in West Africa jointly maintained commercial stations on the coast.

None of the European slave-trading powers maintained an extensive colonial presence in West Africa proper. The Portuguese possessed Angola in the southern half of the continent whence came most of the slaves sent to Brazil. Britain possessed an unimportant colony in Gambia (as France did in neighboring Senegal), and in 1787 a British private group established a settlement for freed slaves and other free blacks in Sierra Leone. Normally, the slave trade was conducted between European agents permanently located at coastal stations and the political authorities of West African states that controlled the land behind the stations, who acted as middlemen in the trade. Large and powerful states, such as Dahomey, could both effectively decree the prices of slaves for considerable periods and deal with interior states that supplied them. They could also acquire slaves by themselves through warfare. Others, like the small "city states" of the Niger Delta, operated in a more competitive environment. In the latter case, by 1815 the British had attained a degree of informal political primacy. Elsewhere, although the European traders possessed fortified stations, they were fortified against other Europeans and not effectively defensible against local African states. European cultural penetration had occurred, but only to a limited extent. Whatever the moral and long-term historical implications of the slave trade, in the eighteenth century it did not lead to much aggressive, formal European imperialism in Africa.

By 1815, the relationship between Britain and West Africa had changed markedly. The growth of other export industries had relegated the sugar-slave complex to a subsidiary position in British trade, letting the humanitarian attack on the slave trade, which began as a minor political movement in the 1770s, bear fruit with Parliament's abolition of the British slave trade in 1807.[5] The West Indian interest, once powerful in the House of Commons, had been unable to protect itself from a combination of abolitionist assault, political opportunism, and strategic considerations arising from the Napoleonic Wars. The situation of British interests in West Africa was therefore uncertain in 1815. The government was now committed to the entire abolitionist ideology and thus to putting down the slave trade — through stationing a permanent naval squadron off the West African coast to intercept slavers, through negotiations with the coastal states, and through pressure on other European countries to ban slave trading effectively. Despite the lack of official British interest in extending direct political control over the West African coast and the fact that Africa had actually lost most of the economic significance that it had had under the old imperial system, the foundations of later imperialism had been laid in this commitment to end the slave trade.

The classic Atlantic "triangular trade" of the eighteenth century thus constituted the central feature of the old imperial system in the Atlantic world. The shipment of trading goods to Africa and their highly profitable exchange for slaves, the transport of slaves to the West Indies via the terrible "middle passage," and the export of sugar and sugar products from the West Indies to Britain made up the sides of the triangle in its simplest form, which was replicated by the French and Dutch. The rest of the system of British trade and colonies consisted largely of supports for this central structure. British Guiana, on the continent of South America, and Bermuda, one of the earliest of English colonies, were in the eighteenth century more or less poor relations of the sugar islands and were associated with their trade. The North American colonies (exclusive of Canada) were also, to a considerable extent, tied to the West Indian sugar economy.

By the eighteenth century South Carolina, Pennsylvania, New York, and most of the New England colonies did the largest portion of their export trade with British (and non-British) colonies in the West Indies, supplying the foodstuffs that were needed to feed the slave populations there but that were uneconomic to grow in preference to sugar. Even colonies such as Virginia and Maryland, which mainly engaged in the tobacco trade directly with England, also exported foodstuffs to the West Indies.[6] One of the prime reasons for the relatively high degree of prosperity enjoyed by the thirteen East Coast colonies in the eighteenth century was their West Indian trade, which created an impetus toward economic modernization, capital accumulation, and the branching out of American merchants into new enterprises, including the slave trade itself. The subsidiary nature of the North American colonies' original commercial roles undoubtedly contributed to the diversification of their economies and to the fundamentally sound business structure that developed there, in contrast to the economy of the British West Indies, which collapsed when its sole product ran into trouble.

The last quarter of the eighteenth century, of course, brought with it an almost total transformation of the connection between North America and the economic framework of the old imperial system. The American Revolution interfered with the West Indian trade of the rebelling colonies, and at the end of the war they were denied free access to British West Indian ports. United States trade turned away from the Caribbean and toward the Mediterranean and northern Europe. In addition, the English textile industry's rapidly increasing demand for raw cotton led, from the 1790s onward, to a major transformation of the agriculture of the southern United States and of the patterns of American trade, paradoxically binding the United States economy by 1815 more closely to Great Britain's than had been the case during the earlier colonial period.

With the detachment of most of its North American colonies in 1783, Britain had been left with a "rump" consisting of Canada, the Maritime Provinces, and Newfoundland. Newfoundland was considered important only because of its proximity to the Grand Banks fisheries. Canada — a huge, underpopulated area that had been Britain's booty from the Seven Years' War (1756-63) — was a directly administered crown colony that, as late as 1800, produced more administrative problems than it seemed to be worth. The French-speaking population of what is today Quebec, guaranteed religious and political rights under the Quebec Act of 1774, created some difficulties on their own, but these were as nothing compared to the problems in relations with both the French Canadians and Great Lakes Indians introduced by the movement of American loyalists fleeing the United States into the area that is today Ontario. The resulting potential for conflict led to the partitioning of Canada into two provinces (French and English speaking) in 1791. Until well into the nineteenth century, however, the economic value of these provinces to Britain was extremely small.[7]

The Atlantic portion of the British empire was, therefore, in 1815 a remnant of a collection of formal colonies that had previously supported the economic structure of the British West Indian trade but had lost their economic coherence with the recent decline of that trade. The American Revolution, damaging as it was to the old system, did not bring the system to an end. Rather, the abolition of the British slave trade in 1807 and the general diversification and expansion of British commerce made both the old imperial system and much of the actual empire obsolescent, while the Industrial Revolution of the late eighteenth century rendered them positively obsolete. The wars of the French Revolution and the Napoleonic Wars (1793-1815) had been fought by Britain originally according to the old principles of commercial warfare, and Britain had picked up new colonies, mostly from France and its allies, all over the world. In 1814-15 it returned many of them, partly paralleling the settlement of 1763 but partly because new colonies had little economic meaning. Most of the areas that were retained — such as Malta, the Ionian Islands, and the Cape Colony in South Africa — were held because of their potential commercial and strategic significance in the broader and more loosely controlled economic world of the nineteenth century.

Empire in the East

In the Indian Ocean and the Orient, British trade and the British imperial presence had grown at a staggering rate in the eighteenth century, but this growth had not centered around a single, all-important trade as in the Atlantic. Therefore, although Britain's eastern imperial involvements changed drastically between 1750 and 1850, no severe break associated with the fate of a particular trade could be discerned around 1800 as it could in the Atlantic world.

If British involvement in the East did not revolve around a single product, it was nonetheless directed primarily toward a single country: India. In the seventeenth century, the English East India Company had come out second best in its lengthy competition with its Dutch rival and had been forced to concentrate on developing trade with India rather than the more desirable Indonesia. By the beginning of the eighteenth century, the English East India Company was the most important trading entity in Bengal and the Coromandel coast; it possessed a formal colony at Bombay, acquired from Portugal, and a long string of trading posts, or "factories," along several Indian coasts. In Bengal, in fact, the company had acquired political paramountcy over quite a large area in the 1690s, having been lured into politics by the economic opportunities presented by the breakup of the Moghul Empire and by the actions of the company's remarkable "governors" there.[8] The East India Company had started in India by following the earlier example of the Portuguese in taking over portions of the Indian Ocean trade, in which India itself was the most important point for the transshipment and exchange of goods such as spices, pepper, porcelain, silks, tea, and cotton. Direct trade with England was supplemented by the so-called country trades, the carrying of goods from one part of the Indian Ocean to another. India's cotton was especially valuable as a product the company could sell anywhere in the world.

The position of Britain and the East India Company in India changed radically in the eighteenth century as a result of several factors. The complete breakup of Moghul control in northern India after 1700 created chaos and a power vacuum that the company, in pursuit of commercial advantage, sought to fill. The company extended its control over Bengal, built up a state around its expanding port at Madras, and made itself, by the second quarter of the eighteenth century, the strongest political force in India. Its "empire" was not seen as such, but it laid the foundation for later official British rule in India.

The second impetus toward change was the accelerated activity of the French, who sought, in the first half of the eighteenth century, to rival and displace the British in India by playing the British company's own political game. By the 1740s, the French Company of the Indies had built up its own powerful system of political alliances and commercial relations. During the War of the Austrian Succession (1740-48) in Europe, French Governor-General Dupleix managed to push the British to the brink of expulsion. The pressure was maintained between wars, and at the start of the Seven Years' War in 1756 the East India Company had clearly lost its preeminence. Only a timely military and political campaign conducted by Robert Clive, an employee of the company – a campaign that culminated in his victory at the Battle of Plassey in 1757 – saved the British position. The end of the Seven Years' War saw Britain once again the major power in India, this time without effective European opposition. But the conflict with France had turned Britain's relationship with India from the more or less private affair of a chartered trading company into a matter of state policy for the British government, and had involved the government in a series of political problems from which it could not extricate itself.

One of the reasons that it could not was the third major factor leading to change in Britain's relationship with India: the growing juncture between the booming commercial economy of England and the business opportunities presented by India's economic strength and political chaos. These opportunities had for years attracted "interlopers" (British merchants acting, illegally, independently from the company) and had tempted the company's agents to do business on their own. It proved to be impossible to stop these activities, in part because public opinion in Britain had turned against chartered monopoly companies. In the period after 1763, the lack of effective controls either within the company or over the private traders made India fair game for British fortune hunters and led to financial problems for the company, many cases of corruption, and incredibly complex political disorders. Prime Minister Lord North was forced in 1770 to take steps to exert government control over the company and over British interests in India and to appoint governors over areas under direct British rule. Despite this, confusion and the making of large fortunes by underhanded means continued, and the British situation in India became an object of attack by the Whigs, desirous in the 1770s of discrediting North's government. This led to the passage in the 1780s of Parliamentary acts bringing the East India Company under an officially appointed board of control; to the impeachment and trial of Warren Hastings, North's governor-general, for corrupt practices; and eventually, in 1786, to

William Pitt's appointment of a "reform" regime in British India under Lord Cornwallis. Cornwallis, not a company man but a general (the loser at Yorktown), made the first real effort to turn the areas of India directly ruled by the company, especially Bengal, into colonies with a British-style government. This new governmental structure was used to alter radically the internal economic structure of Bengal. By 1815, after several wars of conquest, Britain was the unchallenged paramount power in India, directly ruling substantial portions of the sub-continent and indirectly controlling a great deal more.

Elsewhere in the eastern half of the world, British interests expanded rapidly in the eighteenth century, and Britain's formal presence in the East increased vastly in scope during the war with Napoleon. By the end of the century, British merchants had entered heavily into direct trade with China, carrying, among other things, such Indian products as opium. They had broken into trade with Java and other islands in the Dutch East Indies, reversing their defeat of the previous century. Altogether, British influence in the highly integrated commerce of the Indian Ocean became even more preponderant in the late eighteenth century than it was in the Atlantic world. The Napoleonic Wars added a formal colonial dimension to this new preponderance. The British, at war with France's ally the Netherlands, seized key places in the Dutch East Indies. Although most of Indonesia was returned to the Dutch in 1815, the British kept the ports of Penang and Malacca on the Malay Peninsula and the island of Singapore, as well as Ceylon.

In the South Seas, British and French explorers throughout the eighteenth century had rivaled each other's exploits in charting Australia and the Pacific islands. The voyages of Captain James Cook, in particular, had brought the attention of the British public to the South Seas and to their reputed economic possibilities, creating an enthusiasm for overseas development that foreshadowed similar popular fads in the nineteenth century. By 1815, official British contacts with many of the major

Pacific island groups had been made, a certain amount of private trade had developed, and the famous penal colony at Botany Bay in New South Wales had been founded. The acquisition of an Australian colony was not, however, considered a matter of importance in Britain. Australia was merely a convenient site for a penal colony, and none of the other powers had any interest in it.[9]

Other Areas

In surveying British overseas relations in 1815, we have concentrated on long-distance trade and the formal colonial structure that had been a part of the old imperial system. British political and economic connections were of course much more extensive than those that have been described here. Most British trade, both before and after 1815, was with the continent of Europe, and there were places on the continent — such as Lisbon, Hamburg and Livorno — where British informal influence was extremely strong. In addition, a network of naval bases supporting both the navy and the merchant marine had been created around much of the world. To all intents and purposes, Ireland had been a thoroughly exploited colony in the eighteenth century. Even after the union with Great Britain in 1801, Ireland was treated in many ways as a dependency. Although in the following chapters we shall concentrate on the areas conventionally regarded as having been subject to British imperialism, we should remember these additional factors as well.

THE FRENCH COLONIAL EMPIRE

France's effective imperial career started at approximately the same time as that of England and for many of the same reasons. The rapid growth of French seaborne commerce in the seventeenth century was accompanied by formal colonial expansion, especially in the West Indies. Rather more slowly than the British, but in the end no less successfully, the French established themselves in such islands as Guadeloupe and Martinique, where they created slave-worked sugar plantation economies. By the second half of the eighteenth century, the French islands had overtaken the British ones as centers for the production of sugar. The key to the new French position was the colony of St. Domingue, today called Haiti. However, the slave revolution on Haiti in the 1790s and the island's subsequent independence put a stop to the dominance of the French in the sugar trade.[10] In addition, the wars with Britain that commenced in 1793 led to the seizure of many of the French sugar islands. Although the islands were returned in 1815, sugar was no longer the major international trade commodity that it had been. Also, competition from Brazil had developed, so the sugar trade was relegated to fairly minor proportions in French national economic life.

Another product of French expansion in the seventeenth century had been New France, or Canada. In the early eighteenth century, the entire economy of the colony — apart from the largely subsistence agriculture of the French settlers in the St. Lawrence valley — was structured on the fur trade, which required cooperation with a large variety of Indian tribes spread out over an enormous area.[11] The relatively good relations that the French maintained with the Indians followed logically from French dependence on the fur trade and thus on the Indians who procured the fur.

New France was not, however, in any measurable economic sense a success, despite frequent attempts by the French government to experiment with development through an authoritarian political structure centered at Quebec. The colony experienced a certain amount of economic expansion in the eighteenth century together with a considerable rise in population due to natural increase rather than to immigration. But because the fur trade never became sufficiently profitable to pay for the expenses of administration, the colony was a consistent loser as far as the national government was concerned. New France was kept mainly for reasons of prestige and because of hopes that future developments would be more satisfactory, but it was kept on short finances. This led to New France's continued reliance on missionaries in Indian relations and to the inadequacy of its military forces during the Seven Years' War. In the end, when Canada was finally taken by the British in 1759 and formally renounced in 1763, little real regret at the loss was felt in France.

Canada's extension, Louisiana (covering the Mississippi and Missouri valleys), originally seemed more promising. It was claimed in the 1680s as part of the expansive schemes of the middle of Louis XIV's reign, but its development after 1715 came, at least in part, from the harnessing of private capital to colonial enterprise.[12] It was hoped that Louisiana could become a flourishing agricultural colony, with thousands of French settlers, to supply food to the West Indian islands. The Louisiana scheme failed, however, because of a stock panic that drove investors away. By the mid-eighteenth century, although a plantation economy had grown up around New Orleans and a certain amount of river trade had developed, Louisiana had not come close to living up to its potential. Although Spain acquired Louisiana in 1763 at the end of the Seven Years' War, the French remained culturally dominant. The commercial expansion of the Ohio and Mississippi valleys after 1780 led Napoleon, in 1801, to obtain a reversion of Louisiana to France so as to create a new French North American empire. When the impracticality of this idea became clear and the more immediate possibilities of continental European domination presented themselves, Napoleon sold Louisiana to the United States in 1803.

Despite the profitability of many of its West Indian colonies, then, France's "old imperial system" in the Atlantic was not a total success. France's commercial prosperity before 1815 did not depend primarily on colonial ventures. Not only did its internal economy develop at a respectable pace in the eighteenth century, but its foreign trade expanded as well. France retained, at least up to 1800, its preeminence in the manufacture of high-quality and luxury consumer goods, and its trade with the Near East was extensive. Because of the continued power of the

Ottoman Empire, the Near Eastern relationship was not an imperial one, but it laid the groundwork for political and economic domination in the future. The wars of the French Revolution and Napoleon's grand scheme for an eastern empire brought Britain to the region in large force. While French and British occupations of Egypt ceased with the end of the war, the Ottoman Empire had by 1815 begun its political decline and became subject to the imperial attentions of Britain, France, and Russia.

Like all the other European powers, France possessed slaving interests in West Africa in the eighteenth century. It also possessed a real colony in Senegal, although up to 1815 the range of French control was geographically limited and the colony was occasionally occupied by the British. The French slave trade was theoretically ended during the French Revolution, legalized again, and finally outlawed under British pressure after 1815. By 1815, French merchants from Marseilles were beginning to establish themselves in the West African palm oil and peanut trade, but African products were not a large part of overall French trade.

We have already outlined France's early involvement in India. After 1763, although the hope of future expansion of French trade and political influence continued to exist, chances of a large-scale French empire there were essentially nil. France did possess a few commercial enclaves in India and conducted a certain amount of trade through them, but it was only a fraction of the British trade.[13] France also possessed a few islands in the Indian Ocean that continued to develop as plantation colonies, and its trading interests grew in the South Pacific after 1815. Prior to that year, France's expansionary aspirations were mainly continental, not overseas.

THE DUTCH, PORTUGUESE, AND SPANISH EMPIRES

By 1815, the Dutch presence overseas was but a shadow of its former self. The Netherlands, dominated by France throughout nearly a quarter-century of war, had seen its financial holdings and trade routes destroyed and many of its colonies taken by the British.[14] It lost Ceylon and the Cape Colony permanently. In the Caribbean, the Netherlands retained the colony of Surinam and the few islands of the Netherlands Antilles. In West Africa, however, it lost much of its role in trade, parting with most of its trading "castles" and falling behind Britain and France in the newer tropical products. In the East, the Netherlands reacquired control over its Indonesian empire, but its trade with the area in general had declined, despite efforts at expanding coffee sales in Europe. Altogether, the country that had led northern Europe into the age of imperialism in the early seventeenth century no longer seemed capable of substantial expansionary effort overseas.

However, after a depressed period, Dutch commerce bounced back strongly in the post-Napoleonic period. If the Netherlands had held on to Belgium, the continent's first industrialized region, this commercial expansion might have led immediately to industrialization. As it was, Belgium broke away in 1830. The Netherlands retained an essentially commercial and financial economy until its own industrialization in the last third of the nineteenth century. The celebrated Dutch effort after 1830 to rejuvenate, reorganize, and extend the export economy of the Dutch East Indies – the "culture system" that attracted much European attention and had far-reaching effects on Indonesian society – was a consequence of Holland's commercial rebuilding.

By 1815, the premier empires of the first age of European expansion, those of Portugal and Spain, appeared to foreign observers to be fossils. They were still impressive on the map, especially the Spanish empire, but the economic structure upon which they had been built had to a considerable extent collapsed, and the systems of political control that continued to exist did so to less purpose than previously.

Portugal and its colony of Brazil had become practically dependencies of Britain after the start of the Peninsular War in 1807. During the war, the Brazilian landowning elite had become even more inclined to govern themselves than before.

They strongly resisted attempts by the postwar liberal regime at home to reestablish direct Portuguese control. By the nineteenth century, although cultural affinities between Portugal and its largest and wealthiest colony remained, there was little economic reason for Brazil to be subject to even purely formal Portuguese control. Brazil's trade in sugar and, increasingly, in coffee was primarily with northern Europe and conducted mainly by British merchants. In this Portugal could take no part. Its efforts to maintain the forms of direct metropolitan rule made it a nuisance, both to the Brazilian elite and to the British, and it was dispossessed of its colony by Brazil's unilateral declaration of independence in 1822.[15]

The rest of the far-flung system of colonial dependencies that were the legacy of Portugal's era of imperial greatness in the sixteenth century remained more or less intact. But although several of them were substantial trading centers, their contributions to the Portuguese economy at home were minor. Portugal retained some of her tiny holdings on the West African coast, but the old slaving center of Fernando Po, on the Bight of Biafra, had become Spanish in 1778 and eventually passed under informal British control during the post-1807 antislavery campaign. Portugal continued to hold Angola, which had been a major source of slaves for Brazil and the Caribbean in the eighteenth century, but British pressure forced Portugal out of official slave trading. The demand for slaves in the sugar economies of Brazil and, later, Cuba made it profitable to "smuggle" slaves past the British patrols. Individual Portuguese merchants took on the largest share of this illegal trade after 1815 in both Angola and West Africa. Even Angola was forced, however, to alter its economy in the nineteenth century away from slave trading and toward plantation agriculture.

In the Indian Ocean, Portugal had long since ceased to be an important factor in direct trade with Europe. Its possessions of Macao, Timor, and Goa (the last a manufacturing center in India) served as bases for the "country trades" of the integrated Indian Ocean commercial system. As such, they managed to pay for themselves and to yield moderate profits to Portuguese

and half-Portuguese merchants located there, but their contributions to the Portuguese economy itself were exceedingly
modest. Mozambique, in southeastern Africa, remained of
little economic value.

In 1815, the overseas empire of Spain was still, in theory, ter-
ritorially intact, as was the theory of governance under which it
had operated in the eighteenth century.[16] The economic performance of several of Spain's American colonies, Argentina
and Mexico for example, showed encouraging signs of growth.
Yet many observers believed the empire to be on the verge of
collapse, and in fact it did fall apart within a decade. During the
Napoleonic Wars, the colonies had become essentially self-
governing; by 1815, Argentina was effectively independent.
Revolution was expected to spread rapidly.

The expectation of dissolution derived in part from the
realization that, almost from the beginning, Spain itself was
economically inessential to the rest of the empire. Spain maintained an expensive, bureaucratic governmental system in
South and Central America, Mexico, and part of the Caribbean
largely in order to control the silver trade from Peru and Mexico and to monopolize the profitable transoceanic trade that
supported the European settlers in its colonies. It was necessary
to do this because Spain itself produced little that the Spanish
colonials wanted in trade for their products. Thus commerce
would naturally have grown up between the colonies and northern Europe, where trade goods were produced, and Spain
would have been excluded altogether. In fact, there was always
a considerable amount of smuggling, and the landowning elites
of the Spanish colonies were notorious for their willingness to
connive at it. This had led many imperial "projectors" in
England to believe that Spanish colonists would willingly
change masters in the eighteenth century; disputes over
economic policy between the colonial elites and the home
government became increasingly common. But until Spain's
prestige was shattered during the Napoleonic Wars, foreign
observers had been wrong. The colonial elites also recognized
that the Spanish government helped to maintain social order

and the status quo. The ties of Hispanic culture in a largely Indian world also helped to keep the upper classes of Spanish America politically loyal to the home country. Despite the fact that the decline of silver production had greatly reduced the economic significance of the empire for Spain, the home government had, in a fitful and inconsistent way, attempted to readjust the closed economic system to new realities through a certain amount of reform and "liberalization." The process of reform did not progress far. The bureaucratic structure of government and the forcible centering of the empire around Spain continued up to the Napoleonic Wars.

By 1815, the long period in which the Spanish empire had held together without a consensus among its members about economic priorities was just about over. Several factors, many of them purely local, contributed to the wave of independence movements that swept across Spanish America. Of the more general factors, the most important was that the landed and commercial elites of many of the colonies (Peru was an exception) saw no other way to establish the kinds of economic links to the advanced economies of northern Europe that they desired. The elites also saw no other way to structure the domestic societies of their countries in a manner conducive to increases in their profits and their political power. In Mexico, fear by the elite of popular revolution and North American invasion contributed to the movement. In addition, the French Revolution gave the educated elites of Latin America a liberal ideology around which to organize, the Napoleonic Wars weakened Spain's hold and lowered its prestige, and the British Industrial Revolution increased the opportunities for profitable trade open to the colonial landowning classes, if only the obstruction of Spanish rule could be eliminated.

The Spanish empire was therefore tottering at the brink of dissolution in 1815. Although we shall not discuss in detail the movement that resulted in the independence of most of Spain's colonies, we shall consider the role of Britain in the process in the next chapter.

THREE

Economic Modernization and Imperialism, 1815-1860

O NE OF THE MAJOR FORCES changing imperialism and the relationship between Europe and the outside world in the nineteenth century was the Industrial Revolution, which began in Britain and spread to Western Europe. We must therefore begin by summarizing those aspects of British and continental industrialization in the late eighteenth and the nineteenth centuries that most directly affected imperialism.[1]

INDUSTRIALIZATION AND ITS CONSEQUENCES

The central feature of British industrialization was a vastly accelerated use of machinery in manufacturing, which radically increased the productivity of whole industries. In the industry that first underwent modernization in the eighteenth century, cotton, increases in production and exports were little short of astounding, amounting probably to an expansion of several hundred percent. Production and export increases were also large for other major industries: metals, coal, and engineering. By the end of the century, cotton production was far and away Britain's largest export and manufacturing

31

enterprise and was rapidly transforming the society and the physical landscape of the north of England.

In the cotton industry, as in the others, the key to increased production and productivity lay in a series of technological innovations effected as responses to economic pressures on the manufacturing process. In most cases, these were demand pressures. The cotton industry of the north of England, originally a minor adjunct to wool and linen production, was "revolutionized" by the growth of demand for cotton cloth as a convenient commodity in tropical trade and as a cheap material for undergarments and dresses within Britain. Improvements in weaving in the 1730s and a major revolution in spinning after 1760 lowered the price of English-made cotton and increased demand by making cotton even more attractive to merchants and domestic customers. This type of change, repeated in other industries, profoundly altered the patterns of Britain's overseas trade and its relations with both its colonies and noncolonial areas. The innovations in cotton spinning had complicated long-term domestic effects. They simultaneously encouraged the expansion of older modes of production (putting-out and hand-loom weaving) and stimulated further technical innovations, such as the power loom and factory production, that would render the newly expanded older models obsolete early in the next century. This pattern of industrial modernization underlay many of the social effects of industrialization.

England in the late eighteenth and early nineteenth centuries constituted the model for industrialization elsewhere. There was, however, at least one crucial difference. Britain was the first to industrialize. It was not that British industry lacked competitors. India in the eighteenth century offered Britain a good deal of competition in cotton until British hegemony there was used to smash Indian cotton exports. Rather, especially with certain types of manufactured commodities that appealed to mass markets, British technological innovations greatly increased productivity and lowered production costs, permitting British producers to undersell rivals. Being first also gave Britain the advantage of slower economic change than would be experienced by most later industrializing societies, and thus more time for social and political structures to adjust to new circumstances. Also, potential competitors to the British would in the future have to assemble great amounts of capital and industrialize quickly just to be able to compete. In the meantime, of course, Britain was able to stage a further expansion of industrial production and a second technological revolution between 1820 and 1850, thus staying ahead of competitors. On the other hand, in the long run Britain's early lead contained the seeds of later problems. By the 1870s the country was saddled with inferior, small-scale business organization, an older physical plant, and out-of-date managerial techniques. As we shall see, this last legacy of the Industrial Revolution later played an important role in British imperialism.

Results of the Industrial Revolution

Industrialization brought, of course, massive changes in the social structures, the distribution of population, and even the physical appearance of large areas of England.[2] Urban conglomerations, featuring terrible living conditions, appeared in the Midlands and north of England. Changes in social and occupational structures, together with the instability of business conditions and the frequency of industrial depressions, created alarm among traditional status groups. The Industrial Revolution created new social groups, from the economic elite of factory owners, whose existence constituted a threat to the established agrarian and commercial elites, to the urban industrial proletariat. As it happened, the old elite fairly quickly co-opted the new industrial one, but not without creating considerable political and social strain. The new working class, which bore the brunt of the ill effects of change, was not as easily assimilated. Although industrialization did not produce the English urban middle class, it did greatly expand and diversify it. These domestic social changes played a complex part in Britain's imperial history through the effects that they had on domestic politics. We shall return to this point later.

Industrialization as an economic phenomenon more immediately altered Britain's relations with Europe and the world overseas. As we have seen in the preceding chapter, the nature of Europe's, and especially England's, foreign and colonial trade had already undergone major changes even before the effects of the Industrial Revolution made themselves felt in the late eighteenth century. Some of these changes, such as increased foreign demand for cotton cloth, probably helped to cause industrialization, although in general links between colonial expansion and industrialization were probably fairly tenuous.[3] After 1815, with some exceptions, the normal direction of causation was clearly the other way: from change in industry to change in trade patterns. Industrial concerns dominated. While some factors in overseas relations, such as European emigration, were only partly related to industrialization itself, most aspects of those relations had direct and clear connections with industrial production.

This reversal of dominance between trade and manufacturing can be seen in the remarkable change of prevalent economic ideologies in Britain between about 1775 and 1825, from the protectionist ideas of mercantilism to liberal concepts of free trade and free enterprise.[4] Although economic liberalism was in fact a pre-industrial ideology, it was admirably suited to explaining the economic circumstances of an industrializing Britain and to confirming business people's practical perceptions of changed trade conditions. By 1815, business people were aware that the largest profits in overseas trade were not to be made from importing consumables for sale in Britain or for reexport, but rather from the sale of British manufactured goods, especially cotton cloth and metal products, abroad. The difference from the old system was not total: money was still to be made in the carrying trades, and since the wars with France,

Britain's merchant marine was preeminent in the world. But the very expansion of British overseas carrying capacity had made ocean shipping a competitive business. The real profits were to be made by exploiting new industrial productivity through high-volume sales of manufactured goods abroad and industrial raw materials in Britain. As we shall see, liberal free-trade ideas appeared to be most conducive to such sales. By 1815, the balance of the nonagricultural sector of the British economy had shifted decisively from trade to manufacturing, although of course the two activities remained closely linked. We can see immediate repercussions of this change in Britain's relations with two areas: the West African coast and the United States.

British Relations with West Africa

In West Africa, several limits to the extent of European penetration and control had existed in the eighteenth century. These included tropical diseases to which few Europeans had natural immunities. The main limitation was that there had been no good reason for the British or any of the other powers to extend their control. The economic mechanism that brought thousands of slaves annually to the coast, although not perfect, nonetheless worked adequately. In some areas, such as Dahomey, the states with which the Europeans traded had more ability to influence the terms of trade than the slave traders believed desirable. But in most cases, any attempt to increase European control would have created resistance and would have cost far more than it would have been worth. As it was, the supply of slaves was steady and, most importantly, slave prices remained relatively low.[5] The main aim of European traders was to acquire slaves for resale, not to peddle European goods in West Africa. Slaves were cheap in European eyes, because a load of inexpensive trade goods could purchase a large number of valuable slaves. This could occur because, for the most part, the European goods (such as glass beads, cloth, guns, and iron) were regarded by elite segments of slave-trading

African societies as status symbols. In other words, cultural differences in the values assigned trade goods created the basis of profitable intercourse. It was in the interests of European slave traders to see to it that these differences remained intact and that European trade goods remained scarce and therefore viable status symbols. Except in the immediate vicinity of the coastal trading posts, traders were therefore uninterested in spreading European culture either through missionary activity or by other means.

The Industrial Revolution may or may not have been a decisive force in ending the British slave trade (the point is still hotly debated), but it is clear that once the slave trade was illegal, British industrialization stimulated major changes in the commercial economies of West Africa.[6] It did so not only by making West Africa a producer of industrial raw materials, but also through the domestic social changes that it encouraged in Britain. Despite claims to the contrary by abolitionists anxious to push "legitimate trade" as a replacement for the slave trade, few raw materials for British manufacturing were to be found in West Africa. The only important exception in the first half of the nineteenth century was palm oil, used in making soap. The new upper- and middle-class English social strata spawned by the Industrial Revolution after about 1800 turned the use of soap into a criterion of respectability and status. Palm oil was also used in a variety of industrial processes.

Soap was not a major industrial product, however, and in the nineteenth century British traders in West Africa thought of the region as being as much a market for manufactured goods as a producing area. The emphasis gradually shifted to selling as much cotton cloth and ironmongery as possible; palm oil provided a means of paying for these low price, high volume imports. After about 1815, British merchants, unlike the slave traders, had every reason to encourage the spread of Western culture in West Africa as a means of encouraging sales. The maintenance of cultural differences was no longer an advantage, nor were European merchants interested in dealing with a narrow elite market. Rather, they increasingly wanted a mass market oriented toward Western material culture. This change led to accelerated business support of the British missionary societies that had sprung up in the wake of the abolitionist movement, creating the coincidence of the ideas of moral and material "progress" that was to characterize missionary activities for the rest of the century. The slave trade, although sometimes destructive of particular African societies, had normally been accommodated through purely internal modifications in African social organization. In the nineteenth century, even though the importance of West Africa to the economic prosperity of Britain and the rest of Europe had diminished greatly, the foundation of a deliberate program of changing the nature of society and culture in West Africa had been laid.

The nature of the new trade patterns emerging in West Africa also helped to break down traditional social structures. Just as European merchants sought to sell to whole populations rather than to elites, so too did palm oil cultivation prove to be most efficiently conducted by individual peasant families rather than by elite or state structures. Despite continued slave smuggling and attempts at large-scale palm cultivation by states like Dahomey, the conduct of trade continued to change, shaking the economic foundations of the coastal trading states and, over time, bringing those states into conflict with a Britain committed to abolition, "legitimate" trade, and mass markets.

British Relations with the United States

A very different example of overseas economic consequences of British industrialization is provided by the United States. The United States after 1815 possessed a relatively wealthy and expanding economy that had no need for imported social and cultural changes aimed at inculcating modern habits of economic behavior in the population. The United States was therefore an excellent market for British industrial products. This was not, however, the essential basis of the close economic relationship between the two countries in the first half of the nineteenth century. Incipient American manufacturing industries and the fully developed American shipping industry offered competition in the American market, especially from the 1830s on, when the United States government intervened in trade on behalf of American business.[7] The real impetus to extensive Anglo-American trade before 1860 was the growing dependence of the British textile industry on American raw cotton.

The vast expansion of the British textile industry in the late eighteenth century created a demand for raw cotton that far outdistanced existing supplies. In the 1790s — with the development of the cotton gin, the introduction of new strains of cotton, and the opening of new lands in the American South away from the coast — the southern regions of the United States emerged as the major supplier of cotton to the north of England. The Southern economy was dominated by large, single-crop plantations that used slave labor and sold most of their cotton, through highly volatile markets, to English buyers. The South became something of an appendage of the industrial economy of Great Britain, importing large amounts of English products to balance cotton exports.

The Southern plantation economy was, thus, similar to that of the eighteenth-century West Indies, with certain key differences. After 1808, American slave owners could not legally import new slaves and had to rely on the Southern slave population to increase itself. This resulted in higher real labor costs but also in greater independence from the overseas slave market. The American South also possessed a nonplantation, food-producing agricultural sector and economic relations with the industrializing North, making the United States as a whole less dependent on the movement of the British market than the West Indies were in the eighteenth century. A glut on the world's cotton market could cause profits to fall in the South, but an interruption in raw cotton exports, such as that caused by the American Civil War, could create a depression in England.

Most importantly, Britain was in no position after 1815 to exercise predominant political influence over the United States. The Southern landowning class pursued aims in national politics favored by British manufacturers (such as free trade, and no subsidies for Northern business), but it did so in its own interests, not at Britain's behest. The United States' stability and strength prevented the kind of British interference that took place in countries such as Argentina. Even during the American Civil War, despite pro-Southern public opinion in Britain and private assistance to the Confederacy, the British government did not interfere effectively in the South's favor. A rational assessment of costs prevented intervention.

Another important factor in British relations with America was that, except for American tariffs, the United States was an ideal economic partner. Americans possessed a modern material culture, bought British products, produced raw materials, and provided ever-increasing scope for British investment, all without any intervention or expense by the British government. Except during the Civil War, economic relations with Britain were not interrupted by political disorder. Not only was there little opportunity for effective British imperialism in the United States after 1815, but there was also little reason for it.

THE SECOND PHASE OF ECONOMIC MODERNIZATION

One of the most important features of Britain's changing economic relations with the outside world was the high and increasing rate of capital investment abroad that accompanied the "second industrial revolution" after 1820.[8] The second revolution, fueled by capital created during the first period of industrialization, led to rapid improvements in productive techniques, tendencies toward economic concentration, and the triumph of the factory system in the textile industry. New technologies in metallurgy led to mass production of iron and steel. In the 1840s and 1850s industrial expansion focused particularly on the "railroad mania": the rapid building (indeed, over-building) of railways all over the country, which made the railroad the symbol of the new industrial world and gave it a public importance that its actual economic contribution (great though it was) did not justify. Further industrialization was accompanied by population rises and accelerated urbanization. These rapid changes, together with the recurring cycles of economic boom and depression, introduced enormous social dislocations.

By the end of the 1850s, after one of the most spectacular sustained booms in European economic history, the core process of British industrialization was almost complete.[9] Hardly an industry (including agriculture) had escaped some degree of mechanization and improvement in technical efficiency. Britain was covered with railroads and large cities. Many of the political means of social control needed to maintain stability in an industrial society, and the cultural structures and psychological attitudes that supported them, had begun to operate effectively. Most importantly, Britain was even more the undisputed economic leader of the world than it had been in 1815. In production of inexpensive textiles, pig iron, coal, and industrial machinery, it far surpassed the rest of the world put together. While its merchant marine was still challenged by that of the United States, the American challenge would not outlast the Civil War. Finally, as the banking seat of a country with so much capital generated by two complete waves of industrialization, London had become the center of international investment on an unprecedented scale.

An accelerating outflow of investment capital from Britain, a consequence of industrialization, was one of the major economic phenomena of the nineteenth century.[10] It gave impetus to the international spread of industrialization and to the extension of the network of economic relations centering upon the industrial countries that we call the modern "world economy." The capital outflow was fed by a number of sources: the movement of foreign capital through London as an investment center, the reinvestment of commercial earnings, and the investment of domestic industrial profits in foreign areas. Industrial reinvestment at home seemed, especially after the early 1850s, to offer few prospects of the high profits that early stages of industrialization in other countries allowed. Lack of immediate industrial competition abroad and short-sighted family-oriented business management at home led to the avoidance of the unpleasant task of investing in new plants and technologies. Foreign investment seemed more profitable.

Substantial British industrial investment abroad had commenced at the end of the Napoleonic Wars. During the next three decades, it was primarily directed toward the Continent where, together with the emigration of British industrial experts and their new technologies, it helped to set in motion industrial revolutions in Belgium, France, and the German Rhineland. In the 1850s, while British industry enjoyed unprecedented prosperity, France experienced a real industrial takeoff and German industry expanded even more rapidly, especially in metals, with a high degree of intelligent planning by the German states. By the time of the incredible German boom of 1871-73, Germany's industrial base had surpassed that of France. Within twenty years, it would be challenging Britain's.

Many factors lay behind the rise of German industry and the almost simultaneous industrial takeoff in the United States. In both cases, however, the existence of strong economic connections with Britain was of considerable importance. British capital was essential to the first stages of German industrialization (1840-60) and to the intermediate stages of American expansion (1850-80). Britain also provided markets, industrial techniques, and the model of a successful industrializing society. To a great extent, then, Britain spawned the rival industrial economies that would shortly dethrone it from its position of economic primacy.

British investment also, as we have seen, directed itself toward non-European countries, most especially after about 1850, when the economies of Belgium, France, and Germany began to produce their own supplies of capital. The really profitable investment opportunities appeared to lie elsewhere: in the

United States, in several of the Latin American republics, and in the British white-settlement colonies. But before we can examine these cases more closely, we must look at another major factor in Europe's relations with the world overseas in the age of industrialization: emigration.

BRITISH EMIGRATION

As we have seen, industrialization brought with it a substantial amount of occupational and social restructuring. Many social changes, however, were not caused directly by industrialization, although they were often related to it in various ways. One of these changes was the rapid rise in population that most European countries experienced in the late eighteenth and early nineteenth centuries.[11] While France's rate of increase peaked early in the period of economic modernization, Britain's population began increasing early in the eighteenth century, continued its growth during the Industrial Revolution, and expanded until well past the mid-nineteenth century. Other countries followed different patterns.

The nature of nineteenth-century emigration was determined, in general, by population increase and changes in agriculture as well as by industrialization. In Britain, two patterns prevailed, one for England and Scotland and the other for Ireland. Both England and Scotland had experienced considerable internal population movement and emigration to America in the eighteenth century, mainly because of labor displacement due to the continuing reorientation of agriculture toward more efficient and capitalistic forms. Both movement to the cities and overseas emigration continued through the first half of the nineteenth century and provided a steady stream of migrants to the United States, Canada, Australia, and eventually New Zealand. In the nineteenth century, the stream of rural emigrants was joined by a heterogeneous urban and semi-urban stream of skilled workers and lower-middle-class persons motivated by industrial depressions and occupational obsolescence. This postindustrial emigration was also mainly directed to the United States and the white dominions, but less exclusively so. It tended to be directed to areas of industrial and commercial expansion and was especially stimulated by local booms, such as the California and Australian gold rushes of the 1850s and 1860s.

Irish emigration followed a somewhat different pattern. Except for the Protestant Scotch-Irish of Ulster, there was comparatively little Irish emigration in the eighteenth century because of the absence of agricultural change and the poverty of the rural population, most of whom were too poor to migrate. Large-scale emigration commenced in the nineteenth century, reaching massive proportions after the great potato famine of the late 1840s. Rural overpopulation, tied to periodic crop failures, created the motive for emigration; the increasing requirement for unskilled labor in industrializing areas, the opportunity; and the development of cheap transport, the means.[12] Irish people moved in large numbers to the new industrial cities of the north of England from about 1800. The development of industry in America and especially the many road-, canal- and railroad-building projects there, with their large requirements for unskilled labor, made the United States the major goal of Irish emigration from the 1840s onward.

FRANCE AND ALGERIA

In contrast to British emigration, that of France was neither large nor, with one major exception, significant for later French and imperial history. France's relatively low birthrate and its small-proprietor agricultural system did not drive out large numbers of people. Industrial areas attracted migrants from the 1830s, however, and modest numbers of French people were attracted by the opportunities offered in newly developed areas abroad. There was one important case, however, of large-scale French emigration in the nineteenth century: Algeria.

The Algerian coast had long been the location of Muslim city-states — nominally parts of the Ottoman Empire but practically independent — that were centers of trade between Africa and Europe and also centers of piracy. Algiers was the most important of these cities. Early in the nineteenth century, first the United States and then France moved to end the piracy of the Barbary Coast, which interfered with the expanding trade of the Mediterranean and Atlantic.[13] By 1820, the United States had dropped out of North African affairs. France, however, had a direct commercial interest in expanding Mediterranean trade contacts and in developing the area directly across from its southern coast. By 1820, France had stamped out most of the last vestiges of North African piracy and had established political dominance over many of the North African states.

The progression from informal paramountcy to formal empire in Algeria was essentially a matter of domestic French politics, although economic interest played a role. In 1827, an incident arising from the strained relations between France and Algiers was taken by the reactionary government of King Charles X as a pretext for a blockade and thereafter a direct attempt to conquer Algiers. The government's main objective was to use foreign adventure and imperialism to create loyalty to itself among the French middle classes, much as Napoleon had done. Algiers was therefore occupied in 1830. The conquest of the surrounding hinterland proved difficult and expensive, and the war did not prevent the liberal revolution that overthrew Charles X later in 1830. This demonstration of the political inadequacy of imperialism did not, however, end the French adventure in Algeria. The various governments of Louis Philippe (1830-48) believed that they required overseas successes in order to maintain popularity, and in the politics of competing economic interest groups that characterized the July Monarchy, the advantages of patronage through contracts and concessions in Algeria were overwhelmingly obvious. The French army, once established in the area, generated a momentum toward further conquest practically on its own.

A ferocious guerrilla war raged in the Algerian hinterland throughout the 1830s and 1840s. The French found it easy to conquer towns and cities and to rule them indirectly through traditional elites, but it was difficult to defeat the independent agricultural Berbers and to occupy their mountain valleys. Effective resistance was led and maintained under the legendary Abd-el-Kadr.

By the 1840s, without particular encouragement, several thousand French people had already been drawn to Algeria to take advantage of opportunities in trade and government. In order to solidify the French occupation of the hinterland, a policy was now adopted by General Bugeaud, the governor, in which French settlers, particularly peasants, were encouraged to move to Algeria as agricultural colonists. Land was made available cheaply, thus attracting settlers from poorer parts of rural France who might otherwise have moved to cities. Immediately after the 1848 revolution, the government also dispatched unemployed Parisians to Algeria. Under Bugeaud and his successors, land was systematically seized from the Algerian population and assigned to French *colons*. Algeria was politically reorganized under a centralized government in which the French settlers monopolized most civil rights and became a privileged class. Algeria became a magnet attracting emigrants from France and, throughout the century, an exception to the general rule of relatively low French overseas emigration.

The bloody military subjugation of Algeria was largely complete by 1848, but the nature of the settlers' impingement upon the Algerian population required the constant maintenance of a large French army there. Its position in Algeria provided the army with an overseas support base that contributed to its independence in politics, while the settlers had, because of their own position, every reason to support a repressive policy toward the indigenous population. The seeds of the Algerian revolution of the 1950s and 1960s were therefore sown deep in the nineteenth century.

Emigration was a major aspect of European overseas expansion in the nineteenth century, although it played different roles in different countries. We shall discuss the effects of German and Italian emigration on imperialism in a later chapter.

Emigration was caused by a multitude of social, economic, and political factors, not simply by the onset of industrialization. But as industrialization progressed, the factors that induced (and limited) emigration and the social changes associated with industrialization became inextricably mixed. One important product of British emigration was the formation of the self-governing white-settlement colonies – the "dominions."

THE BRITISH DOMINIONS

Although systematic "decolonization" is usually regarded as a phenomenon of the post-1945 period, Britain in fact pioneered the decolonization process in the nineteenth century in its dealings with its white colonies: Canada, Australia, and New Zealand. It perhaps tells us something about the nature of late European imperialism that the process by which the British Empire could be disestablished was put together even before that empire reached its widest physical extent.

Canada

We have already seen how Canada developed after the American Revolution into two communities: a French-speaking one in Lower Canada (Quebec) and an English-speaking one, expanding and fed by emigration from Britain and the United States, to the west in Upper Canada. After the formal division of Canada into two provinces in 1791, each was ruled by an essentially autocratic British government. In Upper Canada, however, the spread-out nature of settlement and the political expectations of immigrants created a tendency toward self-rule and thus a tension with the nature of colonial government. Together with social conflicts and (in Upper Canada) ethnic resentment, this made for great potential instability in Canada.[14] The proximity of the United States was also an upsetting factor: many people moved back and forth between the United States and Upper Canada, and the United States became an increasingly important trading partner for the emerging Canadian economy in the second quarter of the nineteenth century. These factors helped to keep the economic connection of Canada to Britain fairly loose. The growth of Canadian export agriculture made Canadians chafe under close British rule. The growth of Canadian industries led to calls for protection against British imports, especially when Canadian wheat exports lost their protected market in Britain. On the other hand, the periodic aggressive expansiveness of the United States also acted to keep the populations of both English- and French-speaking Canada attached to Britain for protection. The United States' attempt to invade Canada in 1812 and 1813 was not soon forgotten.

In the 1830s, a series of rebellions took place in both Lower and Upper Canada, the former impelled partly by fear of the growing size and wealth of the English-speaking population, and the latter aimed partly at acquiring self-rule. In 1838, the British government dispatched Lord Durham, a Liberal politician and radical ideologue, to be special governor of both provinces. Durham lasted only five months in office before being recalled. Upon his return he submitted the famous "Durham report," which recommended changes in Canada's governmental structure and which became the model, if not exactly the blueprint, for the decolonization of Canada and the other white dependencies.[15]

The genesis of the ideas in the Durham report lies in the emergence of liberalism in Britain in the nineteenth century, and thus indirectly in the general modernization of British society that produced ideological liberalism. In the course of economic development in the nineteenth century, liberalism — with its doctrines of representative government (which allowed new social and economic interests to influence government policy), free enterprise, and free trade (both suited to a rapidly expanding economy that could not be contained by mercantilist restrictions) — had become increasingly the dominant ideology of the commercial and industrial elites in Britain and of much of the middle class. In 1830, the Whig (later Liberal) party had come to power on a moderate liberal platform, and in 1832 it had passed the Great Reform Act, a major step toward real representative government. This had been followed by a spate of new reform legislation, which had both established the groundwork of a new liberal state and displayed many of the contradictions in classical liberalism. The most important of the latter was that, although most liberals favored as inactive (and inexpensive) a government as possible, it was increasingly clear that active governmental intervention in society and the economy was needed in order to create the conditions of free enterprise and to deal with increasingly complex social problems.

In 1833 and 1838, the Liberals, under radical prodding, had abolished slavery in the British West Indies.[16] This had been done in a worthy cause, but it had necessarily involved the most unliberal action of removing the legislative power of the Jamaican Assembly and transforming Jamaica into a directly ruled colony. The Durham report, suggesting that the solution to Britain's problems in Canada was the enactment of self-rule, appeared to liberals to be a reaffirmation of a belief that liberal ideas could in fact be applied to the governance of empire.

The essence of the Durham report was the unification of the two provinces of Canada into one colony and the granting of internal self-rule to a Canadian parliament elected by each province equally. A Canadian parliament was in fact established in Montreal, although the ethnic identities of the separate provinces were not submerged as Durham had wanted. In the early 1840s, during a period of political turmoil in Canada, the British administration showed incredible forebearance in order to make the system of local responsibility and parliamentary government work. The new system did not spare Britain headaches and administrative expense. But it was consonant with liberal ideology, and although the unitary government had a tendency toward deadlock and inefficiency, under it Canada prospered economically from the late 1840s into the 1860s.

The next result of the decolonization process begun by the Durham report was the British North America Act of 1867, which granted Canada practical independence, except in foreign affairs and defense. The act was the result of initiatives by Canadian politicians, who sought complete home rule, among other reasons, in order to establish tariffs against British and United States industrial competition. Despite this, independence was granted largely on the terms desired by the Canadians: a federal, parliamentary system; a head of state with limited powers appointed by the British crown; and complete internal autonomy. The reservation of foreign affairs and defense by Britain was included partly at Canadian insistence. It involved a considerable obligation by Britain over the next few years — for example, in putting down the Red River rebellion in Manitoba (1867-70) and in protecting Canadian interests against the United States.

Why did Britain permit such rapid decolonization of Canada? For various reasons that appeared so obvious in the 1850s and 1860s that they were seldom seriously debated. The dominant liberal economic ideology held that formal colonies, unless justified by special circumstances, were useless. Such thinking seldom led by itself to actual decolonization, but it suggested the form that responses to colonial problems might take if no strong interest group in Britain was concerned to maintain a colonial attachment. The case for decolonization in Canada was in fact overwhelming in terms of mid-Victorian political and economic thought. Canadian autonomy, while it involved political responsibilities for Britain, put a clear limit on them and the expenses they might entail. Canada might (and did) impose tariffs, but at the same time it presented rich opportunities for British investment that more than made up for the inconvenience of tariffs. Moreover, unlike the later case of Irish home rule, political gains could accrue to few major parties or interest groups at home by preventing practical Canadian independence. Decolonization was thus Britain's "natural" policy.

Australia and New Zealand

Australia and New Zealand went through a similar process, although without even the presence of rebellion to encourage action. Up to the early 1830s, New South Wales was a marginal

penal colony with few resources, little trade, and few white inhabitants. Britain had a claim to the entire Australian continent
but had done little about it. In the late 1830s and 1840s, New
South Wales developed an agricultural economy able to attract
voluntary settlers as well as prisoners. Small settlements had
started in other areas and in New Zealand, but altogether, Britain's presence in the region was not overwhelming.[17]

The rapid growth of European demand for foodstuffs and
raw textiles around mid-century and the Australian gold rush of
the 1850s were the making of Britain's Australasian colonies.
But even before this, Australia and New Zealand had become a
focus of colonialist interest because of the writings of Edward
Gibbon Wakefield. Wakefield had become a colonial "authority" in England because of a fictional account of New South
Wales he had written in 1829. In 1833, he propounded a general
scheme for colonial settlement and development. Wakefield's
scheme caught the public fancy, in part because of skillful propaganda by backers of Wakefield who hoped to make money
through him, but also in part because Wakefield's ideas were
connected to currently popular utopian social thought and appealed to people looking for a way to reconcile economic
growth with a social order threatened in the 1830s by rapid
social change.[18] Wakefield's imperialist theory thus served as a
basis for a limited consensus among disparate social segments,
a function that imperialism would be used to perform more and
more as the century went on.

The essence of Wakefield's scheme was the steady and
planned development of efficient agriculture in temperate areas
such as southern Australia and New Zealand, mainly by highly
capitalized colonial companies backed politically by the British
government. The companies would develop export agriculture,
recruiting laborers among the poorer classes of British rural and
urban society under long-term contracts. Smaller plots of land
would be sold at high prices, so as to make poorer immigrants
work for a considerable period of time for the companies
before they could buy farmsteads. This would supposedly

avoid the typical colonial problem of labor shortages and high wage rates due to the attractiveness of "free" frontier regions and ensure that frontier settlers were experienced in colonial agriculture. Wakefield's controlled colonial economy would become profitable very quickly and help to relieve Britain's population pressure without creating an unstable society overseas that would be difficult to govern.

The Wakefield "system" had a great deal to recommend it. Social conflict in Britain in the 1830s gave the scheme political appeal, while Wakefield's emphasis on capital investment and organization made good sense — although the idea of controlling the frontier was impractical. Wakefield was the catalyst for a number of colonial ventures in the late 1830s and 1840s, including at least one by Germany.[19] Among the more successful of these were the company that colonized South Australia and the New Zealand Association, which established the first large-scale white settlements in New Zealand in 1840.

The New Zealand Association, to which Wakefield belonged, had both the political connections necessary to get Britain to declare sovereignty over New Zealand and the capital to establish profitable agriculture. It also managed to push aside the native Maori population. It did not, however, succeed in controlling the settlement of New Zealand.[20] Other companies and settlers moved in during the 1850s and demanded self-government. Originally, New Zealand had been placed administratively under New South Wales, and then directly under the Colonial Office, recently separated from the War Office. The demands for self-government in New Zealand conflicted with the interests of the politically influential development companies, but in the end the settlers won out. They did so because of Canada's example, because the prevailing ideology in England was in their favor, and because self-rule seemed less burdensome for the British taxpayer. Effective internal decolonization occurred in 1856. The first discovery of gold in 1853 brought some increase in population and prosperity to New Zealand, but it was the discovery of further gold fields and the wide spread of commercial sheep grazing in the 1860s that turned New Zealand into a major trading partner of Great Britain and a goal for emigration. In the process, the native Maori were displaced after hard resistance, although they were not exterminated. In the political sphere, New Zealand became increasingly independent until in 1907 it attained dominion status on the same terms as Canada.

Developments in Australia were at once more varied and more spectacular.[21] By 1850, settlements had been made in all of Australia's later states, and New South Wales had become a more or less substantial agricultural producing area, specializing in wool production. In 1851, veins of gold were struck in the "outback" of New South Wales and near Melbourne, ushering in the Australian gold rush. The population of Victoria, now a separate province, doubled in a few months. Although the immediate effects of the gold rush wore off within a few years, the capital generated in the 1850s led to a boom in agriculture and mining and to the rapid industrialization and urbanization of the areas around Sydney and Melbourne. Australia quickly became a major and preferred location for British investment and immigration.

The rapid economic development of the Australian territories brought with it problems of public order and government and a number of social conflicts, especially over the importation of Chinese labor. Although the solutions to these problems were not obvious, the means of solving them was by now taken for granted: responsible self-government. All of the criteria and motives established in the Canadian model for self-government were present in Australia as well. To the British, the potential financial and domestic political cost of trying to govern Australia directly appeared too high. Almost as a matter of routine, most of the Australian provinces were set up as separate, self-governing colonies in the 1850s. Subsequent efforts at confederation failed until the 1890s, when the rise of Japanese power provided an encouragement to unity. New Zealand remained aloof, but in 1900 a federation of the rest of the colonies was effected, followed over the next few years by the assumption by the federal government of defense and foreign relations functions and eventually of imperial control of many South Pacific islands.

The Limits of Decolonization

With achievement of practical independence, the white dominions of Great Britain ceased to be formal dependencies. The remaining relationship with Britain was, from the British standpoint, ideal (except for the dominions' tendency toward tariff protection). Like the United States, they were politically stable trading partners and investment areas that cost the British government little to maintain. Even with tariffs, they were a bargain. On the other hand, formal colonization, with its economic and political costs to Britain, tended up to the 1870s to be regarded as a deviation from the ideal.

It is, however, clear that the ideal British trading partner was a country with a substantial population of European culture — preferably northern European. According to standard British attitudes, only such people could be expected to behave in an economically rational manner. "Colored" peoples, on the other hand, would have to be guided into economic and political rationality. The dimensions of this guidance and the role of European governments in affording it were uncertain. Did less-than-optimal political, economic, and cultural conditions justify direct political intervention in, say, West Africa? In any event, the tendency to identify a country's level of economic capability (and thus its readiness for self-rule) with its possession of an overwhelming white (and preferably English-speaking) population ensured that the British model of decolonization would only be applied to colonies like Canada, Australia, and New Zealand.

LATIN AMERICA

Latin America in the nineteenth century maintained a set of relations with Europe so complicated that they have defied categorization by most historians and theorists of imperialism. All of Latin America except for the Guiana colonies and the Caribbean islands became politically independent in the nineteenth century, mostly in the 1820s.[22] Independence was achieved in most cases by violent revolutions, usually led by property-owning elite groups. The British government and British trading interests supported the movement toward independence in the hope that British trade would benefit from a change in government. In a formal political sense, then, Latin America experienced decolonization in the nineteenth century. On the other hand, it is also clear that most Latin American countries with potential as sources of raw materials, as markets, and as investment areas for the industrializing parts of Europe assumed a kind of dependent position toward Europe — and especially toward Great Britain.

British "Free-Trade Imperialism"

In the early 1950s, Gallagher and Robinson employed the term "free-trade imperialism" to denote a type of international political and economic regime established by Britain in the first half of the nineteenth century in various parts of the world, particularly in Latin America, and the ideology that accompanied it.[23] "Free-trade imperialism" is viewed by those who find it in Britain's relations with Latin America mainly in two forms: as a system of conscious British policy aims and methods, and as a reality of international economics. The existence of both forms has been disputed, especially by D.C.M. Platt.[24] In its first form, British "free-trade imperialism" is held to have been an advocacy of a free-trade policy for the whole world as a conscious mask for British economic interests. Before 1850, with no international industrial competition to speak of, British exporters naturally favored an ideology and a foreign policy which sought, in the name of progress and civilization, to remove all barriers to the free passage of manufactured goods and raw materials. Marginally successful trading interests often used the free-trade ideology to attempt to get the British government to back them when they got into trouble. In certain gross cases, such as the Opium Wars with China, "free trade" was employed in the most hypocritical manner. These, however, were exceptions that occurred only when overwhelmingly important British interests — political and military as well as economic — were involved. Normally, the connections between particular British actions and "deeper" ideological currents were somewhat more problematic.

It was indeed true that the British government traditionally attempted to support British merchants abroad and to assist them in finding new and better markets. This support intensified throughout the nineteenth century. It resulted in the revitalization of the Board of Trade, the establishment of the consular service, and the evolution of what became almost a standardized military response to direct threats to British property. These do not, however, in themselves constitute adherence to a conscious imperialist ideology hiding behind free-trade theory. The ideology of "free-trade imperialism" is held to have centered around the idea of Britain as the "workshop of the world," which should specialize in industrial production while everyone else produced raw materials.[25] Statements to this effect can be found in manufacturers' speeches, but there is little evidence that such statements constituted an ideology or produced a formal theory of economic empire. Even under Lord Palmerston, the most interventionist of all mid-Victorian British ministers, government use of force to support economic interests remained sporadic and highly particular in incidence.

The Importance of British Investment

The term "free-trade imperialism" does not even accurately describe the economic dependency of Latin America on Britain through most of the nineteenth century. Investment, rather than trade, was the real key.[26] Before the 1840s, the main concern of most British business people with connections to South America was to develop the continent as a marketing area. The most fruitful fields were, as we have seen, Brazil and Argentina. In both cases, British merchants soon encountered severe limits on the possible expansion of exports. Demand for many of the manufactured goods in which Britain specialized (such as heavy textiles) either did not exist or was satiated, given the small size and wealth of Latin American populations. Rather, interest grew in investment in Latin America, which would create profits and new markets by expanding the productive capacities of the American republics as exporters to Britain.

In Argentina and Brazil in the second quarter of the nineteenth century — and later in certain other countries such as Chile, Bolivia, Uruguay, and Mexico — the British economic presence expanded fairly continuously, centering around large-scale investments of capital and the immigration of British business people to help manage it. Although the actual number of British immigrants to Latin America was never large, they were of vital significance in the establishment of new industries, many of them dependent upon the British economy. In Argentina, for example, British immigrants in the 1830s and 1840s pioneered in the sheep- and cattle-raising businesses. The latter became, with large British capital investment and the invention of the refrigerated ship, Argentina's largest export industry after the 1860s and Britain's main source of meat. Later in the century, newer and larger immigrant groups entered Argentina — Germans, French, and above all Italians. These newcomers partially displaced British immigrants from their primary position, but this did not change the British orientation of Argentina's economy. Finance and shipping remained largely in British hands throughout the period of rapid Argentine economic development up to the First World War.

The heavy involvement of British (and to a lesser extent, French) economic interests in Argentina was a major factor in the repeated foreign political interventions in Argentina. The most spectacular of these, the blockade of Buenos Aires by the British and French from 1845 to 1847, was occasioned by the dictator Rosas' adoption of tariff protection and by fears for the security of particular British and French economic interests. The main concern of British policy toward Argentina was to see that the complex of British economic interests, especially investments, was not substantially damaged either by unfriendly Argentine governments or by segments of Argentine society that the government could not control. Long-term British policy, to the extent that there was one, favored the establishment in Argentina of the kind of stable political regime that existed in the United States.

The relationship of Britain — and later Western Europe and the United States — to the most "progressive" Latin American countries thus took on much more the character of informal, although not unconscious, economic domination than it did of formal, consistent political interference. This economic domination was a by-product of European industrialization, which turned portions of Latin America into a periphery of a largely European industrial center within the expanding world economy. Economic development in Argentina or Brazil meant, almost by definition, a tightening of economic links with Europe and an increase in the extent to which the fortunes of local business and the lives of inhabitants were influenced — at times controlled — by events occurring in European markets. Since Britain was the first industrialized country, it was the first to become the center to Latin America's periphery, acting simultaneously as primary exporter, importer, and source of capital. This growth of economic dependency made whatever economic and political conditions prevailed in Britain affect the informal Latin American dependencies, without a reciprocal influence except where economic and political conditions in Britain elicited it. Since it was essential for political parties in Britain, largely regardless of their composition, to seek the support of business interests and of middle-class opinion after 1832, British governments tended to undertake sporadic political actions in Latin America to support British economic interests there in the name of "free trade," without formal colonial involvement that would have engendered domestic opposition.

French Involvement

British industrial and financial dominance did not, of course, last forever. Even before full-scale industrialization in other European countries, British trade and investment supremacy was challenged in Latin America and elsewhere. The first real challenge came in the 1830s and 1840s from France, although, except in the Near East, it was economically a relatively weak challenge until late in the nineteenth century.[27] French bankers did, however, make direct investments in Mexico, Argentina, Brazil, and other countries and lent money to Latin American governments. Small French merchant and banking communities appeared in major Latin American urban centers, their prestige enhanced by the importance of France as the cultural model for Latin American elites. The French government also attempted, on the whole less successfully than the British, to intervene in Latin American politics — particularly in Mexico and Argentina. French economic penetration of Latin America increased greatly during the period of rapid French industrialization in the 1850s and 1860s.

Despite the similarity between France's and Britain's economic positions in Latin America, there was one spectacular instance of a difference: France's attempt to conquer Mexico between 1862 and 1867. The domestic political contexts of imperialism in Britain and France underlay the difference. When the Mexican government defaulted on its debts to European banks, the British and French governments agreed to a naval demonstration at Vera Cruz in 1861, taking advantage of the preoccupation of the United States with its civil war. Such a limited action was within the range of normal British responses to this kind of problem, although only barely. But the government of Napoleon III, which was looking for a foreign venture that would appeal to domestic nationalist feeling and create new opportunities for French business, pushed the dispute further than the British were willing to go in order to create the pretext for an invasion of Mexico in 1862. The story of the initial French successes, the setting up of the Austrian puppet-ruler Maximilian as emperor, and the eventual failure of the French due to republican resistance and pressure from the United States is well known.[28] For our purposes, the interesting point is that a fairly common international financial incident, which would normally in the case of Britain alone have led to no more than a naval demonstration, resulted in a full-scale imperialist attack because of French domestic politics, especially the need perceived by Napoleon III for internal consensus based on external aggression.

After the mid-1870s, other countries besides Britain and France became deeply involved in the economies of the Latin American countries. The effects of the "dependency" relationship between Latin America and Europe on the direction of Latin American economic development became increasingly pronounced. Among the major historical questions that arise with respect to the later period are the issue of the extent to which economic dependency retarded full, balanced economic development in Latin America and also the question of the extent to which "dependent elites" in the Latin America states helped to maintain their countries' dependency. We shall turn to these questions in chapter 5.

INDIA: THE EXCEPTION

Our discussions of Latin America, Algeria, and the white dominions have covered the dominant modes of European imperialism before 1860 and their relationships to broader economic and social developments. We have seen that France diverged from the standard imperial ideology that was in force in Britain between 1815 and 1860, mainly for domestic political reasons. But just as Britain led Europe in establishing the fashion in economic theory throughout the nineteenth century, so too did the most prominent current concepts in British thought on colonies and policy toward the underdeveloped world set the model for imperial thought elsewhere. In "progressive" economic circles throughout Europe before 1860 or 1870, French colonialism in Algeria appeared to be a severe aberration.

There did exist accepted deviations from the norm. One of these was the Dutch "culture system" of direct colonial rule, investment, and economic development that the government of the Netherlands applied to Indonesia — particularly Java — from 1830 onward. This system aroused considerable comment, mostly favorable, in economic circles even though it went against the dominant theme in colonial thought, which was to devalue direct colonial rule as an instrument of economic modernization. But the classic, and by far most important, case of an early nineteenth-century colonial development that went almost completely against the ideological currents of the time without overtly challenging them was British India.

British-Indian Relations in the Early Nineteenth Century

By 1815, Britain had extended its paramountcy in India into the central plains by subduing the warlike Mahratta nation. Until the early nineteenth century, there was some justice to the adage that the British empire in India had been acquired in a fit of absence of mind. By the end of the Mahratta wars, however, this was patently untrue. Although there existed no central strategy, or even intention, in London to expand the East India Company's control, and although the fiction was maintained of Britain's being drawn unwillingly into situations that could only be resolved by taking power, the expansion of British India displayed in fact a high degree of purposeful motivation and systematic planning by authorities in India. In addition, the home authorities forced on British India an increasingly authoritarian and centralized system of control throughout the first half of the century. The reasons for these developments, so contrary to early nineteenth-century colonial orthodoxy, lay in the peculiarities of Britain's relationship with India.[29]

One aspect of this relationship arose from a combination of British political control in India and the Industrial Revolution. In the late eighteenth and early nineteenth centuries, it became British policy to reduce the export of cotton cloth from India, up until then the world's largest cotton producer. Indian cotton competed with British cotton, which could not be permitted. A combination of British economic policy and the availability of cheap Manchester cotton turned India into a major importer of cotton cloth and an exporter of raw cotton — in other words, an economic dependency of Britain. Unlike the situation in many colonies, there really was a good reason for British control over India; an ignoble reason, perhaps, but a reason for all that.

The reduction of Indian export industries created a number of severe dilemmas for the British. The Indian economy could only be controlled if British power could be strongly maintained, and this required expenditures on military forces that the home government was unwilling to make. The cost of the East India Company administration and army had to be met out of the company's tax receipts. But cutting off valuable cotton exports reduced potential tax revenues, both from export taxes and land taxes.

The answer to the dilemma was found in a number of ways. Starting with Cornwallis' tax reform in Bengal in the 1790s, tax reform and bureaucratization of the financial system occurred in areas of direct company control. With respect to the "native states" in one way or another "allied" to the British, a succession of governors-general pushed hard to increase financial contributions to the company by pressuring Indian rulers to place their tax systems under British supervision, by exacting levies of troops or funds to support them, and by annexing recalcitrant native states whenever pretexts presented themselves. This last policy reached its height under the most "reforming" of pre-Mutiny governors, Lord Dalhousie (1848-1856), and helped to touch off the Mutiny itself. Some of the motives for British India's territorial expansion into the Punjab (in modern Pakistan) probably derived from the Indian government's desire to exact "contributions" and "reparations" and to extend its tax base. The need for revenue also justified another nineteenth-century anomaly: at the height of the free-trade period in Britain, British India charged import duties in order to keep its government solvent.

Company Reforms

Starting in the 1830s, the East India Company sponsored a comprehensive program of social and economic development in India that had the intended effect of tying India more closely to the outside world and increasing its trade. The ultimate reason for the project was to increase company revenue, but this was to be done by turning India into the kind of economic partner most desired according to mid-nineteenth century economic thinking without simultaneously creating Indian economic competition.[30] This program was largely the product of a remarkable group of liberal political reformers and economists, both inside the East India Company's central apparatus in England and outside of it. The group — which included economist James Mill, historian Thomas Babington Macaulay, and civil servant C.E. Trevelyan — was supported by a host of company employees recruited according to a merit system and specifically trained for their jobs at the company's educational institution at Haileybury. Ever since the 1780s, the government controlled company had been considered a reformist institution in British politics. Partly because of that and partly because of its new, talented, middle-class bureaucracy, the company and its captive "laboratory" in India had attracted the close interest of reformist liberals and utilitarians who, among other things, wanted to demonstrate liberalism in action. In the 1830s, the company, under strong prodding from the Whig-Liberal governments after the Reform Act of 1832 and from Macaulay on the Board of Control and the governor-general's council, instituted an ambitious program of railroad building, port construction, Western-style educational reform, and civil service reconstruction. Successful attempts were also made to abolish aspects of Indian culture that Europeans found distasteful, such as *suttee* (widow-burning).

The Role of Opium

Planned social change and economic development, however, could only be regarded as a long-term solution to the British governmental dilemma in India. In the short run, it was necessary to encourage export industries that could be rapidly developed, that would not compete with British products, and that produced agricultural profits — the last so that the land tax could be raised. Tea eventually played this role, especially after the annexation of the highlands near Nepal. But in the first half of the nineteenth century, the British depended mainly upon opium.

Opium had been produced in India and exported for some time. With the occupation of India by the British, the East India Company and private traders recognized the product's potential for expanding its own market and began to buy opium for export to England. An epidemic of opium-taking began that lasted throughout the first half of the nineteenth century, brought profits to the company, and contributed to the solvency of the Indian government. But when opium's addictive properties became apparent soon after 1800, it became impolitic for the company to push opium exports to Britain openly. So it turned to developing the Chinese market. Opium was essentially "dumped" on the market in Canton from the 1820s onward. Its widespread use led to rapid increases in demand in the 1830s, and the opium merchants accordingly encouraged the production of more opium in India.

In the late 1830s the government of China decided to act. Its motives were complex. Along with a genuine concern about the effects of opium addiction on the population went the feeling that opium was the entering wedge of a vast and undesired European commercial and cultural penetration of China.[31] The Chinese government dispatched a special commissioner to

Canton who forbade the importation of opium and burned the supplies already in warehouses. The Indian and British governments responded by going to war (1839-42), since the export of opium to China was the basis of Indian solvency and could not be interfered with. The matter was put, however, before the British public as being "really" one of future general trade expansion with China. According to this view, the backward Chinese government was merely making an issue of the opium trade in order to prevent the advent of "free trade" and "civilization" in China. It was therefore under the banners of two of the preeminent slogans of nineteenth-century liberalism that Britain and India entered the Opium War against China. The war resulted in a defeat for China, the British occupation of Hong Kong, and partial Chinese acceptance of freer trade. China's defeat also marked the beginning of penetration into the country, to which we shall return in chapter 5.

The Mystique of India

With a functioning export economy, a fiscal system that was normally self-supporting, and what seemed to be a stable governmental structure, India had by mid-century fully taken up the role it was to play for several later generations: it had become the backbone of British power in the East in a political as well as an economic sense.[32] Britain's need for overwhelming military force in India had led to the Company's creation of the Indian army, a large and efficient fighting force that had attained a size of 278,000 men by 1857 (only about 45,000 of whom were Europeans). The Indian army and navy normally cost the British taxpayer not one shilling to maintain, since they were supported by the Indian revenue system. And yet the Indian army could be used not only to maintain and expand the British position in India but also to support British interests elsewhere in Asia and Africa. The Indian army did much of Britain's fighting in China, Persia, and Ethiopia, and before 1858 it was the Indian navy that gave Britain its informal paramountcy in Zanzibar and the East African coast. In other words, although India was never as essential to the well-being of Britain as British imaginations made it out to be, India did possess real value to Britain and was well worth protecting.

By the 1850s, a mystique of India was already thoroughly developed in British public opinion. It was composed of elements of reality and fiction, tied together by a kind of romantic wishful thinking that glossed over inconsistencies. India had appeal as the land of the strange and unusual. In Wilkie Collins' popular novel *The Moonstone* (1868), as in dozens of others, this appeal is manifest. The importance of India as a trading partner and a financially self-supporting strategic base also made up part of the mystique.

One reason for public exaggeration of India's importance was the growing belief, from the late 1830s on, that Russia constituted an immediate threat to British control in India. If India were threatened, then it had to be important. The Russian "threat" was actually based upon a few tentative and uncoordinated Russian military and diplomatic probes into eastern Persia and Afghanistan. Russia was under no circumstances capable of either occupying India or doing anything with the country if occupied. But it was very much in the interest of the British official elite in India to refer as much as possible to the Russian threat to justify certain of their policies — particularly the expansion to the northwest which in the 1830s and 1840s brought the area that is today Pakistan under British control. This expansion originally grew out of the desire to secure India's frontiers and to annex new sources of revenue. By the 1840s, however, many officials in India had managed to convince themselves of the reality of the Russian threat.[33]

The northwest expansion also led to the Indian government's attempt to secure Afghanistan as a puppet state in 1840-41 and to Britain's first major Indian disaster in the nineteenth century. A large Indian army force that had occupied Kabul was forced to withdraw in 1842 and then practically wiped out on the way home. The Kabul fiasco left Afghanistan independent and discredited British arms in India, but it did not put a stop to expansion. Although the home government attempted to restrain the company's Indian administration, it was faced with a constant series of *faits accomplis* as Indian governments broadened their control over border areas and annexed "allied" states. In these new areas—the Punjab (modern Pakistan), and Oudh (in north-central India, annexed in 1856)—British administration was direct and authoritarian.

The mystique of India—an amalgam of romantic economic and strategic elements—was not accepted by everyone in Britain, especially by liberals. What brought the liberals over to the support of a very illiberal despotism in India was the idea of India as the most promising new frontier in the expansion of "civilization" and progress. The comprehensive development program begun by the Company in the 1830s had not only accomplished impressive engineering feats by the 1850s, it had also been highly publicized in Britain as a justification for British imperial rule. Britain was aiding the Indians by leading them socially, culturally, and technologically into the modern world. This view corresponded well with the missionary-abolitionist impulse of Victorian Britain, and eventually evolved into the idea of imperial "trusteeship" in the twentieth century. From the 1840s onward, India also became an area of intense missionary activity, which many Company officials strongly supported as an aid to British rule and the development program. In the 1850s, many officers of the Bengal army attempted to encourage their troops to adopt Christianity—an obviously unwise move that was to have dire consequences in 1857.[34]

The Indian Mutiny

The mystique of India managed, therefore, to combine appeals to practically every important segment of British society. Little political use was as yet made of the mystique; that would await Disraeli in the 1870s. But even in the 1850s, so thoroughly developed was the India mystique that the British presence in the subcontinent had become an important part of middle- and upper-class English people's conceptions of themselves and of their society. It was thus a direct challenge to the whole structure of British social and cultural conceptions and self-esteem that confronted the British public when the news first arrived of a massive mutiny in the Bengal army in May 1857. As further reports came in of massacres of British garrisons and British women and children, the initial shock to British self-confidence turned to an almost hysterical anger, mirrored in the attitudes of British troops dispatched to put down what was soon a full-scale rebellion in north central India.[35]

The Indian Mutiny was a consequence of most of the directions in British Indian policy that we have discussed. The modernization program threatened both Muslim and Hindu status groups and offended the sensibilities of the masses. The increasing cultural pressure placed on the Bengal army, combined with the almost incredible insensitivity of its British officers, did a great deal to bring on the original mutiny among the troops. The disaster in Afghanistan demonstrated that the British were not invincible (and often not even competent), while the reckless policy of annexing central Indian states on flimsy pretexts destroyed all illusions about the ultimate purposes of the British in India. The rebellion's immediate cause was a mutiny of Indian troops at several garrisons along the middle Ganges created by a fear that new cartridges dispatched from Britain were soaked in animal grease (which was probably true) and that this was a British plot to defile both Hindus and Muslims when the ends of the cartridges were bitten off. The last suspicion was not correct, but given the recent British attack on Indian cultures, it was not unreasonable. The greased cartridge issue created a grievance that allowed disparate groups to rebel in concert. It summarized the feelings of many Indians about British rule and brought to the surface the deepest of resentments.

Whatever the reason for the initial mutiny, it soon spread. Whole regiments of troops killed their European officers, marched to Delhi, which was sacked and turned into the mutineers' capital, and besieged the remaining European troops along the Ganges in a few forts — one of which, Cawnpore, surrendered only to have its garrison and dependents brutally massacred. Many of the native states of central India joined the rebellion — especially those obviously next in line for annexation. Britain's hold on the subcontinent seemed very loose indeed.

British rule was saved by a variety of factors. The rebellion did not spread beyond part of the Bengal army. This — and the tying down of mutineers in sieges before the various British garrisons — allowed the disunity and lack of command structure of the rebellion to do their work. The initial advantages of surprise were not followed up, the other sections of the Indian army were brought against the rebels, and large reinforcements began arriving from Britain by the end of the summer of 1857. Throughout the first half of 1858, British armies rampaged through central India, relieving sieges, pushing back mutineers and the armies of the rebel states, and in the process conducting a hideous massacre in the villages and towns through which they passed. It was not so much the Mutiny itself as the atrocities committed on both sides that made 1857 a particular source of bitterness between Indians and Britons for the next century.

Results of the Mutiny

In 1858, with the suppression of the rebellion, the British masters of the subcontinent were forced to take stock of their position. It was necessary first to end the excesses of the British military against the Indian population. This was done by the home government and the governor-general, Lord Canning, whose wise policy of "clemency" earned him a nickname and the hatred of much of the British population of India. Formally, at least, the stage was set for a sort of reconciliation, although an uneasy one.

Several administrative changes followed from the Great Mutiny. Much of the blame for the Mutiny was cast (probably incorrectly) upon the anomalous position of the East India Company. In 1858 the Company was deprived of its political functions and the Indian government was placed directly under the British government. The program of radical cultural change was replaced by a new view of development. While many of the programs instituted earlier were continued, especially the public works projects, their aims and the spirit in which they were conducted altered considerably. No longer were the elite classes of India to be made over rapidly into Europeans; neither were they to be given any substantial share in the conduct of political and economic affairs. The British worked diligently over the next decades to establish an effective government bureaucracy in India on highly technocratic and authoritarian lines.[36] The operation of the bureaucracy (staffed by the new Indian Civil Service) required the training of Indians to fill lower and middle governmental positions and analogous ranks of the educated professions. But the Civil Service, like other aspects of elite Indian social life, was to be segregated. The Indian Civil Service was established in such a way that Indians could not in practice enter higher, policymaking levels. While other areas of imperial society in India were not so thoroughly closed, approximations of this pattern abounded and were supported by an accelerated immigration of English personnel to fill new management jobs. Thus the economic development and partial Westernization of India continued, but led immediately to perceptions of alienation by Western-educated Indians — a circumstance of great import for the future.

EXPLORATION AND IMPERIALISM

The exploration of areas previously unknown to Europeans has, since the fifteenth century, played an important role in the history of European imperialism. Obviously, most of the constituent segments of the "old" empires were places explored during and after the fifteenth century. Even in the early periods of imperialism, however, exploration played another role: it attracted public attention in Europe, often much more effectively

than did the later processes of conquest and economic exploitation. Explorers could easily be represented as heroes and their
exploits could be conveyed in the continually popular genre of
travel literature. The popular image of explorers and exploration was evidence of the development of European public opinion and could be used to serve political and economic ends.

In the late eighteenth and nineteenth centuries, exploration
and travel literature retained its public popularity and its potential connections with politics. The heroes of exploration,
however, were endowed with new qualities consistent with the
values and ideologies of a radically altered society. In Britain
especially, explorers became major symbols that few subsequent media creations have been able to match. Explorers
played a role in bringing on the great wave of imperial expansion in the second half of the nineteenth century, although
perhaps not a preeminent one.

The prototype of the modern explorer-hero was Captain
James Cook (1728-79).[37] As commander of three British
government expeditions to the Pacific, Cook became an immensely popular figure throughout Europe. His reputation,
though merited in many respects, was probably out of proportion to the immediate significance of his work. His voyages
(1768-79) were models of seamanship and, except for the last,
exploratory strategy. Cook visited Tahiti; explored, charted,
and claimed New Zealand and eastern Australia; brought scien-
tists to examine Pacific flora, fauna, and ethnography; explored the Antarctic region; and explored Hawaii and the
northern Pacific. In the long run, this was important and highly
impressive under any circumstances. The immediate objects of
his voyages — the observation of the transit of Venus in 1769
and the discovery of the Northwest Passage on his last
voyage — were not attained (though not through Cook's fault).
Cook's voyages did not lead immediately to colonization (except perhaps for New South Wales), and Cook's and his
associates' reports of the economic potential of the Pacific
islands were vastly inflated — a common failing among

nineteenth-century explorers as well. This is not to diminish Cook's personal stature and importance in Pacific history, but only to indicate that his reputation was based on the way in which his image corresponded to the predominant ideologies of the late eighteenth century, not really on his achievements.

The cult of Captain Cook had many dimensions, more or less correlated with several major currents of popular thought. Cook's humble origins, lack of formal education, and struggle to advance to officer grade from the enlisted ranks of the navy appealed to new liberal beliefs in the "career open to talent." Despite Cook's rather limited scientific knowledge, he was represented as a self-made scientist, much like Benjamin Franklin, thus corresponding to the popular vogue of practical science. Cook obviously appealed to British nationalists. Most strangely, Cook became a hero of the fervent new humanitarian movement — in most of whose concerns he took no apparent interest. He was an unusually humane and thoughtful ship's captain, but that was all. However, his accounts of his dealings with non-Europeans could be — and were — used as examples of proper "enlightened" relations between "civilized" and "uncivilized" peoples.

The pattern of the humanitarian explorer-hero was further developed in Britain, France, and Germany in conjunction with the exploration of Africa and the growth of the abolitionist movement. Mungo Park (1771-1806), a young Scottish physician who reached the Niger River in 1796 after a harrowing journey at the behest of the African Association, was the next popular explorer.[38] His account of his travels was well written, engagingly ingenuous, and modest; it emphasized the emerging popular virtues of duty and self-effacement. Park also became a hero of the "legitimate trade" movement, an aspect of abolitionism. According to the legitimate trade argument, the best way to end the slave trade in West Africa was to establish alternative forms of trade with Europe — a role palm oil eventually played on the coast. Despite the fact that Park's account of the Niger region was not exactly encouraging about economic possibilities, his visit was seized upon as a step in opening the interior of West Africa to legitimate commerce. Park was eventually killed in 1806 while leading another expedition down the Niger.

The nineteenth century saw a host of explorers of a similar sort — many of them medical doctors like Park, many directly or indirectly connected to the growing British missionary societies, some of them national as well as humanitarian heroes. Alexander von Humboldt (1769-1859) set a new literary and scientific standard for travelers, although he cannot properly be regarded as an explorer of regions previously unknown to Europeans. With Humboldt and several, mostly German, contemporaries, the scientific study of geography became a part of the ethos of exploration, and what can be regarded as an explorers' career pattern emerged.

The culminating figure in pre-1870 exploration — the person who, more than any other, consciously drew together in his own person the elements of geographic discovery as a public activity — was the Scottish explorer, missionary, and physician, David Livingstone (1813-1873).[39] In his long and often extraordinarily difficult journeys in south, central and east Africa in the 1850s and 1860s, Livingstone revealed an immense amount about African geography to Europeans. It was, however, his conscious use of his explorations in his published works and speeches in Britain and his (possibly unconscious) development of his public personality as a martyr to the cause of civilization and antislavery that gave him his greatest importance in the history of imperialism. Livingstone's work, coming at a time when the abolitionist movement was at its peak of popularity, helped to direct this influential segment of British popular sentiment toward Africa and toward European interference there. While Livingstone was not a conscious imperialist, his insistence on the need for intervention in Africa on moral grounds paved the way for future imperial expansion. Many of the famous explorers of the late nineteenth century — Stanley, Peters, to some extent even Joseph Thomson on his last journeys — were much more thoroughgoing imperialists than Livingstone, but none was as able as Livingstone to engage popular attention and the forces of humanitarianism. Livingstone and humanitarianism did not cause late Victorian imperialism. They did, however, help to create an ideological and political context for imperialism, giving an acceptable justification for expansion into areas which were at that time not economically worth the effort of occupying.

FOUR

The European Origins of the "New Imperialism," 1860-1900

O NE OF THE MAJOR ISSUES IN the historiography of nineteenth-century imperialism concerns the nature of the relationship between the era of "informal" imperialism during the first two-thirds of the century and the period of rapid formal imperial expansion — the "New Imperialism" — that followed. Whatever the change was that occurred in the 1860s and 1870s, it was clearly a relative one. Informal modes of imperialism did not cease, and of course formal expansion had taken place earlier in the century. The New Imperialism was rather a matter of the amount of colonial expansion and also a matter of changing attitudes and ideologies.[1]

REASONS FOR THE NEW IMPERIALISM

The traditional conception of the New Imperialism was that it resulted from the appearance of essentially new forces in Europe that suddenly directed European energies into overseas colonization and into other forms of conscious imperialism. The nature of these forces has been disputed, but the facts of a real break with the immediate past and of a European origin for

75

the New Imperialism were generally accepted by historians until the 1950s — as indeed they were by most Europeans in the late nineteenth century itself.

Most contemporaries of the new imperial expansion tended to view it as a result of recent economic and diplomatic changes. Joseph Chamberlain (British colonial secretary from 1895 to 1903), for example, argued that formal imperialism was necessary for Britain because of the relative decline of the British share of the world's export trade and the rise of German, American, and French economic competition.[2] Unless Britain acquired secure colonial markets for its industrial products and secure sources of raw materials, the other industrial states would take them for themselves and would precipitate a more rapid decline of British business, power, and standards of living. The foreign economic threat was intensified by Germany's rise as a great military and political power after 1871, its adoption of tariff protection in 1879, its acquisition of a colonial empire in 1884-85, and its building of a powerful navy after 1898. If protective measures (through empire-building) were not taken, Britain's economy would disintegrate and it would be replaced as the paramount world power by Germany, or possibly the United States.

In Germany and France, basically similar ideas were given different slants. German imperialists argued that Britain's world power position gave the British unfair advantages on international markets, thus limiting Germany's economic growth and threatening its security. French imperialists argued similarly.[3] But generally, the need for colonies and secure trading areas was seen as a result of recent changes in the European and world economies and in the balance of power.

To express the prevailing view of what the New Imperialism was does not, however, explain why it appeared. The very change in attitudes that allowed such views to become popular from the 1870s onward represents a break with the past, not an explanation. Why did prevailing conceptions, and thus policies, change? As we saw in chapter 1, there are several classic answers to this question.

Marxist Explanations

To most Marxist historians and analysts, including Lenin, late Victorian imperialism was a consequence of the stage of economic development to which Western Europe had progressed by the late nineteenth century. The increasingly crisis prone capitalist economy had caused a flight of capital overseas, and the new monopoly capitalists invented the nationalistic and strategic elements of imperialist theory in order to hoodwink public and governmental opinion so as to get European governments to bear the burden of securing overseas investments.[4] Imperialism was thus merely another form of the same phenomenon that produced national and international cartels, and in the end would prove even more futile than these attempts to solve the inevitable crisis of capitalism. Neither cartels nor imperialism could permanently alleviate the chaos that lay at the heart of capitalism, nor could they stave off the proletarian revolution. Imperialism was particularly ineffective because the political means employed in its fulfillment led to international tension and war. Although the intentions of organized capital were largely international, the political means available were merely national, thus creating a fatal contradiction.

When world war finally came in 1914, many Marxists naturally expected that a capitalist collapse and a workers' revolution would follow immediately. However, the workers of the Western European countries showed themselves to be no more immune to patriotic and imperialist appeals than anyone else, and the capitalistic economies showed more resilience than anyone (including the capitalists) had expected. Marxists, especially Lenin, began to turn away from the idea of the great imperialist war as the crisis of capitalism and toward the "world revolution" concept. According to this view, capitalism's life in

Europe and the United States was unnaturally prolonged by maintaining apparently high standards of living for workers there at the expense of overseas workers.[5] Revolution would thus in the end commence outside of Western Europe and spread to the industrialized countries.

The classic Marxist theories of late nineteenth-century imperialism have evidence to support them. The flight of capital from Europe was a very real phenomenon. Lenin's view of the origins of imperialism was similar to that of many imperialists and business people at the time. To them, imperial expansion was a possible solution to the problem of the "overproduction" that seemed to cause depressions, especially the severe one that commenced in 1873. The behavior of many business people who invested overseas and their attempts to get their governments to back them up (as for example in the case of Cecil Rhodes in South Africa) seem to correspond rather well to Lenin's model.

On the other hand, most of the classic Marxist accounts tend to fail when they are applied to the complexities of real imperialist expansion in specific parts of the world. In Africa (exclusive of South Africa), for example, the amount of capital investment by Europeans was quite small both before and after the partitions of the 1880s and 1890s, and the companies involved in commerce there were small and politically insignificant.[6] Although some of these companies did in fact act in the manner prescribed by Lenin, their abilities to get their governments to support them cannot be explained by their own tiny influence in domestic politics. Other, ultimately more important, factors were at work, factors of which the tropical trading companies were able to take advantage.

Other Theories

Other major theories purporting to explain the New Imperialism concentrate on the "other factors" that Lenin considered to be merely extensions of the underlying economic causes. For example, J.A. Hobson, an English liberal writing at the time of the fierce debate on imperialism during the Boer War, emphasized changes in European social structures and attitudes as well as capital flow, although his analysis of the flight of capital and the rise of monopoly capitalism influenced Lenin.[7] Hobson's view of imperialism extended beyond the aims of monopoly capitalists to other elite groups, although he suggested that British elites in particular showed increasing signs of amalgamation with each other. Each of Britain's major elites had something to gain from imperial expansion: big business wanted public and governmental support to secure overseas investments against competition, government officials wanted more jobs, military officers desired promotion, and the landed upper classes — threatened by a decline in income and status — wanted opportunities for employment for their sons.[8] The elite in general also wanted to use imperialism as a means of rallying the support of the working class through nationalist appeals, thus heading off the trade union movement and incipient socialism. To Hobson, as to Lenin, the rapid turn to imperialism in the late nineteenth century was also a result of closely spaced economic depressions that adversely affected many elite groups. Hobson's explanation for imperialism suffers from many of the same problems of evidence that Lenin's does and is on the whole less consistent, but it does take a greater number of social factors into account.

In his work on imperialism just after World War I, the economist Joseph Schumpeter took a different view. He concentrated on psychological factors, emphasizing the rabid nationalism and the irrational goals that seemed to characterize imperialism.[9] These he explained partly as a result of the pressures of modern society which required an outlet or catharsis, and partly as a product of the premodern, barbarous psychological traits of the old aristocracies of Europe. The latter, deprived of their traditional scope for action and military aggression, turned to modern colonial empires for substitutes. Although Schumpeter's ideas shared a great deal of social analysis with Hobson's, the two theories diverged on the relationship of capitalism to imperialism. Schumpeter argued that imperialism was an "atavism," a social and psychological throwback to an earlier age, and had nothing to do with modern capitalism.

Schumpeter's theory, unfortunately, is difficult to prove or disprove. In many countries the old elites clearly had a hand in imperial policy, but it is very difficult to find an example in which theirs was the predominant role. In Belgium, for example, the old aristocracy seems for the most part to have been anti-imperialist, while the main exponents of empire were King Leopold's business associates and the middle class in general.[10] Nevertheless, Schumpeter did bring to the fore an important component of the imperialist movements of the late nineteenth century: their emotional public character, often involving the eliciting of mass hysteria that could at times (perhaps including 1914) drag the European governments into actions they might not otherwise have undertaken.

There is also a whole tradition of diplomatic explanations of imperialism which seek to explain it as a response to the breakdown of the "concert of Europe" caused by German unification.[11] According to this view, the imperial explosion of the 1880s was created by the desire of European states for compensation for losses in the new structure of international relations. We shall examine this view in later chapters.

As we have seen in the introduction, a new school of historians has recently appeared which has, in a sense, combined and transcended the approaches of Lenin, Hobson, and Schumpeter and has focused attention on changes in European social structures as the prime causes of the New Imperialism. Most of these historians have concentrated on the "social imperialist" arguments of people like Joseph Chamberlain, which they interpret as attempts to secure government support for business and other elite interests (not primarily in the form of colonies) by use of the imperial question, and also as attempts to head off the rise of socialism.[12]

The "social imperialism" analyses are best discussed in individual national contexts. In general, however, we can say that although this school has succeeded in linking the different social, economic, and political factors behind imperialism in Europe and has given a coherent explanation of why the New Imperialism appeared to constitute a discontinuity with the past, there are certain weaknesses in its approach. It seems likely that, in many cases, the importance of the social imperialist element in the motivations of policymakers and the seriousness with which politicians advanced social-imperialist ideas have been exaggerated. More fundamentally, the social-imperialist historians, like many Marxists, probably overvalue the imperatives of position within a social structure as an explanation of motives. Not all members of a particular elite group perceived social change and behaved in the same ways in the 1880s. A whole social realm of politics intervenes between the general structure of a society and the formal government actions of that society, and it is difficult to show that the political realm is entirely controlled by basic social structure.

Imperialism and Political Fragmentation

The approach that we shall take toward the domestic roots of the New Imperialism is based upon an extension of the social imperialist analysis. It will be argued that, while social and economic changes in Europe had a great deal to do with the New Imperialism, its distinctive features — the things that made it "new" — were mostly the results of long-term political development. Many, but not all, of these developments resulted from major socioeconomic changes, but the intermediate area of political change was where the conscious motive for imperialism lay. And politics can have a historical character of its own quite apart from socioeconomic changes. Political ideologies developed in response to particular economic conditions can continue to affect politics long after the economic conditions change.

The New Imperialism most emphatically did not mean a change in the gradual extension of economic connections from the "center" of the industrial countries to an overseas "periphery." Informal influence remained part of Europe's

normal relations with the world overseas and displayed
remarkable continuity with the past. What constituted the New
Imperialism was rather something laid, as it were, over the top
of this layer of informal or economic imperialism — a series of
newly dominant ideologies, attitudes, motives, and political actions directed, in part, toward formal imperial expansion.
These new political factors were responses to a wide variety of
pressures placed by the circumstances of the times upon European political systems, pressures which were not always derived
directly from Europe's overseas involvements. It was the fact
that much of the New Imperialism was the product of initial
and not-very-successful reactions to temporary domestic
political problems that gave it its curious sense of unreality and
self-contradiction when applied to policymaking, and helped to
guarantee that European rule in the colonies seized in the late
nineteenth century would last such an astoundingly short time.

Many of the socioeconomic changes and political problems
that encouraged European politicians to turn to imperialism in
the 1870s and 1880s were specific to particular countries, but
some were quite general. Of the latter, probably the most important was the problem of political fragmentation, experienced by practically all modernizing societies in the last two
hundred years. In the nineteenth century, political systems
faced with increasingly difficult social and economic conditions
also began to confront the perplexing problem that — with more
and more interest groups clamoring for attention, with elite
groups splintering and multiplying, and with more people par-
ticipating in politics — it was becoming difficult to achieve consensus about national politics and to undertake consistent
political action. And yet, because an industrializing society continually generates new social problems and new interest groups
making demands on government, political action was continually required. Political parties and other elite groups had to
accede to at least some of the demands for action. Yet they
found it difficult to decide which to choose, since they were
likely to have to pay some kind of political price no matter how
they acted.

Political fragmentation was recognized everywhere in Western Europe in the nineteenth century and regarded by politicians as a serious development. This recognition went through different stages in different countries. In Britain, in the period from about 1828 to 1848, the political system displayed many classical signs of fragmentation (conflicting elite groups calling for popular support, the entry of new groups into political participation, and so forth). The effects of fragmentation were, however, dealt with relatively efficiently through the rapid evolution of representative political institutions, by the transformation of the parties into bodies that integrated divergent social and economic interests, and by the whole set of social attitudes and cultural traits that made up Victorian culture and that helped to create an ideological basis for consensus in the 1850s and 1860s.[13] Commencing with the unstable economic situation of the 1860s and the confused social conditions of the 1870s, the British political system again showed severe signs of fragmentation as neither Victorian political institutions nor Victorian ideology proved capable of creating a support base for decisive political action. Disraeli unveiled a policy of imperialism in the 1870s in large part as a means of overcoming the political fragmentation that he perceived as a threat to orderly government and to social peace in Britain.

The causes of fragmentation in France and Germany in the 1870s differed somewhat. France experienced the chaos that followed a lost war, together with the social and political conflicts of a rapidly industrializing country. Germany experienced the latter, in addition to the political effects of imperfect national unification. In both cases, as in Britain, these conditions led politicians to espouse already existing, and very similar, ideologies of imperialism, around which it was hoped that a degree of consensus could be created.

Of course, many of the parties, governments, and interest groups that, sooner or later, came to employ imperialism in domestic politics had specific concerns, often economic ones, that they desired to advance. In some cases, such as the British interest in South Africa, these concerns far outweighed considerations of basic problems of domestic politics. But these exceptions were rare. In most cases in which important interest groups adopted imperialist platforms, they did so mainly in order to create a consensus behind some policy that was only (at best) tangentially related to formal overseas empire. Once again, from the standpoint taken here, late Victorian imperialism was mostly a political reaction to a political change that was in turn the result of rapid socioeconomic change. But the connection between socioeconomic change and imperialism was usually not direct, and this mediation of politics strongly determined Europe's late colonial history. The opportunity of using imperialism in this way was provided by the pre-existence of imperialist ideologies that could be quickly worked together into apparently coherent wholes, and also by the growing number of contacts that European countries had with the overseas world.

This approach has implications for the question of continuity in imperialism. In our sense, the New Imperialism was really something new, not so much because the actual relations between Europe and the overseas world underwent a sharp change in the 1870s, or even because the ideologies of imperialism in Europe changed greatly (at least as far as their separate elements were concerned). What made the difference was the change in the political context of imperialism in Europe, in the use to which imperialist ideologies were put, and in the increased intensity with which particular interest groups with overseas concerns could place pressure on parties and governments that had committed themselves, for largely internal political reasons, to general imperialist goals. Thus, economic relations between Europeans and indigenous elites in soon-to-be-colonized areas — which many historians have emphasized as a *cause* of the New Imperialism — become instead a secondary force helping to determine the *direction* of imperial expansion. Changes in international relations can be seen, not really as direct causes of imperialism, but as additional pressures on fragmenting European political systems that, together with other pressures, encouraged politicians to try imperialism as a means of building consensus.

The specific socioeconomic phenomena that created or exacerbated political fragmentation in Europe in the late nineteenth century varied somewhat among the major European nations, as did the forces that led directly to imperialism. We shall examine the individual European countries separately in the rest of this chapter. Certain factors, however, appear to have been sufficiently common to most of the states that they turned to imperialism almost simultaneously. The gap between the early and late industrial developers had narrowed considerably by the 1870s, so that the social conflicts experienced at any single time by different Western European states tended increasingly to be similar. The great economic depression of 1873 struck all the industrial countries.[14] Aftershocks of the depression were felt everywhere until the mid-1890s. With respect to the ideology of imperialism, there was a pronounced tendency for the ideas and the language of British imperialism to be borrowed and adapted for use in France, Germany, and Italy. With some exceptions (mainly in Germany), the vocabulary and ideology of imperialism were nearly uniform throughout Europe.

THE NEW IMPERIALISM IN BRITAIN

In 1865, a select committee of the British House of Commons commented, in the course of a report on the extent of official British involvement with West Africa, that "all further extension of territory or assumption of Government, or new treaties offering protection to native tribes, would be inexpedient."[15] The committee recommended that areas which Britain presently ruled in West Africa should be prepared for independence. Only seven years later, Benjamin Disraeli, Conservative leader of the opposition and soon to be prime minister once again, said in his famous "Crystal Palace" speech that:

... there is another and second great object of the Tory party ... [which is] to uphold the Empire of England. ... It has been shown with precise mathematical demonstration that there never was a jewel in the Crown of England so truly costly as the possession of India.[16]

Disraeli went on to argue against Britain's withdrawal from any colony and in favor of imperial "consolidation."

It is of course true that neither of these positions completely represented contemporary thought on colonies. There were imperialists in 1865, and there were certainly plenty of anti-imperialists in 1872. But it is also true that these quotations express substantial political consensus. (In the case of Disraeli's speech, the sentiments probably slightly precede consensus.) They stand on opposite sides of a wide ideological gulf; between them, the age of the New Imperialism in Britain had dawned.

The difference between the climates of opinion in the 1860s and the 1870s was noted (and exaggerated) by observers at the time. To liberals who became imperialists in the 1870s — men like the radical politician Sir Charles Dilke and the historian John Seeley — the New Imperialism was but the next stage in the cultural, economic, and political progress of Britain and therefore also, by an extension that was obvious to them, of the rest of the world. Dilke claimed that a "Greater Britain" already existed beyond the shores of the British Isles: culturally in North America and Australia, and economically throughout the world.[17] British expansion was a lawful aspect of human progress, beneficial to all concerned and involving many humanitarian obligations for Britain. Dilke argued that this Greater Britain should be formalized in cooperative arrangements between states to ensure a more efficient pursuit of "progress."

Dilke's popular, optimistic version of imperialism was, of course, a far cry from the almost hysterical xenophobia of other imperialists, especially later in the century. Almost all British imperialist ideologies, however, shared certain assumptions: that Britain was in the vanguard of real "progress," that Britons were racially or culturally superior to other peoples, and that they had a "duty" to assist the advancement of other peoples and a concomitant right to exploit them. Intellectually, late Victorian imperialism was a collection of characteristic nineteenth-century social ideas carried beyond the limits that had been assumed for them in the 1850s and 1860s. The Victorian intellectual and moral synthesis, British nationalism, the concept of continuous economic development, the new intellectual fad of Darwinism — all of these had their effects on the outward ideological forms taken by the New Imperialism. Except perhaps for Darwinism, there was nothing particularly new in any of this. What was new was their combination into a group of comprehensive imperialist ideologies.

Economic Pressures

None of this, of course, explains why this change in attitude, and subsequently in national policy, occurred. The forces that led to the New Imperialism are to be found neither in the progress of British "civilization" nor in the development of major intellectual trends, but rather, as we have seen, in the response of the British political system to the new conditions of the 1870s. Among the new conditions were the short-term effects of the severe economic depression of 1873, which had followed fifteen years of great economic instability. The post-1873 period saw a reemergence of militant working-class organization and cycles of large strikes. Business people after 1873 in practically every industry suffered from lengthy periods of low profit rates and price deflation.

Long-term problems also became apparent in the 1870s; many were, in fact, exaggerated. Britain, like most other industrial countries, had long since begun to run an unfavorable balance of trade (which was increasingly offset, however, by the income from overseas investments). Much more seriously, British manufacturers in the staple industries of the Industrial Revolution were beginning to experience real competition abroad.[18] The German textiles and metals industries, for example, had by the 1870s surpassed those of Britain in organization and technical efficiency and had wrested most of the German market from the British. Within a quarter century, the

German metals and engineering industries would be producing heavily for the English market as well. Competition was, of course, only to be expected, but it struck at one of the basic assumptions of mid-Victorian economic thought: that Britain was the sole "workshop of the world." And British businesses were not responding well to competition. Stuck with outmoded physical plants and outmoded forms of business organization, British export industry now felt the less favorable effects of being the first to modernize. British industry suffered also from poor economic decision-making. This included a comparative lack of support for technological training and the tendency of financial institutions, which were organizationally separate from heavy industry, to invest abroad rather than in Britain. Britain's increasing export problems became apparent in the 1870s and were confounded with the effects of the post-1873 depression to create a kind of psychological panic in business circles.

It has become customary among historians to ascribe many of the most significant European political developments of the late nineteenth century — especially imperialism — to the effects of the Great Depression.[19] In Britain, as in Germany, business organizations obviously hurt by the adverse economic conditions of the late 1870s were among the most prominent advocates of government action to protect British interests abroad. The matter is complicated by the fact that in Britain, as elsewhere, the commercial enterprises most in need of government support abroad during bad times and most insistent about the establishment of colonies as reserve markets tended to be small, economically marginal, and politically weak. Some big financial and industrial organizations also supported imperial expansion, but seldom for the reasons that they gave publicly. Either their immediate objectives for formal expansion were more limited than they said but unacceptably selfish in the light of public opinion (for example, banks wanting returns on their loans to Egypt in 1882), or else they hoped to use imperialism to encourage governments to do other things that had little to do with the formal imperialism that they outwardly professed. While business conditions in the late nineteenth century may have provided part of the climate and some conscious motives for the New Imperialism, they cannot be regarded as the main immediate cause of imperialism itself. Rather, the depression was one of a number of factors causing political problems in a fragmented polity, problems to which segments of the British political system attempted to respond by turning to imperialism. The depression also unquestionably increased the degree of fragmentation in British politics. But by itself, the post-1873 depression does not explain the great gulf between the anticolonialism predominant in Britain in the mid-nineteenth century and the New Imperialism of the late 1870s and the 1880s.

Political Pressures

Other sources of specific problems in British politics that placed pressure on the political system, required decisive responses without eliciting them, and thus exposed the fragmentation of the system were the international politics of the Bismarckian period and the problem of Ireland. Britain's main diplomatic difficulty was that it was intimately bound up in a series of international problems without possessing, any longer, the resources with which to force adequate solutions.[20] The rise of a united Germany, the weakness of Turkey, and other more minor changes had led to a series of crises, some of them potentially dangerous. Britain, with its lack of firm alliances and with the myth of its power partly devalued by the Crimean War and the Indian Mutiny, could not intervene decisively by itself in, for example, the problems created by Russia's designs on Turkey. Rather, Bismarck in Germany seemed to hold the strings of international relations. Except for Disraeli's highly publicized actions at the Congress of Berlin in 1878, which minimized Russia's gains in its war against Turkey, Britain was usually not able to frame a foreign policy that could be represented, in public at least, as successful.

The Irish "problem" was another important and highly publicized source of pressure on the British political system — more important than international crises because it not only created difficulties that the increasingly fragmented political system could not solve but also was itself a symptom of fragmentation. Fragmentation at the national political level manifested itself primarily in the tendency of social groups and economic interest groups to develop consciousness of themselves as groups, to organize to achieve specific goals stated programmatically, and to withhold political cooperation from other groups that blocked the achievement of these goals. The economic conditions of the 1870s, for instance, encouraged the rapid development of trade unions, which are archetypal fragmentary groups. The agricultural depression of the 1870s caused the landed interests once again to seek protection or support, mainly through the Conservative party. Manufacturing interests organized similarly. Other sources of fragmentation were more deep seated, connected with the growing maturity and complexity of an industrial society. Eventually, means were developed to conduct politics and make national policy under these circumstances: reorganized, comprehensive political parties; new means of mass propaganda; and new ideologies that cut across class lines. But all of this took time, and in the 1870s and 1880s the most immediate difficulty facing politicians was that the old means of political operation — the old party organizations, the means of appealing to the public, the mid-Victorian liberal ideological synthesis — no longer worked very well, no longer could be used to create a consensus among enough competing social and economic groups to afford a consistent basis for politics.[21] These conditions were reflected in the indecisive elections of much of the period, the tendency of parties to split on important issues, and the inability of the governments to undertake needed social reforms (such as a complete national educational system). But the greatest symbol of fragmentation was the Irish question.

Ireland had been a problem for Britain (and vice versa) all through the nineteenth century. In the 1870s, despite the half-measures taken by the first Gladstone ministry (1868-74), organized violent Irish resistance to British rule increased.[22] Equally importantly, Charles Stuart Parnell organized a highly effective party to represent Irish interests in Parliament and at the local level, with the double aim of encouraging further improvement in Ireland's condition and achieving a degree of Irish home rule. Parnell's party became an important factor in British politics, contributing greatly to its increasing turbulence and to its fragmentation. But neither Parnell nor the leaders of the "regular" political establishment were able to figure out what to do next. Parnell's party operated in Parliament as an obstructive force, so as to get the attention of the others. But it was difficult to translate attention into solid political gains for Ireland. The Tory and Liberal governments of the 1870s and 1880s obviously had to work with Parnell, but they could not give the Irish what they wanted (home rule) without offending interests in their own parties and risking internal splits. So Irish policy, for the same reasons as policy on education and defense, remained indecisive — the source of much public controversy, but little definitive action.

Domestic Pressure Groups

One of the ways in which the question of fragmentation touched upon the New Imperialism was that some of the competing interests in politics in the 1870s had vested overseas economic concerns and were already oriented toward more formal kinds of imperialism. Only a few of these interests were particularly influential before 1880, and often this influence was due not to the inherent strength of the interest group, but to the exogenous decision of other political groups to support the interest for their own purposes. The merchant houses trading in palm oil with West Africa, for example, especially the

Hutton firm of Liverpool, faced difficult economic circumstances in the 1870s: a fluctuating supply, heavy competition, and an uncertain market at home. The British government had traditionally supported the palm oil trade in West Africa, in part because of its connection with the ideology of abolition through "legitimate trade." The economic conditions of the 1870s, however, led the British palm oil interests to demand more than previously: British protectorates in West Africa to secure the palm oil mechanism, to reduce "excessive" foreign (German and French) competition, and to reduce the "interference" of African merchants in the development of interior markets.[23]

Also in the 1870s, London financial houses became increasingly concerned about the steadiness and consistency of British governments in "protecting" British investments abroad — particularly those in the securities of foreign governments and in foreign-government-backed development activities such as railroads. It had, of course, been official British policy for years to support such investments. But with the large expansion of these investments after about 1860 and with the economic and political instability of many areas of high investment (such as Egypt), calls upon the government for stronger, more systematic, and more consistent protection became increasingly strident. These calls were reinforced by fears that increasing French and German overseas investment would depress interest rates. The rising availability of non-British investment capital did not always endanger British interests, but it did lead investors from all over Europe into risky purchases (Egyptian government bonds and Suez Canal shares, for example), which in turn led investors to seek security through their respective governments. In many cases, governmental action was publicly justified through the portrayal of particular investments as vital national initiatives.

Yet another source of pressure for some form of imperialism came from associations of manufacturers in export-oriented industries such as textiles and metals — the traditional "backbone" of the British economy — which experienced great difficulties in the international market from the 1870s onward and tended to turn to the government for help. Early on, no comprehensive idea of what sort of support was appropriate had been developed, but many spokesmen of industry called for the opening of "virgin" markets and protection against "unfair" competition. Occasionally even tariff protection was mentioned, although not until the 1890s was there much support for it, and not until Joseph Chamberlain's advocacy of protection in 1903 did it become a major issue. The manufacturing interest in the 1870s was still very loosely organized and vague about what it wanted, and thus by itself could elicit no specific response from the government.

Among the other groups pushing the government for intervention in non-European societies was the highly vocal abolitionist movement, supported by many missionary and religious organizations. Even before the 1870s, abolitionist and missionary influence on the public consciousness had forced governments into action against the internal slave trade in Africa.[24]

The aggregate influence of all the groups pressuring the British governments, both Liberal and Conservative, in the 1870s and 1880s cannot explain the whole reason for the move toward formal imperialism. None of the groups was powerful enough by itself to cause such a move, and there existed as yet no common ground for joint political pressure. Imperialism, *per se,* was still largely an illegitimate ideology in the early 1870s. Something was needed to bring together the different strains of imperialist thought and action and to create the political context for colonial acquisition.

The Turn to Imperialism

Robinson and Gallagher, in their classic work on the partition of Africa, ascribe the partition to the pre-existence in the minds of British officials of a kind of official ideology, developed over the previous few decades, which portrayed the world in terms of a number of strategic priorities necessary for the maintenance of British power and prosperity.[25] These priorities justified intervention in the politics of other countries. According to Robinson and Gallagher, the revolution in Egypt in the early 1880s set off the imperial scramble by threatening the Suez Canal, which in turn threatened (in the minds of the British government and Foreign Office) Britain's "lifeline" to India. In 1882, Gladstone's Liberal government invaded and captured Egypt, ending the revolution of Colonel Arabi Pasha, after the French had held back from joint action. The Egyptian repudiation of foreign debts was the pretext for the intervention. The occupation of Egypt led to British fears for the headwaters of the Nile and also set the French and Germans to seeking compensation through a scramble for African protectorates.

In the debate over the Robinson-Gallagher thesis, it has become clear that the British concern with the Suez Canal was based on an exaggeration of the canal's strategic importance — in other words, upon a myth which held it to be essential to control of India. This myth was, in fact, only a few years old in 1882. It was not a specific element of an old official tradition, although the idea of intervention in general for strategic reasons may have been. The specific myth of the canal's importance was the product of political action in 1875: Prime Minister Benjamin Disraeli's spectacular purchase of the Egyptian government's shares in the Suez Canal Company, which gave Britain effective control over the canal.[26] The takeover of the canal led to lengthy debates in Parliament and a Conservative propaganda campaign in which Disraeli and the Conservatives linked imperialist expansion to British security and prosperity. Disraeli and the Conservatives, soon rivaled by Dilke and other Liberal imperialists, made emotional appeals to public opinion emphasizing strategic factors and romantic images of empire. Disraeli not only pushed through the purchase of the canal for strategic reasons that were unconvincing even to later imperialists, but also linked it to the elaborate mumbo-jumbo of declaring the queen to be empress of India — with appropriate gaudy ceremony.

These fairly harmless gestures were followed, however, by Disraeli's declaration of British control over the Boer republic of the Transvaal in South Africa in 1877. The takeover was initially occasioned by pressure from speculators for direct control over newly discovered diamond mines, but it was also undertaken in order to advance the idea of empire in the British public mind. The price was paid almost immediately. Partly to demonstrate the benefits of British rule to the Boers, British officials in South Africa sent an army to attack the Zulu nation, the Boers' enemy. A large section of the British force ran into the Zulu army at Isandhlwana on January 22, 1879, and was wiped out. In the subsequent war, the British did defeat the Zulu, but got so involved in Zulu affairs that they were led to annex Zululand in 1887. Moreover, the Boers, obviously not sufficiently grateful for British "protection," revolted in 1880 and defeated a British army at Majuba Hill. Britain recognized the independence of the Transvaal once again in 1881. Since Disraeli's Conservatives were no longer in power, it was Gladstone's Liberal government that had to pay the costs of Disraeli's imperialist forays.

Disraeli's imperialism in the 1870s had been initiated in large part for political reasons. Even its failure in South Africa did not dampen the enthusiasm of many politicians and interest groups for imperialism as a domestic political tool. From the political and ideological standpoint, then, the New Imperialism commenced in Britain in the mid-1870s with the deliberate romanticizing of India and the purchase of the Suez Canal, rather than with the occupation of Egypt. The whole set of policy ideas focusing on Suez as the key to India, which Robinson and Gallagher heavily emphasize, was to a great extent derived from Disraeli's use of imperialist ideology during the seven or eight years before 1882.

Why did Disraeli turn toward imperialism? — probably for a variety of reasons, including pressure from individual interest groups and the recognition of apparent short-term strategic opportunities. But the most important factor appears to have been a general political one. Disraeli's government (1874-80), like those of Gladstone immediately preceding and following it, found itself subject to the severe political pressures previously described and without the political means of coping with them. Although the Conservatives had an adequate majority in Parliament, they, like the Liberals, were badly split on almost every issue and therefore unable easily to undertake decisive new policies without fragmenting. Also, their electoral support was uncertain. Their 1874 victory had been due primarily to Liberal splits, and they had no firm constituency except among the declining landed classes — a dangerous situation for a party in a democracy.[27] Disraeli's attempt in 1867 to use sponsorship of democratic reform to attract middle- and lower-class support had not worked as well as he had hoped. He needed some kind of new approach to overcoming social and political fragmentation. Disraeli tried several, one of which was the sponsorship of various forms of social legislation in the 1870s. The most promising approach, however, both to Disraeli and before long to many other politicians, was imperialism.

On the surface, an ideology and a policy of imperialism seemed the ideal way to link together disparate interests and social groups and to create broad public support. The elements of an imperialist ideology were already present, built up over the previous three hundred years and connected with the popular identification of colonies with national self-esteem. A highly emotional imperialist ideology could perhaps overcome seemingly irreconcilable class and interest differences by emphasizing shared images of national greatness and shared fears of dangers to that greatness. Such images could also hide the many internal contradictions that an ideology appealing to so many different groups and interests was bound to contain.

Disraeli and the imperialist politicians, who, so to speak, came out of the closet after Disraeli set the fashion with Suez, also wanted to attract the support of particular social groups and economic interests: the increasingly organized working class, to whom a "social imperialist" policy of securing domestic jobs by overseas market protection might appeal; business and financial interests concerned about foreign competition and the security of overseas investments; and even industrial interests without specific overseas involvements, which could be attracted by the idea of imperialism as a means of controlling economic conditions by preventing gluts and depressions. This last was eventually incorporated into Joseph Chamberlain's scheme for "imperial preference" in 1903.

Disraeli's turn to imperialism, like those of other imperialists in both major parties, was thus in large part motivated by political considerations. Imperialist ideology and overseas economic interests could probably not have brought on such a change by themselves. The large outflow of British capital in the 1870s and 1880s did not bring any new form of imperialism to the areas toward which it was primarily directed: the United States, Latin America, Europe, and India. Formal imperial expansion occurred mainly in the areas of less importance for capital investment. Rather, the political decision to follow an imperialist policy gave concerns with investments in tropical Africa, for example, the means of acquiring government support. From this standpoint, Suez, the annexation of the Transvaal in 1877, and the mystical rigmarole Disraeli performed with the Indian empire really constituted the watershed in the emergence of the New Imperialism. Robinson and Gallagher's "official mind" of imperialism must be understood as part of a much broader and more public ideological imperialism which added to the "official mind" many of its characteristic elements (such as the emphasis on Suez) and gave it the force of popular opinion.

The Growth of Imperialism

Although Disraeli set the fashion for imperialism, others rapidly followed suit when it appeared that imperialism might work as a domestic political ideology. There were, of course, imperialists – Dilke, Seeley, and the like – already scattered throughout the political elite, and they leaped immediately to the cue. Within the Conservative party, some of the younger leaders, such as Lord Randolph Churchill, who were strongly influenced by Disraeli and moderately to the "left" of the party center on social issues, adopted an imperialist posture with alacrity. The more conservative group led by Lord Salisbury that took over leadership of the party in the 1880s did not take as readily to imperialism, although they clearly recognized its domestic appeal and accepted the need to keep up with the other powers. Salisbury, as prime minister in the late 1880s and most of the 1890s, was the most important figure in the imperial rivalries of the period, but he always regarded imperialism as a burden thrust upon him by the situation and by other people's previous decisions.

In Gladstone's Liberal party, a clear but not uniform imperialist segment emerged. Social progressives and democrats such as Dilke already favored an extension of mid-Victorian liberal values to the rest of the world by imperial means. More conservative members of the party – the old-line Whigs led by Lord Hartington – were the political descendants of Palmerston and thus interventionists in foreign relations. They emphasized threats to British power in the world, from Russia and France in the 1870s, and later from Germany.

Joseph Chamberlain, the most important political imperialist of them all, started out as an associate of Dilke in the 1870s but later managed to combine both Liberal imperialist groups and to lead large segments of them out of the party. A nonconformist of middle-class origins, Chamberlain (1836-1914) had made his fortune as a metals manufacturer in Birmingham and had gone into politics in the 1870s as a radical Liberal backed by a Birmingham political machine.[28] His rapid rise in Liberal politics resulted from his ability, demonstrated in Birmingham, to integrate organized business and labor interests into the same political movement. By advocating schemes for municipal public works combined with measures to increase welfare and job security, Chamberlain had overcome local political fragmentation. It was hoped that he could do the same at the national level. Upon his arrival in Parliament, however, Chamberlain discovered that his advocacy of democratic reform and a moderate social welfare policy did not immediately command support throughout the Liberal party and the nation. Another means of creating consensus was needed. In the mid-1880s, after considerable hesitation, he selected Ireland and imperialism to fill this need.

When Gladstone and the Liberals returned to office after the election of 1880, Chamberlain was a coming power in the national party. From the first, Gladstone received considerable imperialist pressure from Chamberlain's radical ally Dilke and from more conservative segments of the party under Hartington. Although a firm anticolonialist himself and having also to deal with strongly anticolonialist segments of the party, Gladstone needed imperialist support in order to stay in power and achieve his major aims: further electoral reform and the "solution" of the Irish problem. This was the political context in which the era of colonial expansion and rivalry began for Britain and in which interest groups with specific advantages to be gained by colonization were able, beyond all normal measures of their power, to get the government to back them up.

This process was related to the increasingly imperialist cast of official thought on foreign policy that Robinson and Gallagher describe, but it was largely parallel to it. While the "official mind" displayed continuity with the past, the public and party political sphere of social life demonstrated a high degree of discontinuity in its shift to an acceptance of formal, aggressive imperialism. The interventionist official mind had, in the past, been given its limits by political factors (and political masters) that tended to pull up short at major military interventions and long-term commitments. Although interventionism was much the same in terms of dictating governmental reactions to economic threats, the political limits had to some extent been lifted. This can be seen in

Britain's intervention in Egypt in 1882, in which the lines of action to be taken were discussed in a fairly traditional context (the need to protect bondholders, sources of cotton, the system of international financial obligations, and so on), but in which the new political setting encouraged a much more extensive intervention.

Chamberlain did not immediately become an imperialist in the early 1880s. He did not decide until about 1884 that his career would prosper better as Gladstone's imperialist, anti-Irish home rule opponent than as his radical lieutenant. Chamberlain therefore shared Gladstone's reluctance about occupying Egypt in 1882 but supported his chief after the decision to invade. However, when the question of rescuing Gordon in the Sudan arose in 1884 and generated great public interest (see chapter 5), Chamberlain began to identify himself actively as an advanced imperialist. In the Conservative party, Randolph Churchill, previously reticent about imperial adventures, performed the same maneuver as Chamberlain. At the same time, between 1884 and 1886, many of these politicians turned opposition to Gladstone's plan for Irish home rule into a crusade which they hoped would, with imperialism, create for them a broad basis of public support. In doing so, the new imperialists managed to disrupt the machinery of politics far worse than Parnell's Irish nationalists had done.

The Liberals, who fell from power in 1885, returned in 1886. Gladstone introduced a comprehensive home rule bill, and the Liberals immediately split. Chamberlain led a large segment, called "Unionists," away from the party in opposition to home rule, causing Gladstone to fall. Eventually, the Unionists aligned themselves with the Conservatives to produce an exceptionally strong political bloc that kept the Conservatives in power for most of the time between 1886 and 1905. The Conservative-Unionist connection laid a strong foundation for an active imperialist policy, which was thought to be essential to Conservative power. During the premierships of Lord Salisbury (1885-86, 1886-92, and 1895-1902), Britain participated in the most active phase of the scramble for Africa, commenced its open rivalry with the other powers in China and the Pacific, and entered into the process of alliance building and confrontation that preceded the First World War. Salisbury himself was not a confirmed imperialist, but if the price of holding the Conservative-Unionist alliance together and broadening its support base was imperialism, he was willing to pay it. In addition, Salisbury was a specialist in foreign affairs and tended to subscribe much more wholeheartedly than, for example, Gladstone to the Foreign Office view of colonial gains as necessary "compensation" to Britain for the advancement of other countries' interests.[29]

We shall discuss imperialism and imperial rivalries in Africa in the next chapter. The 1890s were a crisis period in the partition of Africa as far as the European powers were concerned. Germany and Britain managed to settle most of their territorial disputes there, but in 1898 Britain and France appeared to come close to blows over the French attempt to acquire a base on the Nile at Fashoda. British politicians and public opinion watched developments in Africa closely, and a large part of the national being seemed to be bound up with what was going on there.

The period in which unalloyed imperialism held sway in British politics was fairly short. Two events in particular helped to break the charm of imperialist ideology by demonstrating the dangers of expansion and international rivalry: the Fashoda incident in 1898 and the Boer War (1899-1902). Despite the widespread rethinking of national priorities that both events entailed, they did not result in a total discrediting of imperialism or in a definite turn in some other direction in British foreign policy. Like the Indian Mutiny in 1857, they brought imperialist ideology and imagination more into line with international political reality and caused imperialists to modify their positions considerably.

The Fashoda incident seemed dangerous because of the high public nationalist excitement that it engendered in both countries. Before long, however, the whole affair began to appear ludicrous. The English and the French were required to think seriously about whether control of the Upper Nile was worth a major European war, which it patently was not. Africa and the whole tropical empire were thereby put into clearer perspective. Although Britain in essence "won" the Fashoda confrontation because the French backed down, what they won amounted to very little.[30] Reaction from the shock of Fashoda also helped lead to the development of Britain's informal alliance with France against Germany because it convinced the governments and publics in both Britain and France that they were in more danger from Germany than from each other — in a sense, a conviction even more dangerous than the imperialist assumptions that led to Fashoda.

The genesis of the Boer (or South African) War and its results will be summarized in chapter 5. In Britain, the war created an immense public sensation, splitting the Liberal party and calling into question the whole policy and ideology of imperialism. The hot debate between liberal imperialists and classical anticolonialist free-traders took on considerable urgency as political groups were required to take positions on an actual issue of immediate importance. The fact that the war went badly at first for the British and that it was fought bitterly with high casualties against an essentially European population, helped to cast doubt on the imperialist position. It has often been said that the British won the Boer War but lost the peace, since the eventual result of the war was the establishment of the Boer-dominated self-governing Union of South Africa in 1910. Actually, this was the kind of solution to colonial problems that had, since the Durham report, been seen as the ideal, the New Imperialism notwithstanding. British business interests had been secured in the diamond- and gold-producing areas of the Boer republics, and the threat of nationalization or deliberate anti-industrial reaction by the Boers had been averted. That the eventual solution left the black majority in South Africa at the mercies of the Boers and of unchecked industrialization was something that the imperial ideal could do nothing about. South Africa became an investor's paradise. Even if ideological imperialism did not triumph in the Boer War, economic imperialism certainly did.[31]

THE RISE OF GERMAN IMPERIALISM

Germany's overseas imperialism, cut short by the First World War, displayed many of the same features as imperialism in Britain: the linkage to domestic politics, the peculiarly indirect relationship between economic interests and formal expansion, and the comparatively large gap between ideological conceptions and social realities in the overseas empire.[32] Three phenomena of the nineteenth century in particular underlay the entry of Germany, previously without colonies, into the imperial sweepstakes in the 1880s: emigration, national unification in 1867-71, and (as elsewhere) rapid industrialization and social change. The prevalence of emigration as a feature of German social life up to the 1890s made it a more important factor in imperialism than it was elsewhere in Europe. Early schemes for colonial (and continental) expansion, especially those advanced during the Revolution of 1848, were framed mainly in terms of emigration: overseas colonies would absorb the overflow of "excess" population from Germany while, unlike emigration to the United States, colonies would maintain the emigrants' economic and cultural ties to the homeland. Colonies would also perform the more usual function of stimulating and protecting German overseas trade. Although privately operated German "colonies" were established in many parts of the New World, the idea of a national colonial policy largely fell apart with the collapse of the Revolution of 1848. When colonialism revived in the 1860s and 1870s, it was in the context of the Bismarckian unification of Germany between 1862 and 1871.

Bismarck, although originally a convinced free-trader and anticolonialist, occasionally emitted signs in the 1860s that Germany might acquire colonies. In so doing, Bismarck probably recognized that he might be able to make a broad appeal to a middle class that was usually concerned about emigration, and also that he might be able to appeal to business interests in the National Liberal party whose support he needed before 1871 and among whom colonialism was becoming popular again.

The most important influence on German colonialism was Germany's rapid economic modernization after 1850. Certain new manufacturing interests, especially the metals industry, favored protective tariffs and related policies. They therefore had to work out how to get general support for what they wanted and also what to do if Britain and other countries retaliated with their own tariffs. Colonies figured in both considerations. German merchants in West Africa and the South Seas found themselves in difficulties in the 1870s and turned to colonialism as a means of getting government support. In most cases, however, colonialism was envisaged by business people before the mid-1880s as a possible part of a larger policy of overseas economic expansion; colonialism was useful mainly as a means to some other goal. Politicians and the spokesmen of economic interest groups in Germany, like their British counterparts, were increasingly fascinated by the possibilities of imperialism as a means of creating political consensus. For example, big business might, by backing colonial expansion, acquire lower-middle-class support for policies of tariff and market protection if the two concepts could be linked. This was possible because the term "colony" still retained in Germany the aspect of a settlement for emigrants — an image with wide lower-middle-class appeal.

In the late 1870s, groups in Germany already inclined toward colonialism, many of them for reasons that had little to do with colonies, used the example of British imperialism as the cornerstone of new organizations that were founded to press for German colonial acquisition. These organizations united in the *Kolonialverein* of 1882, which did the primary work of integrating the various types of German imperialist ideology into at least a serviceable patchwork and conducting a public propaganda campaign. The *Kolonialverein* also managed to tie together different segments of the German political order that were interested in imperialism, both those few business concerns that would be directly benefited by the seizure of colonies (especially tropical trading companies in Hamburg and Bremen) and the larger number of political and economic groups primarily interested in the political benefits that subscribing publicly to a popular colonial movement could bring.

But of course Germany was not a parliamentary democracy, and even the most popular movement could not be sure of affecting policy. The *Kolonialverein* and a group of colonial publicists managed to generate a brief middle-class "colonial enthusiasm" in the early and mid-1880s, but the movement's popular depth was questionable and the interest groups that backed it were not powerful enough to force the adoption of a colonial policy. All they could do, essentially, was to present an opportunity for Bismarck to take, if he desired. And in 1884 he did so.

Bismarck's sudden conversion to colonialism in the 1880s has been the subject of considerable historical debate. Were his motives diplomatic? A German grab for colonies might encourage Britain and France to do the same and thus come into mild conflict with each other, preventing them from forming an anti-German bloc in Europe.[33] Was Bismarck merely responding to the pressure of commercial interest groups seeking an extension of the protectionist policies adopted by Germany in 1879? And so forth. Most recent studies of Bismarck have claimed that these were secondary considerations and have concentrated on the political context of Bismarck's decision. Hans-Ulrich Wehler, for example, has interpreted Bismarck's turn to colonialism in terms of "social imperialism," that is, as a means of convincing the German bourgeoisie and perhaps the proletariat that their interests lay in overseas expansion and in maintaining Germany's authoritarian social and political order.[34] When an "ideological consensus" in favor of an "export offensive" and colonial acquisition appeared among business and middle-class groups, Bismarck, according to Wehler, decided to seize a few colonies and to argue that he was doing so in order to protect Germany from economic depression. Bismarck used his new colonial initiative to push various measures of government support for overseas business through the Reichstag in 1884-85 and obtained an increase in prestige through his sponsorship of an international conference on West Africa in Berlin in 1884-85. Bismarck soon became disenchanted with imperialism because it failed to yield the domestic results he desired.

Other historians have emphasized more direct political advantages sought by Bismarck in his support of colonialism, especially the undoing of his archenemies, the left-liberal Progressive party.[35] The Progressives were highly anticolonial and had committed themselves to opposing the new colonial movement. However, the Progressives depended upon lower-middle-class voters, to whom the emigrationist ideal of colonialism was thought to appeal. In sponsoring colonial acquisition, Bismarck encouraged the Progressives to oppose the policy and thus to lose favor with many of their supporters. The Progressives took the bait but probably did not suffer for it as much as Bismarck had hoped.

The mystery of Bismarck's imperialism will never be solved, mainly because Bismarck was probably pursuing multiple ends, and his priorities were unclear. But the majority of the motives attributed to him can be explained, as they can with Disraeli, as reactions to fragmentation and lack of political consensus, as means of creating a broad base of domestic support for his government that was otherwise lacking. It appeared that big business, the trading interest, and lower-middle-class anti-industrial groups — which were often at each other's throats — could be attracted by a colonialist program. Of course, in the long run, both Bismarck and Disraeli were wrong. Imperialism could not provide the kind of consensus they needed, and it involved a greatly heightened probability of war for their respective countries.

At any rate, in the early 1880s all of the ingredients for an active colonial initiative were present in Germany: businesses with immediate motives for seeking colonial expansion, more important economic interests organized to influence policy and motivated to use imperialism to put public pressure on the government, an enthusiastic public colonial movement with a number of defined imperialist ideologies, and — to make the final decision — an effective head of the national government who could be persuaded of the value and limited risk of colonial enterprises. This combination led to a brief but significant spurt of aggrandizement.

In 1883 Bismarck, having previously signaled a turn towards an active overseas intervention by supporting a subsidy for German commercial interests in Samoa, began to make private agreements to support colonial ventures abroad, especially in Southwest Africa and New Guinea. Then in 1884 he declared a protectorate over Southwest Africa after eliciting Britain's renunciation of claims to most of the area; he dispatched a gunboat to claim the coastal regions of what would later be the colonies of Togo and Kamerun; and he declared a protectorate over northeastern New Guinea and adjacent islands as an operating area for a newly-chartered development company. He used his new acquisitions to attack the opposition in the Reichstag and finished the year with the Berlin West African Conference, a minor diplomatic success. In 1885 Bismarck also accepted as a protectorate the coast of present-day Tanzania, which had been claimed for Germany by a private company under the leadership of Carl Peters. Bismarck had not wanted East Africa, which involved him immediately in a dispute with Britain, the sponsor of the sultan of Zanzibar whose coastal territories Peters had claimed. But to have repudiated Peters would have cost Bismarck too much politically, and so he acquiesced, setting off a spectacular competition for interior territories between Germany and Britain.

Germany thus found itself with quite a substantial empire by 1885. The formal empire increased slightly in following years with the acquisition of additional islands in the Pacific, part of Samoa, and the enclave of Kiaochow in China, and with an extension of Kamerun into adjoining French territory in 1911. None of these possessions was generally regarded as economically vital to Germany. Public interest in imperial expansion, which cooled somewhat after 1885 and had to be deliberately restored by propaganda organizations, focused mainly on possible initiatives in noncolonial areas such as the Ottoman Empire.

Most of the hopes of the people who established the colonial empire were disappointed. Bismarck found that the colonies could not be run without considerable government expense and that colonial trading and concession companies on whom Bismarck depended to operate the colonies could not do so. Also, imperial issues showed themselves to be incapable of creating for Bismarck a progovernment consensus. When Bismarck fell from power in 1890, he probably regretted having been involved with colonial expansion. On the other hand, convinced colonialists, organized after 1887 into the German Colonial Society, pressed for more colonial commitment and expansion than Bismarck or any subsequent chancellor was willing to contemplate — especially the establishment of agricultural settlement colonies.

The German colonial empire took permanent economic and political shape only gradually after 1890. None of the African colonies except tiny Togo ever became economically self-supporting. Within Germany itself, the colonial empire played mainly a political role. Colonial issues and scandals provided a continuous source of debate for political parties, which in turn affected German foreign policy to some extent. Although by 1914 most Germans probably believed that the acquisition of colonies had been a good thing, the tangible results of colonization for Germany were, to say the least, meager.

THE EXPANSION OF THE
FRENCH COLONIAL EMPIRE

Classical liberalism, with its inherent aversion to formal colonialism and its worship of free trade, was never as strong an element of nineteenth-century ideology in France as it was in Britain. This was due, among other things, to French traditions of state intervention in the economy, to the highly unstable political history of French liberalism, and to the fact that the free-trade idea, by potentially exposing French industry to the competition of an already industrialized Britain in the first half of the nineteenth century, did not enjoy automatic support from politically liberal business people. But although the ideological basis for anticolonialism was weaker in France than in Britain, so too was self-conscious imperialism. Only a few groups, mostly business and military, consistently favored imperial expansion in the late nineteenth century. The prevailing popular view held that trade and investment overseas were much more important than colonies.[36]

Napoleon III

As in a number of other areas, Napoleon III had been a bit ahead of his time in attempting to use imperial expansion to create a consensus behind his regime between 1850 and 1870. The adventure in Mexico resulted directly from this aim, and expansion in Southeast Asia played at least a minor domestic political role. On the other hand, the initiatives that would extend the French empire in West Africa clear across the continent were originally undertaken by officials on the spot and simply presented to the government as *faits accomplis*.

Louis Faidherbe, an army officer appointed governor of the tiny colony of Senegal in 1854, decided on his own to use Senegal as a base for conquering much of West Africa.[37] Employing his limited military forces, he took advantage of the vagueness of Senegal's territorial boundaries in the interior to pick fights with several of the African states up the Senegal River. He would "pacify" them, establish French garrisons and control, and then encourage further quarrels beyond the new boundaries, each time claiming to his superiors that his actions were necessary in order to secure Senegal's frontiers. Faidherbe's strategy was similar to that of the expansionist British governors of India, both in its military and political pattern and in the fact that its object — undisputed possession of the Sahara and the western Sudanic plains — made little real economic sense. In the early 1860s, Faidherbe had extended his Senegalese base and acquired sufficient military forces from France that he could play the several large states of the Niger region off against each other and penetrate into the interior of Guinea. By the time he left Senegal in 1865, Faidherbe had extended practical French control as far as the Niger.

Faidherbe had not, however, succeeded in making the French West African colony pay for itself. As with most visionary imperialists, he was not fazed by current unprofitability. Faidherbe argued that with proper planning and investment, large-scale agriculture could be established in the Niger basin, thus turning the region into a major trading partner for France. This inflated view of the western Sudan's economic potential influenced French policy for many years. After Faidherbe's departure in 1865, French aggression remained dormant for a time. But France was now, mainly because of Faidherbe's obsession, thoroughly involved in the affairs of the West African interior.

Napoleon III's reign also saw the expansion of French interests in Asia. Here, the central government played a more important role in determining policy than in West Africa, and the business enterprises involved, while not highly significant ones, exerted some influence.[38] (I shall consider French penetration of China later.) Generally, it involved joint action as a junior partner with Britain in seeking free access to the Chinese market, extraterritorial rights for French citizens, and a variety of concessions. France's main interest lay to the south, in an area only theoretically under Chinese sovereignty and not yet, in the 1850s and 1860s, subject to the attentions of any other European power: the coast of Indochina.

French naval forces invaded Cochin-China in 1861 in response, supposedly, to executions of Christians and missionaries. With the grudging acquiescence of the British and the forced approval of China, the French took over several of the provinces of Cochin-China. Thereafter French commercial influence spread. The naval officers administering the French holdings forced protectorate treaties on several other kingdoms, although until the 1880s France made no claim to outright sovereignty over the whole of Indochina.

Under Napoleon III, the French government also actively supported French merchants throughout much of the world, including the South Pacific, parts of the Guinea coast, and Latin America, although it normally stopped well short of colonization. The prime traditional areas of French overseas commercial and political activity remained the Near East and North Africa, which were, unlike other trading areas, regarded as vital to France. In the 1840s and 1850s a substantial amount of private French investment found its way to these areas. Although overall French overseas investments could not compare with Britain's, they kept pace in Egypt and the Ottoman Empire.[39] Napoleon III, with his close ties to the big banking interests, consistently backed them up in the Near East. In 1854, for example, he joined Britain against Russia in the Crimean War, not simply to protect the French interest in the Ottoman Empire against Russian encroachment but also to prevent Britain from obtaining the sole paramount position there.

France's main Near Eastern involvement was with Egypt. Since the rise of Mohammed Ali just after the Napoleonic Wars, France had attempted to develop a special relationship with the Egyptian government. Britain, to whom the Egyptian cotton crop was important, would not allow Egypt to become a French satellite, but a close relationship between France and Egypt existed right up to the British occupation in 1882. In the 1850s and 1860s, Egypt was a prime area for French commercial investment, culminating in the Suez Canal project — a project that was French in inspiration and predominantly French in funding. The British invasion in 1882 thus seemed to many French people to be a direct affront to their country.

The Third Republic

Except for Mexico, Napoleon III's imperialism stopped short of major outright colonial acquisition. It stopped altogether, in any event, with the Franco-Prussian War of 1870-71 and Napoleon's fall from power. The period that followed was marked by political and economic confusion. In the political sphere, the 1870s saw the German occupation and the national resistance, the establishment of a provisional government under Adolphe Thiers, the Paris Commune and its bloody repression, and the bitter and confusing clash of monarchists, Bonapartists, liberals, republicans, and radicals out of which the democratic Third Republic emerged after 1875. With its lack of a popular consensus and of a well-organized party structure, the Third Republic was initially very unstable. Its early politics moved from crisis to crisis; social conflict and religious antagonisms abounded. If ever there was a country whose politicians required means of creating consensus, it was France in the last quarter of the nineteenth century.[40]

Economic conditions in the 1870s also tended toward instability. While the 1850s had been the boom years of full industrialization and the 1860s at worst an unsettled period, the 1870s appeared to be disastrous. The loss of the Franco-Prussian War and the indemnity due Germany threatened the economy in the early 1870s, while the post-1873 world depression created conditions of long-term economic stagnation. This situation exacerbated the social antagonisms already present and made politics and government even more difficult. It also encouraged a movement by major industrial and financial concerns to obtain government support. General opinion in France was traditionally more protectionist than in Britain, no more so than during depressions. As in Germany and Britain, the missionaries and the small trading companies operating in West Africa and the South Pacific were able to take advantage of industry's protectionist sentiment to construct a case for colonial acquisition in their areas of activity.

The procolonial interest group in France was, however, extremely small. It had not been able to persuade the government to retain the protectorate over the Ivory Coast that had been declared in the 1840s. Although humanitarian and commercial groups had established the settlement for freed African slaves at Libreville that later evolved into the French colony of Gabon, further expansion was not pursued. The Catholic missionary interest, although active under Cardinal Lavigerie, could not by itself make much impression on the highly secular post-1875 governments. It was generally recognized in the 1870s that no popular groundswell of support for imperialism existed in France — certainly not to the degree that it did in Britain and Germany. French colonial publicists and organizations do not seem to have made much of an impact on public opinion except perhaps to head off outright anticolonialism. This was done by propaganda that related colonial expansion to the maintenance of France's great power status and economic security. Anticolonialists did attack expansion on various grounds, but until the rise of the Socialist party late in the century they had no organizational foundation for their attack.

Most of the impetus to colonial expansion in the 1880s arose within the French political elite. Pressure came from trading companies, Cardinal Lavigerie, some ideologists, and especially the military, but these only created the context for a political decision. By most accounts, the most important factor in France's entry into the new imperial sweepstakes was Jules Ferry, who was premier between 1880 and 1881 and between 1883 and 1885.

Recent research has tended to downplay the notion that Ferry was the sole originator of modern French imperialism. The existence of the procolonial interests mentioned above has been noted, and it has been argued that there was an informal colonialist "party," or at least sentiment, in the National Assembly.[41] It also seems that Ferry's imperialism was not a deep conviction; he does not appear to have been particularly interested in colonies until the late 1870s. His ideas on colonies were highly unoriginal (colonies would secure trade and open up new markets), derived directly from a few French colonial publicists. Nevertheless, Ferry is still considered the key figure in the New Imperialism in France. If he had not decided to turn French policy toward expansion in 1880 and 1881, it is entirely possible that France's participation in the scramble for Africa and Asia would have been much more modest than it was.

Ferry was one of the leading "Opportunist" republican politicians who succeeded to control of politics after 1875. Like most Opportunists, Ferry was willing to shift his political opinions in search of consensus and stability; his turn to colonialism must be understood in these terms. Ferry was not without convictions. His sponsorship of secularization and reform of the French educational system displayed radical republican convictions and created a dangerous split between Catholics and liberals. In Ferry's sudden interest in colonialism, we see the opportunistic side of his political behavior. He appears to have intended a national colonial policy both as a means of patching up the differences created by the educational reforms and as an avenue of attack on the most obvious political problems of the Third Republic: severe fragmentation at the party level and lack of consensus throughout the system. An active imperialist policy would perhaps unite the various factions of the Opportunist liberals and attach at least some radicals and conservatives to them as well. It might also rally the support of a nationalistic public by showing that France was once again a major power. Such considerations seem to have been far more important to Ferry in the early 1880s than was the pressure of overseas economic interests, although those interests gave him a direction in which to go and an ideology with which to explain the need for overseas expansion.

The actual occasions for France's new turn to imperialism grew out of political and economic situations that predated Ferry's premiership. The key element was France's annexation of Tunisia in 1881. Ever since the early nineteenth century, France had acted as the paramount power and economic influence in Tunis, which still theoretically belonged to the

Ottoman Empire. Great Britain had, however, checked France's ambitions there for strategic reasons, and by the 1870s Italian economic influence was growing rapidly. The Italian government regarded Tunisia as a major development area for the future and as a possible site for extensive European settlement. In the late 1870s, the Italians pushed hard to force the ruler of Tunisia to accept Italian "protection." France naturally moved to counter Italy through diplomacy and in 1878 secretly negotiated an agreement in which Britain acquiesced in whatever France wished to do in Tunisia. In 1881, Ferry decided to exercise France's option and, on almost no pretext at all, dispatched an army from Algeria that conquered the country and forced the Bey of Tunis to sign a treaty of protection. This naturally offended Turkey and outraged Italy, but with British support, France's hold remained secure. Ferry had, in a spectacular move, picked up a new colony for France, although at the expense of driving Italy into a German alliance. French public opinion responded with restrained enthusiasm.

Ferry's other imperialist moves included the final conquest of all Indochina, which required a minor war with China that ended in 1885. France was forestalled from moving into Siam (Thailand) only by British pressure. Perhaps appropriately, Ferry's fall from power in 1885 was occasioned, at least outwardly, by the news of a minor French military reverse in Indochina. Indochina eventually became, after Algeria, France's most important colony and the site of considerable economic development. In the short run, the seizure of Indochina excited little real interest in France; in Asia it further weakened China's prestige and helped to encourage the final British occupation of Burma.

In the 1880s, the French were active in various other places throughout the world. Tahiti was converted from a French protectorate to a colony in 1880, and other acquisitions were made in the South Pacific. In Africa, French activity was especially pronounced. After several years of stalling, the French restarted their advance from Senegal, this time with political, military, and financial support from the French government. Although the initiative in West Africa still came from the military commanders, they also received encouragement from Ferry. The process by which the enormous territories of French West Africa and French Equatorial Africa were conquered is described in chapter 5. In addition, the island of Madagascar was conquered in 1885, partly on the basis of existing French interests there and partly on the basis of armchair geography in Paris.

At the time of Ferry's fall in 1885, France had taken the decisive steps toward a vast expansion of its overseas empire. Although some of France's late nineteenth-century acquisitions (especially Indochina) offered economic opportunities to French people, it is doubtful that the seizure of the majority of them brought any long-term benefit to France. In all probability, Indochina would have been just as much of a benefit under cheaper informal control as it was under full colonial rule. In most places, free access to markets was all that French business people really needed. France's colonial expansion in the 1880s appears to demonstrate both the largely political motivation of the New Imperialism and the economic irrelevance of many of its consequences.

Imperialism did not achieve Ferry's domestic political goals, either. Not only did Ferry fall from power in 1885, but no subsequent French government, political party, or interest group was able to use imperialism as an issue to create support or consensus. Other images and other ideologies were simply stronger and more appealing, and they swamped imperialism in the political marketplace. Occasionally, the empire could produce a diplomatic crisis that could mobilize public opinion and spread nationalist hysteria, but imperialist emotions could not be sustained and the crises themselves proved to be dangerous. During the Fashoda crisis with Britain in 1898-99, for example, the French government encouraged a popular reaction to

British efforts to prevent French control of part of the Upper Nile, and, briefly, the possibility existed of war with Britain. Since the government could not seriously move in this direction, its subsequent backing-down cost both the cabinet and imperialism credibility with the public.

THE PORTUGUESE AND BELGIAN EMPIRES

The "big three" powers of Western Europe — Britain, France, and Germany — were of course not the only entrants in the imperial sweepstakes. Many other states — including two non-European ones, the United States and Japan — made various kinds of expansionary moves in the late nineteenth century. In some countries, such as the Netherlands in the East Indies, late Victorian imperialism took the form of internal reform, more thorough exploitation of territories already possessed, and the final acquisition of control over areas in between zones of previous occupation. Portugal expanded its area of effective control in Angola and Mozambique, reformed and enlarged the colonial administration, and undertook an ambitious program of European settlement and economic development.[42] This was done partly as a means of improving the stagnant Portuguese domestic economy and partly to forestall the very real possibility that the other imperial powers would divide the Portuguese colonies among themselves. The development program and the need to obtain Great Power diplomatic support put the Portuguese empire in an awkward position of economic and political dependence. Right up until the First World War, British and German economic interests vied with each other for concessions in Portuguese Africa and plotted to divide the Portuguese colonies between themselves. In general, Portugal received little benefit from its colonies.

Imperialism in the Low Countries was a fairly significant element of the history of late European expansion. We shall discuss imperial reform in the Netherlands in chapter 6. Although Dutch reform initiatives greatly influenced other colonial powers, much more international attention was paid to Belgian, or rather Belgian-based, overseas expansion in the late nineteenth century.

The Congo Free State, founded in the 1880s by King Leopold of Belgium, did not officially become a Belgian colony until 1908. Belgian investors, however, backed Leopold and his International African Association to a greater extent than those of any other nationality. Belgium in the late nineteenth century was one of the world's major capital investment centers because of the availability of profits from the relatively early Belgian Industrial Revolution. Belgian colonial investments were not limited, in fact, to the Congo. Much of the investment in the German colonial empire, particularly in Kamerun, was Belgian in origin. In any event, middle-class Belgian public opinion regarded the Congo essentially as a Belgian colony, and the Belgian parliament extended loans to the Free State, receiving in 1901 the right to annex it.[43]

The International African Association was originally conceived by Leopold and his associates as a large investment company operating in the apparently virgin territory of the Central African interior. Leopold desperately wanted to make a name for himself, not merely as a figurehead constitutional monarch and a playboy, but also as a successful big businessman like the financiers he so admired. The rapid growth of imperialist attitudes in Western Europe in the 1870s and their attachment to the humanitarian antislavery movement seemed to give Leopold and like-minded Belgian businessmen their opportunity. They represented their association, which was backed by a substantial amount of capital, as the culmination of the "legitimate trade" tendency in abolitionism. The way to end the internal African slave trade and to spread the blessings of European civilization to "darkest Africa" (the expression is that of Henry M. Stanley, the association's most celebrated employee) was to intervene massively in the African economy. Investment would create profitable industries which would in turn swamp the internal slave trade economically and pay for stamping it out militarily. The native population would be drawn to European culture not simply by missionary activity but also by working for the association. Among Leopold's main selling points was the argument that a private, international organization, presided over by the ruler of a little country, would be the ideal agency for colonial expansion. The international organization could pool the resources of the European countries and could undertake colonial development without arousing jealousies among the powers. The association promised to follow free-trade policies wherever it ruled. In terms of prevailing imperialist ideologies, Leopold's case was practically airtight.

Imperialism also played a domestic political role for Leopold, although it was clearly a secondary one. Leopold, whose power in his own country was highly circumscribed, probably hoped that a broad middle-class and business coalition could be formed around imperial expansion, thus giving him a stronger parliamentary power base. This aspect of Leopold's imperialism proved fruitless.

By the early 1880s, Leopold and his cohorts had selected the basin of the Congo River as their field of activity. Their plan was to establish a claim to the Congo waterway, thereby encouraging competition among the European powers to seize areas of their own. Leopold would then take advantage of the resulting international furor to make the case for granting control of all of Central Africa to the "neutral" International African Association.

Events went only approximately according to plan. The association dispatched agents to the Congo, especially Stanley, who established stations in the early 1880s, forced the appropriate treaties from African rulers, and staked a claim against the French and Portuguese. The French government countered by sending Da Brazza to the Congo to establish counterclaims, and by 1884 the race for control of the Congo was on. When Bismarck called the Berlin West African Conference late in 1884 to discuss disputes arising from the scramble for West Africa, attention focused on the Congo basin. The

Conference gave Leopold some, although not all, of what he wanted. He and his company were assigned control of the central portion of the Congo basin, with a narrow access to the sea. All of this was designated the "Congo Free State," with Leopold as sovereign. The interior boundaries of the Free State were not clearly defined and were later worked out through military conquest and treaty-signing competitions between Leopold's agents and their British, French, and German rivals. Leopold had originally wanted control of the upper Nile, but the British seizure of Uganda in the early 1890s deprived him of it. British pressure also prevented Leopold from gaining a wider access to the sea.[44]

In return for its colony, King Leopold's company (now called the International Congo Association) — still representing itself as a philanthropic organization — agreed to maintain free trade, to prevent the sale of liquor and firearms to Africans, and to suppress the slave trade. In pursuance of its real goal of profitable economic development, the association twisted these obligations in a manner that became increasingly blatant with the years. Although lip-service was paid to the free-trade idea, as the association's activities expanded, especially into the mineral rich Katanga (Shaba) area in the 1890s, it acted very effectively to prevent business competition with its area. The association mounted a series of military expeditions under Stanley and others, supposedly to cut off the trade in slaves from the Upper Congo to East Africa but actually to expand control over the eastern interior and to destroy indigenous trade competition. The association destroyed the slave trade but replaced it with the practice that later most inflamed liberal world opinion against the Congo: the exploitation of forced labor. An older form of slavery had in essence been replaced by a newer one, on a much larger scale.

For more than twenty years after its establishment, the Congo was run by the association from Brussels as a large-scale business enterprise. Initially, the association made its profits from preexisting trades such as the ivory trade, which was taken over directly from Muslim slave-traders. The association also introduced new forms of agricultural production, especially rubber-growing. Finally, in the twentieth century the copper mines of Katanga were developed in response to a world-wide increase in demand for copper. All of these industries required large amounts of unskilled labor, as did the building of the railway from the coast to the new capital of Leopoldville (Kinshasa), the construction of Leopoldville itself, and the development of the port facilities at Stanley Pool. As in most new colonies, the amount of labor that could be attracted by the wages the association wanted to pay was limited. Construction projects were often distant from population centers. Although serious abuses in labor "recruitment" occurred in many colonies, those in the Congo were perhaps the worst. They were certainly the most publicized. Leopold's agents, claiming that they were introducing the indigenous population to "useful labor," drafted Africans from all along the Congo and its tributaries and drove them in gangs to construction projects and rubber harvests. Forced labor occasioned high death rates and other shocking abuses.

Despite Leopold's mastery of public relations and his (apparently sincere) efforts to encourage missionary work, when conditions in his empire became public knowledge in the late 1890s, humanitarians and liberal anticolonialists throughout the world took him under attack. Within Belgium, the attack was led by the landed aristocracy, the radicals, and the socialists. In England and elsewhere, the Congo was portrayed as a violation of the moral principles that lay behind the cult of progress, and also as a violation of free trade principles. Although at first the Congo authorities denied the abuses, their defense rang hollow in the face of mounting evidence. By 1903, anticolonialists everywhere could attack colonialism itself and expose its hypocrisy by focusing on the blatant case of the Congo without seeming unpatriotic to their own empires. A whole Congo literature appeared around the turn of the century, of which the best-known example is Joseph Conrad's novella *The Heart of Darkness*. In several countries, Congo reform movements were founded, the most important of which was the British movement led by the radical intellectual E.D. Morel.[45] In Belgium, attacks on Leopold increased.

The crisis came to a head in 1908, when Leopold agreed to give up the Congo to the Belgian government, which did not really want it. Between 1908 and 1914, most of the powers of Europe expected Belgium to renounce all or part of its empire, possibly in favor of Germany. Instead, Belgium held on. In fact, it turned the tables on Germany by picking up the German protectorates of Rwanda and Burundi as League of Nations mandates in 1919. As far as colonial administration went, Belgium followed a policy of authoritarian direct rule and prided itself on its paternalistic social and health policies. There was no real governing ideology of empire, since the Congo was peripheral to domestic Belgian concerns. The handling of economic development was left mostly to large business consortia, of which the *Union miniére,* which ran the Katanga mines, was the most important. Mainly because of Katanga, the Congo was a profitable colony that, until the late 1950s, made few demands on Belgium.

THE ITALIAN EMPIRE AND THE RISE OF ETHIOPIA

The Italian colonial empire was the result of deliberate political decisions in the late nineteenth century.[46] Although Italian expansion took place mostly in areas in which Italian business interests existed, those interests were so marginal that they probably would have been totally ignored had the political opportunities they seemed to create not tempted Italian politicians to follow them up. Italy was not an industrial nation at the start of its imperial career. The reasons for expansion lay not with existing overseas interests but with politics and social conflict at home.

Italy presented a classic picture of political instability in the 1880s and 1890s. Recently unified, geographically diverse, militarily weak, and unsettled in its relations with the Papacy,

Italy was a limited constitutional monarchy with no clear focus of power and no tradition of legitimacy in its national institutions. Its problems of political fragmentation and lack of consensus were stupendous compared to those in other countries. These problems were never successfully solved before World War I. In part, Italian imperialism can be seen as one response to them. The domestic political dimension of Italian imperialism overshadowed any economic ones probably to a larger extent than in any other imperialist country.

Italian merchants had been operating in the Red Sea area since the 1860s, on the coasts of what would later be the colonies of Eritrea and Somalia. In 1880, the Italian government declared an official protectorate over Assab, where an Italian company had purchased a concession. The Italian move was a limited one, intended to protect Italian merchants against exclusion by the British and French. To the extent that Italian politicians and the voting public looked abroad from their domestic political confusion, they looked to Tunisia.

Italian businessmen had played an increasingly important role in Tunisia since mid-century. Italy had real economic and strategic interests there, and its politicians had fondly regarded Tunisia as an informal Italian protectorate. We have seen how France in 1881, with Britain's consent, invaded Tunisia and forced it into the French empire. This set off a howl of displeasure in Italy, shared to a greater or lesser degree by all classes of political participants. The seizure of Tunisia was one of the events that drove Italy into the Triple Alliance with Germany and Austria. It also demonstrated the apparent ability of imperial issues to elicit a single reaction throughout Italy. This lesson, reinforced by the new popularity of imperialism in other countries, was immediately learned by Italian politicians greatly in need of consensus-building devices.

In the late 1870s and 1880s, Italy possessed no means of affording the basis for national political action, and the performances of its governments in foreign affairs, finance, and economic development showed this. Political parties were mere ideological groupings within the Chamber of Deputies. The dominant left liberal "party" was no more than a loose grouping of small circles of politicians who endlessly formed and re-formed governments by promising and withholding support. No government could stay in power long enough to deal with any of Italy's overwhelming financial problems. The fragmentation of parliamentary politics was, of course, largely a reflection of a fragmented Italian society. Italy had no modern tradition of concerted action apart from the nationalist movement of the *Risorgimento,* which was widely regarded as an imposition of the north upon the rest of Italy.

The most important of the liberal politicians who turned to imperialism in the 1880s as a solution to these problems was Francesco Crispi, who was prime minister on several occasions in the 1880s and 1890s. An active and vigorous politician, Crispi was partly responsible for a tendency toward larger and more stable parliamentary blocs in Italian politics. His imperialism must be understood as part of the same consensus-building process. Crispi originally had little concern for Red Sea colonialism and looked at the Tunisian crisis in terms more of diplomatic initiatives in Europe than of African imperialism. Like many of his contemporaries, he absorbed imperialist ideologies from Britain, France, and Germany during the colonial fever of the early 1880s. Influenced by these ideologies, Crispi probably did come to believe that Italian economic growth depended on expanding overseas markets and that one way to create them was through colonies. But his prime concern remained the effect of imperialism on domestic politics.

In the aftermath of Tunisia, Italian governments — to a large extent although not exclusively under the urging of Crispi — began to move to convert their holdings on the Red Sea into a formal empire to offset the public black eye Italian politicians had received in Tunisia. The circumstances for Italian action in the Red Sea area were unusually favorable in the 1880s. The British incursion into Egypt had set off a French effort to obtain compensation. France in particular, and Germany to a lesser extent, were looking for toeholds in northeastern Africa, supposedly so as to prevent total British domination of the region. The Italians had happened to start at Assab first and were able to keep up with the other powers in pressuring local rulers to place themselves under Italian "protection." More importantly, the Mahdist movement in the Sudan had finally succeeded in conquering the whole country by 1885. The Mahdists went on the offensive for the next ten years, attacking Ethiopia, the British- and Italian-occupied ports on the Red Sea, and Egypt. Although they were contained in each case, the Mahdists fully occupied British attention and prevented the British from extending their sway. The Italians and French thus got the opportunity to establish their colonies without strong British interference.

Equally significant was the emergence of Ethiopia as a power in northeastern Africa.[47] After more than two centuries of disunity and weakness, the traditional Coptic Christian country of Ethiopia had begun once again to form into a unitary state in the middle of the nineteenth century. This development was cut short by a British punitive expedition against the Emperor Theodore in 1868, after which the empire broke apart. In the 1870s, however, the ruler of the province of Tigre proclaimed himself emperor as John IV and began the same process of unification and conquest. He was opposed, and occasionally aided, by a number of other rulers, of whom from the 1880s on the most important was Menelek, ruler of Shoa. In the 1880s, the European powers attempted to use the internal divisions of Ethiopia and the rivalry of contenders for the emperorship to obtain a predominance over the country. The Italians tried to get the support of John, who managed in 1884 and 1885 to acquire most of Eritrea. The French, however, seized the main route of access to north central Ethiopia in French Somaliland, and John turned to them and against the Italians. The Italian government and the army command in Eritrea now decided upon outright conquest to turn their holdings into a large interior colony, possibly including all of Ethiopia. Grandiose plans were intimated by Crispi in public, but the actual military advance into the interior was stopped in 1887 by John, who defeated the Italian army and incidentally brought down Crispi's current government.

John was killed in battle with the Mahdists in 1889, and power in Ethiopia shifted to Menelek, who proclaimed himself emperor. The rise of Menelek was regarded in Italy as a guarantee of Italian paramountcy in Ethiopia, since the Italians had supplied him with military equipment. In 1889, Menelek signed the treaty of Wachali (Ucciali) with Italy, which among other things contained arrangements for Italy to handle Ethiopia's foreign relations. The Italian government publicly treated this as tantamount to making Ethiopia an Italian protectorate. When Ethiopian chiefs subsequently visited Italy, the public became wild with excitement over this tangible proof that Italy had at last entered the ranks of the great powers.

Menelek had no intention of letting Italy actually take control of his country or its foreign affairs. He later claimed that the Italians had tricked him at Wachali with different versions of the treaty and that he had not agreed to a protectorate. Actually, he used Italian self-delusion as long as was necessary to hold off the British and French, and then in the 1890s reversed himself in order to protect Ethiopia from the Italians with French support. In 1895, Crispi, then prime minister and faced with a loss of public prestige in the collapse of his imperial policy, dispatched a substantial army to Eritrea to invade Ethiopia. Under constant pressure from Crispi, the commanders of the Italian forces attacked Ethiopia in 1896 before their army was up to full strength and compounded their problems with a series of strategic errors. Menelek defeated them utterly at the battle of Adowa, with enormous Italian losses. Adowa was the greatest military victory of Africans over Europeans during the partition of Africa. Adowa, and Menelek's political skill, guaranteed the independence of Ethiopia and allowed it to pursue some imperial expansion of its own. The Italians were lucky that Menelek was willing to make peace quickly and allow them to keep Eritrea and expand into Somaliland. Menelek secured his access to the sea by arranging for the French to hold it for him by building a railroad from his capital at Addis Ababa to French Somaliland.

The catastrophe at Adowa was the end of Crispi as a politician, but it was not the end of imperialism in Italian politics. The failure in Ethiopia was treated, not as evidence of the illogic of Italian imperialism, but as a result of particular policy mistakes. The lure of imperialism as an integrating force in Italian politics remained strong. The nationalist political movements that expanded after 1900 emphasized it with increasing vigor.

The next round of Italian colonial expansion was directed against Turkey, which seemed to be on the verge of collapse. Many Italian business people pressured the government to move in to guarantee Italy a share of Turkish spoils ahead of time, since the Near East was seen as a prime future market. But again, the main concern was to use imperialism as a means of building broad support for the nationalist organizations that many businessmen favored as a counter to the expanding socialist party and trade unions, and in order to maintain the "centrist" cabinets before 1914. The most important figure in centrist politics, Sidney Sonnino, consciously used imperialism in this way.

The first target was the Turkish province of Libya. Taking advantage of the chaos of revolution in Turkey, Italy trumped up a cause for war in 1911 and captured Libya, a country with little apparent value to any European power.[48] Italy's possession was confirmed by treaty in 1912. Although public reaction was not as enthusiastic as had been hoped, the conquest confirmed the role of imperialism in Italian politics. It set the stage for Italy's designs on Anatolia (Asiatic Turkey) just after the First World War and for the expansionary schemes of Mussolini.

Not all the expansionary states of the late nineteenth and early twentieth centuries have been discussed in this chapter.

Several of the most important — Russia, the United States, and Japan — were not Western European powers and thus are excluded from detailed examination here. In each of these cases, however, similar general trends can be perceived. Imperialism appeared there not simply as an extension of specific economic interests or as a result of the spread of imperialist ideologies, but also as a response to political circumstances that differed in specifics but were often quite similar in general type.

FIVE

The Imperial Scramble, 1880-1910

T HE RIVALRY OF THE MAJOR EUROPEAN countries (and the United States and Japan) for overseas empires was one of the most publicized political phenomena of the period before World War I. We have already examined the origins of this rivalry; in chapter 6, I shall investigate some of its consequences and in chapter 7, I shall attempt to place it in a wider historical context. The present chapter is essentially a narrative of the main events of Western Europe's last period of massive imperial expansion. Some of the events described here are discussed in more detail in the interpretive chapters (4, 6, and 7). For convenience, we shall proceed by continent.

AFRICA

During the age of the New Imperialism, Africa displays, much more completely than any other continent, a close correspondence between the general expansion of European economic, political, and cultural control and the establishment of formal colonial empires. The vast majority of the African landmass was divided among the European powers between 1880 and 1910; earlier instances of informal expansion were followed almost inevitably by colonial conquest, and the further spread of European influences took place largely within a colonial context.

Formal European colonial acquisition began in Africa, as we have seen, well before 1880. In the late 1870s, on the eve of the scramble for Africa, certain areas of the continent were already under direct European control. The French had Algeria, the Senegal colony — recently expanded by Faidherbe, and a kind of assumed paramountcy over the areas that would later be the colonies of the Ivory Coast, Gabon, and a small part of Dahomey. Portugal controlled the coastal regions of Angola and Mozambique and a few small possessions in West Africa. Spain possessed portions of Morocco, while Italy had interests in small areas along the Red Sea. Liberia, an independent state, clung to an identification with the United States as its protection. The rest of the recognized European holdings were British: the Gold Coast, gradually (and unwillingly) taken over by the British government in the course of the century and informally extended into the interior by the British defeat of the Ashanti kingdom in 1874; the colony of Lagos, seized as a support for Christian Yoruba states and as a base for suppressing the slave trade; and South Africa, including the old Cape Colony, Natal (without Zululand until 1887), and the Boer states of Transvaal and the Orange Free State — the last two of which, annexed in 1877, would regain their independence by war in 1881. There were no other formal British colonies, although the British had for some years exercised various forms of informal political and naval control over most of the Guinea coast and, more recently, over Zanzibar. The primary reasons for the British presence in each of the cases were the suppression of the slave trade and the protection of British trade.[1]

The Occupation of Egypt

We have already looked at some of the explanations for the drastic political changes that commenced in the late 1870s, leaving only two sub-Saharan African states independent by 1902.

In most of these explanations, the occupation of Egypt in 1882 plays an important role. We have already seen that Egypt, with its modernizing but bankrupt government, came under the financial control of Britain and France in the late 1870s. A nationalist resistance movement under Col. Arabi Pasha arose in response. Arabi took over the government in 1881-82, reduced foreign control, and threatened to repudiate the national debt.[2] This upset European investors and their governments. In 1882, the British and French dispatched fleets to Alexandria, using the pretext of a riot there. Gladstone's government attempted to arrange a joint Anglo-French intervention in Egypt, but the French — and later the Italians — refused to cooperate. After bombardment of Alexandria failed to make Arabi change his policies, the British invaded Egypt in September 1882, defeated and captured Arabi, and occupied the country.

The British intended the occupation of Egypt to be temporary. They used their new position to reorganize the Egyptian government, to improve its finances (and thus its ability to pay its debts), and to increase their control over the Suez Canal. Although arrangements were made with France and Germany to continue joint international supervision of Egyptian finances, it soon became apparent that the British intended to retain the upper hand and to remain for a long time — a decision formalized by Lord Salisbury's government in 1887. Britain retained "informal" control of Egypt until the outbreak of World War I, when the khedive, nominally a Turkish official, was deposed and replaced by a British-appointed native Egyptian royal dynasty under British "protection." The British removed the protectorate in 1922. Egypt became theoretically an independent state but under strong British influence (and usually under partial military occupation) right up to the nationalist revolution of 1952.

The British occupation of Egypt involved Britain much more strongly than before in the affairs of Egypt's own colonial empire in the Sudan and the Red Sea. Supposedly in order to protect the Suez route to India, Britain occupied a series of Red Sea ports previously held by Egypt. This injected Britain into the chaotic politics of the Ethiopian region. In the Sudan, a nationalist, fundamentalist revolt against Egyptian rule appeared in the early 1880s led by Mohammed Ahmed, who proclaimed himself the Mahdi.[3] The revolt was primarily a response to rapacious tax-collecting by Egypt, to the assumption of power by an Egyptian bureaucracy in Khartoum, and to the antislavery policies that had earlier been forced by Britain on the Egyptian government. Beset by the British occupation, Egypt faced the Mahdi ineffectively. A British-led Egyptian army was destroyed by the Mahdi in 1883. He then went on the offensive, attacking Egyptian posts on the Nile and threatening Khartoum and the British Red Sea ports. At this juncture Gladstone decided to evacuate the Sudan and required the Egyptian government to appoint General Charles Gordon, former governor of the southern Sudan and a hero of the English antislavery movement, as governor-general of the Sudan to do the job. This was a gesture to public opinion, since Gordon was a highly popular figure. Gordon, however, was committed to British imperial expansion in furtherance of humanitarian goals. He decided to remain in Khartoum rather than evacuate it. He allowed himself to be besieged in 1884, expecting that the government would be forced to send a relief expedition and thus conquer the Sudan while rescuing him. Gladstone did eventually send an army, but it arrived at Khartoum in January 1885 too late to save Gordon. The British then left the Sudan to the Mahdist state until 1896, committing themselves only to defending Egypt from Mahdist attack.

Controlling the Upper Nile

Another consequence of the occupation of Egypt was a rivalry, rather mysterious in its logic even for the participants, for control of the Upper Nile. We have already examined some of the ideological and psychological motivation behind this rivalry and need only summarize the events here.[4] In a sense, the Mahdists for a while did the British a favor since they effectively neutralized the middle Nile and refused to come under the sway of any European power. It would have been better, of course, had the Mahdist state not been so aggressively expansionary itself, but between them, the British, Ethiopians, and Italians found that the Mahdist threat could be contained. Unfortunately, the unsettled condition of Ethiopia in the 1880s gave several European powers — especially Britain, France, and Italy — the opportunity to attempt to carve out spheres of influence or actual colonies. Britain's formal aim, which was to prevent a potentially hostile European state from getting control of the source of the Blue Nile, reflected an exaggerated emphasis on the security of the water supply on which Egypt depended. The Italian aims we have seen. The French were interested in securing access to new markets in northeastern Africa, in acquiring a handle on policy in Egypt, and in preventing a complete British takeover of that quarter of Africa. Nothing perhaps better illustrates the unreality of imperialist aims during the scramble for Africa than the preoccupation with the headwaters of the Nile, a preoccupation due almost totally to ideologies of empire derived from European politics. In any event, the success of Ethiopia in asserting its independence against the Italians, together with the British destruction of the Mahdist state in 1896-98, restored a kind of balance in the region. The British, French, and Italians occupied the Somali and Eritrean territories around Ethiopia, while in theory Britain and Egypt shared a "condominium" over the Sudan after 1898.

The British conquest of the Sudan in the 1890s, while it was billed in public as revenge for Gordon, was in fact the result of a British desire to eliminate a source of unrest in northeastern Africa. Even more importantly, it was the product of another of those semifanciful "strategic" conflicts with which late Victorian imperialism abounded. The French, pushing rapidly across West Africa and the northern part of the Congo basin in the 1890s, had extended their claims into the vicinity of the upper Nile.[5] In order to assert France's continued importance in Egypt and in Africa generally, the French government dispatched a small military expedition from Equatorial Africa to the southern Sudan in 1896 under the leadership of a Captain Marchand. As we have seen, this expedition arrived at Fashoda on the Nile in 1898. Meanwhile, news of the Marchand expedition, together with other factors, spurred Lord Salisbury's Conservative government to send an army to the Sudan to build a railroad south and to head off the French. On the way, the army wiped out the Mahdist state in several pitched battles, inaugurating the condominium. The British force met the already arrived French at Fashoda in 1898, setting off the Fashoda crisis discussed in the previous chapter. The French subsequently retreated, leaving the whole of Sudan to the British.

The Partition of East Africa

The race for control of the Nile was not, however, limited to the northeastern corner of the continent. It also — in part, at least — affected the partition of East Africa. Europeans looking for the source of the Nile and for likely areas for trade or missionary work — men such as Livingstone, Burton, and Speke — had explored the interior of East Africa up to the lakes region since the 1850s and had directed a considerable amount of European public attention to the area. More important than exploration itself, however, were the effects of the economic and political expansion into the East African interior of the Sultanate of Zanzibar.[6]

In the 1840s Zanzibar, under a new and aggressive dynasty, began asserting its preeminence over the Muslim Swahili-speaking trading cities of the East African coast. In the process, Zanzibar became a minor imperial power in its own right. At the same time, Zanzibari traders moved extensively into the interior, expanding the slave and ivory trades and increasing their control over them. This made Zanzibar a prime object of abolitionist attack in Europe from the 1850s onward. At the same time, however, the island began to assume a new importance in Indian Ocean trade. Not only was there a vast increase in the ivory trade (which, because ivory was transported by slaves, meant an increase in the slave trade), but also the Zanzibari government introduced the large-scale growing of cloves. Since British India was the center of Indian Ocean trade, the commercial growth of Zanzibar meant that it came increasingly under the economic sway of Britain. Up to the 1880s, British merchants carried on most of Zanzibar's overseas commerce. British consular officials, backed by the navy, began exerting growing influence over Zanzibari politics, and by the 1860s they were actually deposing sultans and selecting new ones. Thus Zanzibar, at the very time that it was becoming a minor imperial power in its own right, increasingly became an informal dependency of a major power. The abolitionist view of Zanzibar therefore came to have political significance. Humanitarian groups, prompted especially by Livingstone and other missionary-explorers, put heavy pressure on the British government in the 1860s and 1870s to force Zanzibar to stop slaving. The slave trade, although (unwillingly) outlawed by Zanzibar, did not in fact come to an end until the 1890s.

The British position in Zanzibar was taken in the 1870s as evidence of a general British sphere of influence over all of East Africa north of Mozambique, a circumstance that disturbed none of the other European powers until the 1880s – even though German trade with Zanzibar became nearly as large as that of the British by 1885. The situation changed drastically with the entry of the German colonial entrepreneur Carl Peters in 1884.[7] Acting with the reluctant permission of Bismarck, Peters signed a series of rather dubious treaties with chiefs in the hinterland of the coast opposite Zanzibar. Bismarck used these treaties to claim German sovereignty in the area. Bismarck's main motive in so doing, despite strong reservations about East Africa, was probably to maintain his procolonial image in domestic politics. But as Bismarck had predicted, Peters' actions set off a heated competition for control of East Africa, as that area suddenly came to be viewed in terms of European imperialist ideology and the Nile controversy. East Africa, was represented in public and in the councils of government as the route to the Nile's headwaters, for which Germany, Britain,

Portugal, and even the Congo Free State were in competition. According to hysterical imperialists in Britain, Egypt would be at the mercy of the power that controlled the sources of the Nile and thus could divert its waters. This was, of course, nonsense. Even ignoring the risk of war that such a project would have entailed and the astronomical expenses involved, a state successfully diverting the Nile would have ruined its citizens' investments in Egypt, which were what the state wanted to protect in the first place. But the obvious silliness of the "strategic" argument for control of East Africa did not prevent governments, politicians, and publicists representing special interests from using it extensively as an excuse for seizing East African colonies.

The actual reasons were more varied. Peters and his business associates believed that they could make money by monopolizing East African trade. Peters also wanted to use his East African exploits to create a political career for himself. William MacKinnon, the founder of the rival Imperial British East African Company (IBEAC), thought that a railroad through what would later be called Kenya could open up the fertile and heavily-populated area north and east of Lake Victoria.[8] In any event, the "strategic" importance of East Africa was largely a means of influencing public opinion and government officials already used to thinking in specious strategic terms.

The actual scramble for East Africa was complicated. British and German agents raced against each other in 1889-90 to sign treaties of protection with Buganda, the key state of the later Uganda, where warring political parties were already oriented toward different European missions there. This rivalry was cut short in 1890 by a treaty between Britain and Germany delineating boundaries and spheres of influence in East Africa. Britain got Uganda and the general area of Kenya as its sphere. Capt. Frederick Lugard, working for IBEAC, led a military force that intervened in a civil war raging in the kingdom of Buganda; in effect, he conquered the country and several neighboring provinces. In 1892-93, an extensive debate raged in

Britain about whether Uganda should be annexed. The Uganda issue was the occasion for a showdown between imperialists and anti-imperialists in both parliamentary parties.[9] In the end, in 1894, Uganda was taken over as a protectorate and subsequently expanded by conquest to fill the entire British sphere of influence. Britain annexed the area between Uganda and the Indian Ocean, later called Kenya, in order to provide access to Uganda. In the 1890s, IBEAC began the construction of a railway from the coast at Mombasa to Uganda, with much of the expense borne by the home government. The "lunatic expense," as it has been called, seemed to many observers to epitomize the lack of logic of late Victorian imperialism. Kenya required rapid economic development in order to pay for the railroad. From 1903 onward, the development policy in Kenya centered around alienating the lands of the indigenous peoples of the southcentral highlands and encouraging white European and South African settlers to take them over. White settlement thus became the distinctive feature of colonialism and economic development in Kenya.

Britain also became the formal protector of Zanzibar, which was, however, forced to give up to Germany its sovereignty over the mainland coast. The protectorate of German East Africa (the continental part of present-day Tanzania plus Rwanda and Burundi) existed until the First World War. It was never an economic success, but it had a profound effect on the inhabitants of many of its regions. One major effect was the spread of Swahili as a spoken language throughout East Africa, a development fostered by the adoption of Swahili rather than German as the standard language of the colony.[10]

West Africa

The activities of King Leopold and the International African Association in the Congo region have already been discussed. In the 1890s, the Free State competed strongly with the other powers, expanding its holdings to the north and east and into Katanga.

In West Africa we have already examined the general course of French expansion from Senegal. The expansion resulted from the relations with the larger western Sudan states established earlier by Faidherbe and from the impetus toward exploiting those relations created by the French political situation in the 1880s.[11] As we have seen, the western Sudan was represented to the French public as a potentially valuable market, and later as a route to the Upper Nile. The French colonial army swept rapidly eastward from Senegal in the 1880s and early 1890s, defeating the Muslim states along the Niger (many of which had themselves expanded earlier in the century during a series of religious revivals) and pushing toward Lake Chad. Because of the geography of the western Sudan and the large areas there under the sway of individual states, the French interior expansion moved swiftly and spectacularly.

In Guinea, which France had been threatening for some time, the conquest was a great deal slower. Although the British had agreed in the early 1880s to the general boundaries of the French sphere of control there, actual French occupation was fiercely resisted until well into the 1890s, especially by the forces of the Guinean national leader Samori Touré. In the Ivory Coast, where French economic interests were paramount in coastal trade and which had previously been briefly an official French protectorate, the declaration of French control was an easy step, followed by military occupation from north and south in the 1880s to stake France's claim to a connection with the French Sudanic empire. Farther east on the West African coast, the French protected the small trading state of Porto Novo against its larger (and less tractable) neighbor, Dahomey. In 1894, motivated by the northward expansion of the Germans from their new colony of Togo to the west and by the British advance in Yorubaland to the east, the French intervened in a dispute between Porto Novo and Dahomey and sent an army that conquered Dahomey after fierce resistance.

In Equatorial Africa, the explorations of Brazza and others were used as the basis of France's claim to a belt of colonies north of the Congo River which restrained the claims of the new Congo state.[12] Small French military forces occupied the area and pushed toward Lake Chad, where in the late 1890s they made contact with the forces coming from the west. The French had successfully hemmed in the British and German coastal colonies. In the course of their campaigns just after 1900 against the slave trader Rabeh, who had attempted to found a new state around Lake Chad in the ancient kingdom of Kanem, the French occupied the rest of the central Sudan. On the map, their new empire looked impressive. The British had, however, clearly taken the most immediately profitable parts of West Africa: Nigeria and the Gold Coast. Lord Salisbury referred to the French colonies as having "rather light soils," by which he meant that a large portion of the French West African empire was made up of the Sahara Desert.[13]

The British seizures in West Africa were more modest in extent. They grew out of previous British involvement in the region.[14] Sierra Leone, established as a refuge for freed slaves in the eighteenth century, had by stages become a British colony in the nineteenth. The main effect of the scramble for Africa in the 1880s was to define the colony's boundaries. The Gold Coast (present-day Ghana) had in essence already been occupied. In the 1820s, as we have seen, the British government had taken over control of the British forts along the Gold Coast. Officials there had attempted to convert this control into a protectorate and had been defeated by the powerful Ashanti Confederation in the interior. The forts had reverted to private control, but an informal protectorate had emerged all the same, thus generally worsening relations with the Ashanti. In the 1860s, due to astute politicking by the coastal Fante people and the influence of missionary societies, Britain officially assumed responsibility for the coast. This led immediately to the Ashanti War of 1874, in which the defeat of the Ashanti placed the central interior of the Gold Coast in a recognized British sphere of influence. In the 1880s, the British moved to solidify their control and to occupy areas to the north before the French did. In

1896 the British again defeated the Ashanti, and in 1901 the
Ashanti Confederation was annexed into the Gold Coast proper. We shall discuss the conquest and occupation of the various
regions of Nigeria in chapter 6.

The other main imperial claimant in West Africa (apart from
some minor activity by Portugal and Spain) was Germany,
which in a sense set off the coastal scramble by declaring protectorates over Togo and the Cameroons in 1884.[15] As we have
seen, Bismarck was not anxious for large German colonies in
the interior of Africa. In West Africa he reined in the officials
sent to administer the two new protectorates. Within a short
while, however, officials and interest groups at the coast were
arguing that coastal colonies made no economic sense if they
did not control their hinterlands. In the 1890s, therefore, the
Germans joined in the race to extend "effective occupation"
into the interior. They had few resources, however. In the end,
Togo was left as a small enclave (although at least twice as large
as could be economically exploited), while Kamerun (the German colony in the Cameroons) incorporated a large interior territory, much of which, however, could not be developed effectively from the Cameroons coast.

Southern Africa

The southern portion of the African continent was a continuous focus of European imperialist attention during the late
nineteenth century, mainly because important economic interests were at stake there. Much the same processes by which
domestic European politics and economic interests interacted
to influence the direction of imperialism elsewhere occurred
with respect to southern Africa. Because of the proven mineral
resources of the region, however, there was less need to advance
a "strategic" significance for it, at least as far as convinced imperialists in most European countries were concerned.

It had been strategic considerations that had caused Britain
to retain control of the formerly Dutch Cape Colony after the
Napoleonic Wars. Thereafter, the growth and expansion of the

Dutch (Boer or Afrikaner) population to the east into Natal and to the northeast into the Transvaal had created much difficulty for the British colonial administrators.[16] At each stage of the Afrikaner expansion, their extremely large demands for land and labor brought them into conflict with African populations. The British government would occasionally attempt to restrain the Afrikaners but would fail to do so, and in the end would back them up. In this way Natal was eventually annexed by Britain. In the 1830s and 1840s, Afrikaners pushing beyond the range of British authority established the independent settlements that became the Transvaal and the Orange Free State. The British authorities in the Cape Colony had attempted to establish sovereignty over the Boer republics, but in 1852 the British cabinet refused to allow the sovereignty to continue. In the meantime, both the Afrikaners and the British government had run up against the powerful Zulu nation.

The situation in South Africa was radically altered in the 1870s by the discovery of diamonds, first in areas (soon annexed by the British) adjacent to the Boer republics and then in the Afrikaner lands themselves. These discoveries immediately attracted investors and prospectors from all over the world, turned Cape Town into an important commercial city, and began the influx of non-Boers into the republics. We have already seen how Disraeli, responding in part to business pressure, annexed the Transvaal in 1877, only to become embroiled in wars with the Zulu (1879-80) and Afrikaners (1880-81). In 1881, Gladstone renounced British sovereignty over the Transvaal once again. In the 1880s, however, the discovery of gold in the Transvaal caused a gold rush, further immigration, and large-scale change in South Africa. It also brought big capital to the Cape Colony. One of the main instigators of what followed was Cecil Rhodes (1853-1901).

Rhodes was perhaps the most remarkable of the late Victorian imperialists.[17] The son of a clergyman, Rhodes was sent to South Africa in 1870 to make his fortune — which he did within two years, thanks to his shrewd dealings during the diamond boom. Throughout the 1870s and early 1880s, Rhodes divided his time between helping to form the De Beers diamond monopoly and attending Oxford. In the 1880s he branched out into politics, becoming the leader of an expansionary, pro-business party in the Cape Colony parliament and, in 1890, prime minister of the now self-governing colony. In the 1880s Rhodes also, as a private individual, formed a consortium, later chartered as the British South Africa Company, to "develop" the area later known as Rhodesia (Zambia and Zimbabwe). In connection with his role in De Beers and his design for Rhodesia, Rhodes also insinuated himself into British politics, eventually developing close relations with Joseph Chamberlain.

Rhodes was ruthless and often unethical, and he was perfectly capable of using imperialist appeals he knew to be exaggerated in order to enhance his political and business interests. On the other hand, he appears truly to have been imbued with a romantic notion of the destiny of the British Empire as the key to the progress of mankind. His frequent allusions to such a destiny in his speeches and writings could be dismissed as a cover for his material aims, but his establishment in his will of the Rhodes scholarships as a means of informally extending the empire probably demonstrates his sincerity. Rhodes' idea of a "Cape-to-Cairo" railway through territory completely under the British flag was undoubtedly in part a scheme to attract public support for declaring British control over the part of Central Africa in which the South Africa Company wanted to expand. On the other hand, Rhodes, hard-headed businessman though he was, appears to have been genuinely attached to this extremely dubious project. Rhodes was, in short, an enigma and thus a perfect symbol of late European imperialism.

Rhodes and the businessmen and politicians associated with him decided in the 1880s that the Boer republics would have to come under the British flag. Many Afrikaners, however, experienced a heightened sense of Boer nationalism as they contemplated the threat to their agrarian culture that economic change and the possibility of a British takeover represented.

These feelings led to support for a conservative nationalist movement headed by Paul Kruger, the president of the Transvaal during the second South African War. Although a substantial Boer elite group opposed Kruger and accepted economic change, even this group was put off by the aggressiveness of the Rhodes faction. Rhodes, on the other hand, found increased official British support, especially after Chamberlain became colonial secretary in 1895. Chamberlain and Rhodes both saw the South Africa Company's seizure of Rhodesia in the 1890s as a step in outflanking the Afrikaners as well as a means of annexing a mineral-rich area. The Afrikaners in turn acted increasingly independently of Britain, restricting immigration into the Transvaal, limiting the civil rights of non-Afrikaners, restricting the financial activities of foreign businesses, and arranging to have a new railroad built to the sea through Portuguese Mozambique rather than through British territory. They gave Chamberlain and Rhodes a weapon to use against them by seeking and receiving support from Germany. Rhodes and Chamberlain were personally not anti-German; both in fact believed that Germany and Britain should cooperate in overseas expansion.[18] But when the German government made weapons and loans available to the Afrikaner republics, British anti-Boer groups led by Rhodes and Chamberlain were able to attach the South African issue to the threat of German expansion and thus to all the fears of foreign competition and impending economic disaster that had been current in Britain for the previous twenty years.

The crisis began when Rhodes, then Cape Colony prime minister, secretly dispatched a South Africa Company force into the Transvaal in 1895 in order to support a non-Boer uprising in Johannesburg. The "Jameson Raid," named after its leader Dr. Leander Starr Jameson, failed totally. The Transvaal government arrested the raiders and turned them over to the British, who tried Jameson and put him in jail. Rhodes, although acquitted (wrongly) of complicity, saw his political career ended and spent his last few years in the development of

Rhodesia. But the Jameson raid made the aims of all sides clear. The Boer nationalists were pushed to more extreme measures and to closer links to Germany while Chamberlain and the Cape authorities committed themselves privately to creating the pretext for annexation. This was forthcoming over the issue of civil rights for foreigners in the Transvaal. The Boers rejected a British demand on this subject, and Britain went to war against the republics in 1899. The struggle began well for the Boers, who won most of the initial victories, and created a panic in Britain. We have already discussed the domestic British repercussions of the conflict. After a gruelling guerrilla war, the British won in 1902 but almost immediately decided to return autonomy to the republics. Eventually, in 1910, the two Boer states, Natal, and the Cape Colony were united by act of Parliament into the self-governing Union of South Africa.

Morocco

In previous chapters we have discussed the occupation by Europeans of every part of North Africa except Morocco. Morocco, a very old Muslim kingdom, had been an object of European attack since the fourteenth century. Many of its northern port towns were occupied by European powers. But during the height of the scramble for Africa in the 1880s and 1890s, it had not been taken over by any single power, mainly because an actual conquest of the politically fragmented country would have required an expensive military effort and because no single European state was overwhelmingly preeminent there. France and Spain both had long-standing designs on the country. Both of these nations, as well as Britain and Germany, vied with each other to extend investments and government loans in Morocco at the end of the century. To most observers, it seemed just a matter of time before Morocco would be "protected" by somebody.[19]

By 1904, French economic influence in Morocco had expanded to the extent that France was beginning to exercise political paramountcy. Germany, as part of a larger diplomatic strategy, protested and moved to assert its own position. Britain, in return for French acknowledgement of British control in Egypt, unexpectedly recognized a French sphere of influence in Morocco, while France and Spain worked out an arrangement whereby Spain got predominance over the northern and southern extremities of the country. A diplomatic crisis ensued. An international conference at Algeciras in 1906, while awarding a general predominance in political influence over the Moroccan sultan to France, guaranteed free economic access to all powers. Subsequently, the French greatly expanded their political influence. In 1911, Germany protested against the obvious French intention of annexing Morocco by sending a gunboat to Agadir and encouraging Moroccan resistance to the French. Another crisis followed, which was resolved when all of the powers agreed to a French takeover of most of Morocco. Germany received an extension of Kamerun in equatorial Africa, which was actually what the German government had wanted. The Moroccan sultan was forced to sign a treaty of protection with France in 1912. Since the sultan controlled only part of his country, the French and Spaniards subsequently had to dispatch large forces to conquer their protectorates. In the 1920s they had to send even larger armies to put down the extensive Rif rebellion.

THE MIDDLE EAST AND ASIA

While Africa was the scene of most of the formal European colonization in the late nineteenth century, the Middle East and Asia were also areas of great interest.

The Middle East

In the Middle East, the Ottoman Empire still held sway over most of its former territories, although in one way or another the Turks were deprived of control of their African territories by 1912. The European powers expected the imminent collapse of Turkey all through the nineteenth century and sought to be in position to pick up the pieces. But before 1914, the pieces did not fall quite as easily as expected. Instead, Turkey underwent a revolution in 1908-9 that brought a group of modernizing army officers to power.[20] Although the new government was faced with the same heavy interference with its internal administration and finances as the old, it was much more successful in playing the British off against the Germans. The Turks' major mistake was to enter World War I on the side of Germany in 1915. Although they fought much better than had been expected, the war brought the revolt of many of their Arab subjects and, in the end, the partitioning of much of their empire into mandates assigned to the victorious powers under the League of Nations.

Iran, or Persia as it was then known in Europe, had been subject to a double outside pressure throughout the nineteenth century.[21] From the north, the Russians pushed their control into the southern Caucasus and Turkestan. While Persia had been able to resist them to an extent, it had lost most of its northern border territories. From the south and east, it also came under pressure from the British in India. British policy in India had always encompassed economic penetration into Iran. In the nineteenth century, expansionist tendencies in the Indian government, enhanced by the Russian threat to take over all Persia (a threat far more real than the much-publicized Russian craving for India), led to direct British military intervention in Persia on several occasions. By the end of the nineteenth century, southern Iran was under the economic and political sway of British India, while the northern territories came under considerable Russian influence. Revolution in Persia in the early twentieth century did not improve the country's posture of independence.

In 1907, as Russia and Britain found themselves with similar diplomatic concerns in Europe, the two countries divided Iran into spheres of "commercial" interest. The Russians got the northern portion, where they proceeded to exercise political control, while Britain reserved part of the south as a market area. The British region did not include the oil-producing areas on the Persian Gulf that were shortly thereafter developed. As a result, Britain took the opportunity provided by the First World War and the Bolshevik Revolution to occupy the whole south of Iran and to nullify the Russian concession. After World War I, Iran entered European political calculations mainly as a source of oil.

India

Much of the political history of southern Asia is tied up with that of British India. The control of Indian foreign policy came much more strictly under the British cabinet because of the post-Mutiny reorganization and because of the extension of the telegraph to India. No longer could governors-general (now viceroys) or subordinate officials invade neighboring lands on their own authority and get away with it.[22] British India proper stopped expanding at its previous rate; there were no major annexations except that of Burma in the 1880s, and that was something of a special case. Nevertheless, the Indian government did attempt to gain indirect control over nearby states as a means of advancing India's economic policies and as a way of maintaining political stability on India's borders. Nepal remained an Indian satellite, Tibet became one, southern Iran remained under Indian control, and a large number of Indian Ocean islands were treated as Indian dependencies. After years of maintaining India's boundaries with Afghanistan at the Khyber Pass, the British in 1878 invaded the country in response to the pro-Russian policies of the Afghan government. Unlike the first Afghan War, the second (1878-79) was won by the Indian army. A pro-British ruler was placed on the throne, and parts of the Afghan border were annexed. Various other, more minor examples of expansion occurred, but altogether the range of British India's foreign policy contracted during the late nineteenth century.

Within India, British economic development policy continued to foster rapid technological change and rapid population increase. These changes transformed the face of India. But they also created severe social problems, such as periodic mass famines, with which the British could not really deal. The expansion of educational opportunities created a large, Western-educated elite and middle-class group which, however, other British policies tended to exclude from a share in government and from access to high positions in politics and business. It is therefore not surprising that new anti-British nationalist movements expanded rapidly in the late nineteenth century. Of these, the most effective was the Indian National Congress, formed in 1885.[23] The British responded with grudging reform and coercion, blindly repeating their experience in Ireland. During the period of Liberal government in Britain between 1905 and the First World War, new coercion acts were advanced in conjunction with the Morley-Minto reforms. The latter included a limited derogation of power to advisory councils in India, including the Viceroy's council, and a limited amount of Indian representation on them. The reforms did not go very far and, as we shall see in chapter 8, they did nothing to stop the growth of the independence movement.

Southeast Asia and the Pacific

We have already seen how the European powers partitioned much of Southeast Asia in the 1880s. Singapore and parts of Malaya had belonged to Britain since early in the nineteenth century; at the end of the century the exploitation of Malaya's rubber resources began. The rest of the partition commenced with France's conquest of Indochina in the 1880s, which encouraged the British to annex Burma. Siam (Thailand) retained its independence mainly by playing the British and the French off against one another.[24]

In the Pacific, a great deal of annexing occurred during the 1880s and 1890s, precipitated mainly by Germany's seizure of northeastern New Guinea, the Bismarcks, the Marshalls, and the Carolines in 1884-85. This led the British, acting largely in support of Australian and New Zealand traders, to claim numbers of islands. This in turn led to some international disputes, especially in Samoa, where British, Australian, New Zealand, German, and American business interests had been active for many years. The attempts by German consuls in the 1870s to use indigenous Samoan political disputes to create a German protectorate brought British and American resistance. The dispute was resolved by the declaration of a three-power condominium over Samoa and finally, in 1900, by a division of the island group between Germany and the United States, the British pulling out entirely.[25]

China

Primary European interest in Asia centered on China. Until the rise of Japan in the latter part of the nineteenth century, China was the most powerful Asian state — a country that held sway, sometimes in theory but often in practice, over a multitude of areas outside its ethnic boundaries. As a non-Christian country, China attracted missionary attention. More importantly, China was a large country, a manufacturing and industrial center with the world's largest population into which business interests all over Europe and America wanted to penetrate.[26] But economic reality was no more the sole motivating force behind European imperialism in China than it was elsewhere. Economic imagination, supplemented by the same kind of fascination with the exotic and the emergence of a patently unjustified sense of European racial and cultural superiority that we have seen at work in the case of India, operated on European views of China. By the second half of the nineteenth century, the "markets of China" had taken the place of the "markets of Latin America" in the mythology of European economic expansion. If only the obstructive Chinese government could be made more cooperative, if only China's traditional isolationist policies could be changed, and if only the Chinese market could be opened up, economic prosperity in Europe could be assured for decades. Behind the reality of China's economic potential, in other words, lay a myth which made China, like Africa and other areas, an element of late nineteenth-century European imperialist ideology.

In the wake of the Opium War (1839-42), the major European powers rapidly emulated Britain in seeking economic concessions from China. Although European trade in China was still restricted by law, the scope for it greatly enlarged in the 1840s and 1850s. European trade and missionary activities increased, especially in South China. When the Chinese government attempted to resist the increasing threat to its control, Britain and France went to war in 1856-60 and obtained even more concessions: wider trading rights, extraterritoriality for their citizens, more rights for missionaries, control of Shanghai, and so on. The United States took the opportunity to obtain some of the same privileges from China, while Russia received not only trading privileges but also Chinese recognition of Russia's occupation of the area north of Manchuria. In the 1860s, the Chinese gave up control of their customs collection to foreigners, although not to foreign governments. In 1864 the Chinese government and the foreign communities in Shanghai put down the T'ai P'ing rebellion, a popular movement combining elements of Christianity and traditional Chinese culture that had controlled much of southern China for over a decade.[27]

Between the 1860s and the 1890s, China was assailed continually by new outside pressures without undergoing a major political change in response to them. A number of able and ruthless conservatives came to the fore in the imperial government. The most prominent was the empress dowager, Tzu Hsi, who dominated the government periodically until 1901. The increasing presence of Europeans in the Chinese economy, their manifest military and technological superiority, and the rapid spread of Christianity and other aspects of European culture in China all discredited the government and created great forces for social change, but the government made only limited efforts to modernize China's administrative and military machinery. As a result, foreign governments found it increasingly easy to intervene in support of their nationals in China. At the same time, the overseas demand for labor and the new business opportunities engendered by the expansion of the world economy led to an exodus of Chinese that reached huge proportions by the 1870s, turning the Chinese — as opposed to their government — into one of the great expansionary peoples of the nineteenth century.

From about the middle of the 1870s, as European imperial rivalries became more intense, the Chinese government found itself besieged with demands for particular concessions from European governments, which used as excuses the many incidents that inevitably occurred in the course of European penetration. Britain and Germany became rivals over the question of which should "advise" and equip new units of the Chinese military. All the major European powers pressed the services of their banks as money-lenders and as builders of railroads. The situation finally came to a head in the 1890s, in part because of the appearance of Japan on the scene as an imperialist power in its own right.

In 1894, Japan went to war with China over Japan's claim to control Korea, which was theoretically a Chinese possession. The new Western-style Japanese army soundly beat the Chinese, and China had to sign a humiliating peace treaty giving Korea and the Liaotung peninsula to Japan and requiring reparations and many new economic concessions. This was a signal for all the other powers to demand "compensation."[28] Russia and France forced Japan to withdraw from the Liaotung peninsula, which fell under Russian control. All of the powers vied with each other to lend the reparations money to China in return for even more concessions. In 1897, Germany employed a pretext to occupy Kiaochow on the Shantung peninsula as compensation for the Russian gains and as a means of securing a monopoly for German mining investments in Shantung. Britain and France immediately seized ports to compensate themselves. Despite United States efforts to secure general free trade, China appeared to become a theater of major imperial conflict.

Within the Chinese government, a reformist group had slowly been making its influence felt. Under the stimulus of foreign pressure, the reformists essentially took over in the late 1890s and began a wholesale modernization of the civil service and military. In 1899, however, the dowager empress and other conservatives staged a *coup d'etat*, assumed control after executing some of the reformers, and planned a massive attack on the foreigners. Their hands were forced, probably before they were ready, by the actions of a popular antiforeign society called "Boxers" by the Europeans. The Boxers began a campaign of terror against Christians in order to encourage European reprisals. In 1900, mounting tension led to a popular antiforeign uprising, the Boxer Rebellion, sponsored and led by the Chinese government. The Boxers laid siege to the foreign embassies in Peking. The foreign powers responded with an expeditionary force that raised the siege, sacked Peking, and occupied much of northeastern China.

The aftermath included even more concessions, but also a falling-out between Russia and Japan over control of Manchuria and the area west of Korea. This led, in 1904, to war between the two powers, decisively won by Japan in 1905. Japan subsequently increased its influence over much of northeastern China, formally annexing Korea in 1910. Within China, the conservatives lost control and, despite attempts at radical reforms, the authority of the central government slowly collapsed. For the first time, leadership in China was taken over by Western-oriented, often Christian reformers, mostly from the south, of whom the most important was Sun Yat-sen (1866-1925). In 1911-12, a highly complex revolution occurred, in which the last emperor was deposed and a republic declared.[29] Although the republican government, eventually led by Sun, managed to acquire some independence of the Europeans, Japanese, and Americans, central authority remained extremely precarious and effectively collapsed by the 1920s.

Japan

The most remarkable event in Asia in the late nineteenth century was the rise of Japan to world power status, a subject that lies beyond the scope of this book.[30] Japan, threatened in the 1850s and 1860s with forcible inclusion within the Western-dominated world economy and with reduction to the status of an informal possession of the Europeans, reacted (after a protracted and violent internal revolution) by attempting to integrate Western technology and economic organization into Japanese culture. So successfully did Japan accomplish this feat that it became an economic, naval, and military power capable of joining in the carving up of China. Japan's entry into the ranks of imperial status was due to a number of factors, including domestic political conflicts and the desire to ensure Japan a substantial share of its most obvious markets and sources of raw materials.

The United States

The United States had maintained an official presence in China since early in the nineteenth century and had not been behind-hand in obtaining concessions when other states had done so. On the whole, however, the United States had not been in the forefront of imperialism in Asia and the Pacific, even after it forcibly "opened up" Japan in the 1850s. This changed in the 1890s with the growth of aggressive imperialism as a significant political ideology in the United States, which allowed business and other interests to direct American power overseas.[31] The United States annexed the Hawaiian islands in 1898 at the insistence of Americans who had overthrown the indigenous government in 1894 but who got their desired annexation only when they were able to put across a "strategic" argument based on the need to protect American access to Chinese markets. Also in 1898, during the Spanish-American War, the United States seized Manila and at the end of the war secured the entire Philippines and Guam from Spain. American imperialists justified these acquisitions on strategic grounds that in turn depended on the semimyth of the Chinese market. The United States had to fight a bloody and expensive guerrilla war in the Philippines after 1900 in order to keep a possession of little real value to it. This lack of value was recognized comparatively quickly, and American policy oriented itself toward eventual autonomy for the Philippines.

LATIN AMERICA

Of the three main continental theaters (outside Europe) of imperialist competition in the late nineteenth and early twentieth centuries, Latin America experienced the least direct political interference and the smallest amount of formal colonial expansion. The major offender in both respects was the United States. The United States' policy of treating Latin America as its own particular sphere of influence helped, however, to inhibit the European powers.

It should be emphasized that the lower level of formal imperial activity did not mean that Latin America became any less economically dependent on the outside world or that limited political intervention in support of European interests came to an end—quite the contrary. Both the movement of capital from a depressed European economy between 1873 and 1896 and the subsequent rapid expansion of a European-centered world economy brought many areas of Latin America into much closer connections with Europe and the United States and made them more dependent upon economic decisions arrived at in Europe.[32] This process of integration with the industrial world constituted a continuation of developments that had been occurring throughout the nineteenth century. The major changes at the end of the century resulted mainly from an acceleration of European investment and from the strong entry of the United States into the economy of much of Latin America. Most of the other forms of imperialist impingement upon Latin America were incidental to this major development.

Both Brazil and Argentina experienced strong tendencies toward industrialization in the latter part of the nineteenth century. Decades of large foreign investment in export industries, heavy European immigration, and the accumulation of capital by indigenous elite groups led to the creation of new industries and the growth of markets for domestic products. Yet unlike the United States, the larger Latin American republics did not leave the economic periphery of the world economy and enter the industrial center. Political interference by the industrial world had little to do with this. By 1900, the larger Latin American states had acquired sufficient strength and stability to be able to withstand the most blatant forms of foreign pressure. Mexico, between 1914 and 1917, felt the military weight of the United States but in fact managed to absorb it without excessive difficulty despite the fact that a revolution was going on. The United States and the European powers of course exerted subtler political influences, but very often at such cross-purposes that where some political stability existed, these influences could be played off against each other. The situation was different in the smaller countries. Weakness and political instability invited direct foreign control in the Caribbean and Central American republics. The United States took the lead here partly for "strategic" reasons (as in Panama) and partly to forestall other powers, particularly Germany, from occupying territory in the Caribbean. But in the larger states, the main foreign impingement was economic. Most explanations of the role of the outside world in preventing Latin American industrialization focus, not on the political actions of the industrial states, but on the private sectors of the industrial economies.

According to most versions of neo-Marxian "dependency theory," the leaders of European and United States finance deliberately promoted an international division of labor that left the manufacturing and financial center in Europe and the United States and caused the Latin American countries to specialize in raw materials and consumer goods exports, which are inherently less profitable.[33] This arrangement removed a critical amount of capital from Latin America just at the time, 1880-1914, when it was most needed for full industrialization. Economic development therefore did not reach its full extent, and the Latin American economies – and therefore the Latin American societies – remained dependent upon external forces.

It should be pointed out that dependency theory has concentrated primarily on questions of capital flow and secondarily on the location of the decision-making center in the late nineteenth-century economic situation of Latin America. In fact, the extension of the world economy and its continuing integration simultaneously made most industrial countries increasingly dependent on foreign markets, sources of raw materials, and sometimes even capital. "Dependency," in its general sense, is a characteristic of practically all members of the modern world economy. The problem for Latin America, as for much of the emerging "Third World" in the twentieth century, was that economic decisions in the world economy were made in the financial markets, company boardrooms, and to some extent government offices of the industrial countries. It was at these centers that capital, managerial talent, and control of demand factors were lodged. Since business decision-makers sought to maximize profits, they quite naturally operated so as to draw the bulk of the profits to themselves, mostly for reinvestment. As the world economy became even more closely integrated in the early twentieth century with the appearance of multinational corporations, it became even more difficult for countries such as Argentina, Brazil, and Mexico to influence the decision-making process. Only action by Latin American governments could have counterbalanced the effects of the external location of the decision-making structures. Except in Mexico from about 1917, such intervention by governments did not occur until the Second World War, and then not effectively until international cartels of the governments of primary-goods-producing countries appeared in the 1960s.

Compared to these major developments in Latin America's economic relations with the industrial countries, the more overt political forms of imperialism were less important. The United States, while an imperialist power itself, acted to check the schemes of other powers. The larger Latin American states were capable, in any event, of effective resistance, as the United States learned during its invasion of Mexico in 1916-17. Latin American states learned to play the powers off against one another. The United States took over several small Caribbean and Central American countries, apart from the temporary occupation of Cuba and the permanent seizure of Puerto Rico after the Spanish American War (Haiti, 1915; Dominican Republic, 1916; Nicaragua, 1912). But except for Theodore Roosevelt's forcible creation of Panama so as to build the Panama Canal, these seizures were not undertaken in support of politically important business interests.[34] Rather, they generally resulted from political instabilities that threatened small United States economic interests and created the possibility of European intervention that would supposedly have threatened the Panama Canal. On the whole, even United States imperialism in Latin America tended to be temporary and ineffective.

The tardiness of Latin American governments in taking effective action in the world economy was due primarily to causes other than conscious European and United States political imperialism. Latin American governments tended to be unstable, having to confront socioeconomic change with fewer resources of any kind than European governments did. The most stable Latin American governments of all, such as that of Porfirio Diaz in Mexico (1877-1910), were often run by people who received great personal benefits from the unimpaired investment of foreign capital in their countries — in other words, by economic "collaborators." The ending of the unequal economic relationship between Latin America and the rest of the industrial-centered world economy thus had to await further political development in the Latin American states.

The only important case of external aggression in Latin America in the period of the imperial scramble of the late nineteenth century was that of the United States' seizure of Cuba and Puerto Rico from Spain in 1898.[35] The origins and consequences of the Spanish-American War lie somewhat beyond the scope of this book. The development of American imperialism in the 1890s, however, appears to have resulted from patterns of domestic politics and overseas economic involvement that closely followed European models. The United States experienced its own New Imperialism in the late nineteenth century mainly because of the same desires to create consensus and combat political fragmentation that affected European imperialism. But because the United States had developed effective means of conducting politics in a complex modern society (through broadly based parties and broadly appealing ideologies), the political requirement for such phenomena as imperialism was correspondingly smaller than in Europe. Moreover, although United States businesses possessed important interests in Latin America, the United States economy remained largely self-oriented. Its most important external connections were with Europe. Thus in almost every respect, formal imperialism was a much less important phenomenon in the United States than it was in Europe and had a vastly smaller effect on the policies of the United States over a long period of time.

SIX

Colonial Systems in Operation, 1880-1940

I N THIS CHAPTER WE SHALL DISCUSS the impact of formal colonial rule on parts of the non-European world in the modern era. Late European imperialism, as we have seen, encompassed a great deal more than the establishment of new colonial regimes. It included political aspects of the expansion of the world economy as well as political and ideological developments in Europe. Often, in fact, once a colony had been acquired and secured from other nations' designs, its economic development ceased to be of much interest to the public. Quite apart, however, from their roles in the history of imperialism, both the new colonies of the late nineteenth century and the older ones that experienced reorganization during the same period played important historical parts as agents of change and as influences on the structure of the modern world. Much of the politics, economics, and social conditions of the majority of the present members of the United Nations was shaped by their colonial experiences. We cannot summarize the colonial histories of all of these countries. Instead, we shall review some of the major issues and general conditions of colonial rule, and then we shall discuss the nature and consequences of colonialism in three representative colonies.

THE IMPACT OF COLONIAL RULE:
MAJOR QUESTIONS

In the last twenty-five years, certain major questions have dominated the literature on the colonial periods in the histories of newly independent countries. What effect, in the long run, did the colonial interval have on the political development of these countries? Until not long ago, it was normally assumed in the industrial countries that colonial rule had an overwhelmingly important effect in encouraging political change.[1] The standard notion of decolonization before World War II was that independence would come when the colonial governments had totally converted indigenous political systems to European models. (Even policies of indirect rule were oriented in this way.) Accordingly, when decolonization occurred with unexpected rapidity after 1945, the political difficulties experienced by many new nations were ascribed to the untimely cutting-short of the period of colonial tutelage, which left many premodern elements in place in these countries' political systems. As far as the assumed goal of political development (Western-style democracy) was concerned, colonial rule was assumed to have brought about nearly all positive elements of change. Its frequent lack of success in achieving the goal was thus due mainly to the shortness of the colonial period. In fact, as we shall see, this view was largely an apology for colonial rule, framed in the last days of empire. The political effect of colonialism was great, but so were its limitations, and its impact was very complex.

The impact of colonial rule on economic, social, and cultural change was even more complicated. While colonial administrations fostered socioeconomic "development" on the European model, the idea that such changes could be in any sense total was seldom seriously entertained. Colonial administrations could attempt to impose European political forms, but almost all colonial authorities agreed that more general societal changes were matters of adaptation and possibly of new creation and were thus highly complex phenomena. And so they were. It has become increasingly clear that colonial rule was only one of many factors for change in the histories of Third World countries.[2] All colonial governments, of course, made economic development one of their prime objectives. And yet often, try as they might, they failed to alter basic production patterns in the ways they had intended. Many of the economic and social effects of colonial rule were entirely unexpected by the colonial authorities. One of the reasons for this was that the colonial authorities were not the only ones concerned. Private European businesses and indigenous social and economic structures also affected what happened to colonial economies. Official economic policy was not the same as economic reality.

Many other questions are debated in the literature. Did colonial rule encourage healthy economic development, or did it warp natural economic change to make colonies permanently dependent on the industrialized countries? Did colonial rule help or hinder the evolution of peasant economies? Did white European settlement in such colonies as Kenya and Southern Rhodesia accelerate or misdirect economic change? Did colonial rule effectively "Westernize" colonial cultures, and if so, was this a good thing? We shall discuss these questions later, when we examine specific colonies.

FOUNDATIONS AND CONSEQUENCES OF COLONIAL POLICY

Although colonial policies were not the only forces for change in European colonies, they were sufficiently significant that we should examine general patterns in them and compare them as they were formulated in different colonies. Certain conditions under which policy was established and applied in many areas helped to determine not just the ways in which the colonial governments operated, but also the effects of colonialism on indigenous societies.

The Problem of Financial Solvency

Perhaps the most important and general of these conditions was the financial insolvency of colonial governments. In all of the early European colonial empires, it had been taken for granted that colonies had to pay the costs of their own administrations and if possible render a surplus to the home government. This had not always been the case in reality (New France, for example, had continually run a deficit), but exceptions were rare. Unprofitable colonies conveyed little prestige in the seventeenth and eighteenth centuries. At the end of the nineteenth century, however, most major European powers possessed some overseas territories that did not pay for their governments, and others that barely did so. This awkward situation was the result of many circumstances, of which the most important was that much of the imperial acquisition in the 1880s and 1890s had taken place in the atmosphere of economic unreality that we examined in chapter 4. In the hysteria of imperial expansion, ideological rather than dispassionate economic considerations had often prevailed.

This is not to say that economics had nothing to do with late Victorian expansion. We have seen that economic conditions in Europe and Europe's economic connections overseas strongly influenced the direction of European imperialism. Occasionally, for example in South Africa, very real and specific economic interests predominated among the causes of imperial takeover. Some colonies in the late nineteenth century incorporated successful commercial economies. But even this did not necessarily guarantee fiscal solvency for the colonial administration. In the German colony of Kamerun in West Africa, for example, several trading and development companies did reasonably well, especially those eligible for official mail contracts, other hidden subsidies, land grants, assistance in displacing African commercial "middlemen," and permission to impress labor.[3] And yet the tiny German administration there was always in deficit and had, right up to 1914, to be supported by annual subventions from the home government. Bismarck's expectation that the trading companies would assume the minimal costs of government was disappointed when those costs skyrocketed because of the need for "effective occupation." The trading companies begged out of their commitments, and the government was left holding the bag. Kamerun's aggregate economic record (before 1914) was mixed. Companies building railroads made money, mainly because of government interest guarantees. One large land concession company went bankrupt, but another, heavily backed by Belgian capital, made a considerable profit. But none of this made any difference for the government. In attempting to create the conditions for profitable economic development, the administration found its expenses continually increasing faster than its revenues.

This sort of pattern was constantly repeated in the newer colonies of most of the imperial powers. Many colonies, including the majority of French African territories and a number of British colonies such as Gambia, were even less able to support profitable enterprise than was Kamerun. Even when a colony managed to balance its accounts, as was customary in the British colonies, it could do so only by drastically restricting government activities. There were, of course, exceptions, such as Rhodesia, but not many.

The financial inadequacies of colonial governments had a great many effects. Although most colonies were acquired and held by force, this force was seldom overwhelming — mainly because of finances. For the most part colonial rule, although authoritarian, was not totalitarian because it could not afford to be. It was based mainly on a temporary superiority in military technology and political organization.[4] Undoubtedly, had any major European state wanted to mass its strength in any of its overseas territories, it could have effected practically any change that it desired. But no European power did; rather, because of the economic insignificance of most colonies, the desire to spend as little as possible on them, and the financial weakness of colonial administrations, most colonies were operated on a shoestring. This required the adoption of a great many expedients.

Political Consequences of Colonialism

One of these expedients was "indirect rule." Although the theory of indirect rule was later elevated by Lord Lugard (governor of Nigeria, 1912-19) into a programmatic doctrine, indirect rule was originally nothing more than the necessary practice of colonial authorities almost everywhere.[5] Regardless of governmental theory or administrative style, colonial administrators had to depend heavily on the assistance of the peoples they ruled. In most cases, dependence extended beyond the employment of Africans and Asians in the lower ranks of government to the cooptation of pre-existing political organizations. In some cases, in fact, even social structures that had previously been unimportant or that had strongly resisted the Europeans were seized upon as agents of administration. In addition, most colonial administrations found it easier to buy off indigenous elites with a share of power than to attempt to suppress them by force. This, of course, involved dangers. An unsuppressed elite could always lead a revolt, which was what happened in the 1920s during the Rif revolt in Spanish and French Morocco.[6] Usually, however, cooptation was successful. The colonial powers normally failed when they were prevented from offering adequate political and economic inducement, for example by the existence of a large white-settler population. It was not accidental that colonial officials tended to dislike white settlement, which limited their options, or that the first serious post-World War II violent resistance experienced by the British in Africa came in Kenya, dominated by its white farming class.

Dependence of the colonial rulers on the ruled took many forms. Although not strictly a colony after 1910, South Africa presents one end of the scale of approaches to the control of non-European peoples.[7] It was a complicated case. On the one hand, the South African War (1899-1902) ultimately resulted in almost complete autonomy for the white inhabitants of South Africa and an agreement by the British to respect Afrikaner cultural integrity in return for Afrikaner acceptance of full economic development. On the other hand, relations between the government and the black population exhibited the most extreme form of control and lack of dependence on indigenous social structures. And yet, even in South Africa, some cooptation was necessary. For example, although the central political structure of the Zulu nation was broken up by the British in the 1880s, both the British and later the South African governments found it expedient to support a fragmented system of Zulu chiefships and to protect Zulu culture and national identity. Other indigenous ethnic groups and political organizations were also maintained in a dependent status. This policy gave the white authorities the ability to hold out incentives to a legitimate but ethnically-divided elite, which helped to prevent the growth of modern resistance organizations among Africans. Thus even in a repressive colonial society unusually able to afford overwhelming predominance, indirect manipulation of traditional structures was found to be useful.

It has been argued that one of the reasons for the political instability of many former colonies after independence, especially in Africa, was that the colonial governments had done little to promote the development of a qualified governmental and business leadership.[8] There is a considerable amount of truth to this accusation in many cases, but often the reality was much more complicated. Except in certain areas (such as the Belgian Congo) where economic activity was sufficiently extensive to attract lower- and middle-level managerial personnel from Europe, colonial authorities and businesses had to recruit them from the indigenous population and to educate them. In practically every colony, a Western-educated elite grew up around the colonial administration and European commercial enterprises. In most cases (India was a major exception), this elite was indeed not large enough to take on all governmental and commercial functions immediately upon independence, but this was a relatively temporary phenomenon and probably not a major contributor to instability. The Western-educated elite would have been larger and better trained had it not been for two factors: the comparative poverty of the colonial governments, which curtailed their support of education and restricted the number of government positions open to qualified candidates, and the fact that colonial authorities often came to consider their Western-educated subordinates to be a threat to European rule. Connected with the latter was often a personal bias against non-Europeans who attempted to follow Western customs and held European-type jobs. The apprehension of "Westernized" elites as effective opponents was sufficiently justified, especially in India from the late nineteenth century.[9] By the time of the First World War, in many colonies there was an emphasis on keeping the new, nontraditional indigenous elite subordinate in position and limited in size, and also a tendency to confer higher status on the traditional elites. In many places, of which India is an example, colonial governments in the twentieth century emphasized traditional structures ever more strongly and played traditional elites off against one another and against the Western-educated elites as nationalist resistance grew.

In many places, then, the political legacy of colonial rule was not so much the lack of an indigenous political leadership as it was the presence of too fragmented and heterogeneous a political leadership. Political structures that in a "normal" (independent) system might have modified themselves or been totally eliminated were juxtaposed against truly modern structures.[10] Political fragmentation was deliberately encouraged by the colonial authorities as a means of maintaining control, whether or not they disguised this policy as "indirect rule." Thus, colonial rule helped practically to guarantee political instability upon the withdrawal of the European authorities after World War II. Such instability was not universal and a great many other factors helped to contribute to it. It can moreover be argued that a weak colonial government at least left some indigenous political structures standing, which a strong government would not have done. We need not condemn weak colonial rule on account of its weakness, but we do have to take note of the historical consequences of that weakness.

The Creation of Dependent Economies

One important result of colonialism in many areas was the creation of dependent economies: economies that could not function at the national level without the heavy participation (and usually direction) of the imperial metropole.[11] Economic organizations in the European countries, whether governmental or private, would make the decisions and attempt to carry them out, while the colony itself would have little input into the process. Not all colonial economies became so dependent (South Africa, for example), but in many cases colonial rule brought an exaggeration of the kind of dependency that we discussed with respect to the Latin American economies. As in Latin America, so in the actual colonial empires there appeared dependent economic elites that were frequently the same as the coopted political elites. Dependency could extend below the elite level. In the Gold Coast (Ghana) and Nigeria, colonial rule and economic penetration encouraged the growth of middle-class social groups undertaking the management of small capitalist businesses and leading the way (much more effectively than any social planning by the colonial governments) toward the adaptation of traditional society to the modern world.[12] These middle-class groups were "dependent" in varying degrees. Gold Coast cocoa farmers were at the mercy of international forces over which they had little control. Employees of European firms in places like Lagos and Accra were even more directly dependent. Nigerian market-women, however, whose occupation predated colonial rule, were not so thoroughly under European control. The Nigerian colonial

government could influence their economic behavior only indirectly through taxation policy, which led in the 1920s to great
political resentment.

One highly significant economic consequence of colonial rule
was regional economic integration.[13] In many areas — for example, in large parts of Central Africa — national or regional
economies cannot be said to have existed in the modern sense
before the imposition of colonial rule. In other areas — the Gold
Coast, for example — already existing large-scale regional
economies were simply taken over and partly adapted to European uses. In either case, the impact of colonial economic
policies often had profound and long-lasting consequences.

Both the economic conditions in newly-acquired colonies in
the late nineteenth century and their attractiveness to European
investors varied enormously. Some colonies, including several
in French West and Equatorial Africa, attracted almost no
financial interest except from a few small business people willing to establish themselves outside of France. Others with rich
mineral resources, such as Northern Rhodesia (Zambia) and
the Katanga (Shaba) province of the Belgian Congo (Zaïre), attracted investment easily. Places like South Africa would have
experienced heavy investment regardless of the presence of colonial government — which was dispensed with after 1910
anyway. In most cases, the major segments of European
business were generally unwilling to jump into colonial
investment.

The making of colonial economic policy was a complex and
varied process, usually involving interaction between the central colonial authorities in the European countries and the
colonial governments overseas. Big business interests, in the
comparatively few instances in which they were concerned with
colonial policy, could influence decisions in both places. Small
traders and business people in the colonies were usually ignored
by the central colonial departments but could often exert considerable influence overseas. Governments also responded to

domestic political requirements and to prevailing imperialist ideologies in making colonial economic policy. For example, just after 1900 the German government helped to sponsor a scheme for creating peasant production of cotton in Togo. The scheme resulted partly from pressure by the textile industry, but partly also from an official desire to demonstrate that the colonies could fulfill the role assigned to them by economic theories of colonialism prevalent in Germany.[14] The Togo cotton program failed, as did many similar schemes in other colonies (for example, the post-World War II British groundnut scheme in Tanganyika). Of all the factors influencing colonial economic development policy, however, probably the most important was the need for revenues to make the colonies fiscally self-supporting.

In most cases, the key to colonial solvency was seen to be in the encouragement of European capital investment in the colonies and in the creation of colonial labor forces. In both of these activities, the administrations of the individual colonies took a leading role. The preferred sources of capital were the larger European financial institutions. Since this kind of capital did not usually flow readily to the colonies, governments were forced to coax it out. British and German authorities, for example, made large concessions of land and other privileges in the late nineteenth century to colonial companies in order to encourage investment.[15] This policy seldom worked well. Companies would often not live up to their commitments, and it became customary even in areas where investment was not especially risky for companies to insist on land concessions, tax exemptions, monopolies, interest guarantees, and sometimes disguised forced labor. So unsatisfactory was the direct concession policy that by 1914 in most colonies it was being superseded by another, less distinct policy that emphasized the role of the colonial governments as the directors and initiators of economic change. This newer approach was still primarily oriented toward developing exports, but it seemed to open a

larger range of developmental options. The new policy direction was usually associated with the emergence of professional
colonial services in most of the imperial countries.[16]

Many aspects of early-twentieth-century political and social
policy in the European colonies were in fact closely related to
the colonial administrations' assumption of economic direction
without having an abundance of resources to allow them to do
so. The British cult of indirect rule had this kind of economic
aspect: it favored gradual economic development through the
cooperative adaptation of traditional political and economic
structures to export production as the surest road to solvency.
In the German colonies, one basis of "humanitarian" policies of
protecting indigenous societies was a concern for preserving
small-scale trade and peasant agriculture as a part of government economic development policy. Encouragement of small-
scale peasant agriculture did not preclude industrial-type
development where that might be appropriate, but in most
cases it was thought that this would occur more naturally and
successfully later, when the colonial economy and population
were ready.

One of the major accomplishments of colonial rule in many
countries was the building of transportation facilities such as
railroads and harbors — large capital-intensive projects that
could not be left entirely to private initiative. Sometimes,
however, the expectations attached to these projects were
unreasonably high. Before the First World War especially,
many officials believed that the extension of railroads into areas
of subsistence agriculture would stimulate peasant export production almost by itself.[17] Sometimes this would happen, but
more often, successful economic modernization required a
whole set of complementary economic changes. Colonialists'
faith in public works projects as generators of economic change
lasted a long time and, like many other colonial ideas, eventually merged with postindependence concepts of economic
development.

There were, of course, factors in development policy peculiar to individual colonies. In Kenya, for example, decisions taken in the early twentieth century by the British government and Sir Charles Eliot, Commissioner of the British East Africa protectorate, led to a policy of encouraging white agricultural settlement in the highlands around Nairobi.[18] This policy displaced the Kikuyu, the largest African ethnic group in the area, from their farmlands and created a high degree of racial antagonism that culminated in the Mau Mau revolt of the early 1950s. On the whole, white-settlement policies went against the assumptions of most British (and non-British) colonial officials after about 1900. Officials tended to think that white settlement was inefficient and would interfere with proper economic and social development. This so-called official "humanitarian" view often clashed with an alternative, "frontier-agriculture" conception, which was itself an extension of earlier thinking about such white-settlement colonies as Australia, Canada, and New Zealand. In German East Africa before 1914, both types of colonial policy and both types of colonial reality (settler plantations vs. African peasant agriculture) were juxtaposed and the subjects of a running political feud within the colony and in Germany.[19]

We have seen that one of the consequences of colonial rule was the creation of dependent economies in many of the European colonies. It is, however, difficult to determine how much of this was due specifically to colonialism and how much to the extension of the growing world economy into colonial areas, in part, although not exclusively, through the medium of colonial development policy. Most colonial economic policies were of course intended to facilitate the integration of the colonies with the world economy. Did colonial rule simply act as the conduit of economic forces, or did the peculiar conditions of colonization have some special effect of their own? No universal answer can be given to this question, but examples can be cited in which the colonial situation clearly exaggerated the dependence of large sectors of indigenous economies — not only on international markets, but also on specific European enterprises.

In the Gold Coast (Ghana), government policy encouraged the adoption of cocoa farming by peasant proprietors, who were supported by a modest transportation network to allow them to get their products to market.[20] The government also, however, sanctioned a virtual monopoly on cocoa buying by a consortium of British business houses which allowed the consortium to fix the price of cocoa within the colony. The consortium could cushion itself against the effects of changes in the international market by reaping large profits in times of high prices without passing much of the profit on to the growers. This was permitted partly as a benefit to British business, but even more, it was supposed to attract capital. As it happened, however, the bulk of the real capital investment load was borne by the highly efficient African cocoa farmers themselves, who invested their time and savings in new plantings and went into debt to the consortium. In the case of the Gold Coast, the existence of colonial rule led to a lack of optimization in an effective export industry that the colonial authorities otherwise encouraged.

Similar patterns of economic deviation and dependency were found in many other colonial areas, especially where the peasant-agriculture model was followed. More than that it is difficult to say about the overall economic effects of colonialism on a worldwide basis without resorting entirely to ideological pronouncements. The colonial experience was so varied that the actual role that colonial rule played must be assessed case by case.

STYLES AND STRUCTURES OF COLONIAL RULE

A great deal has been written about the administrative structures of the European colonial empires and about the various theories and policies according to which they operated. Significant as these aspects of imperialism were, however, it must be kept in mind that they were not the only factors involved in the colonial situation and that they were usually less important than those which we have already discussed.

Colonial administrative structures and theories were in fact remarkably similar among the colonial powers. Certain countries with long colonial experience and substantial imperial reputations — especially Britain and the Netherlands — set a relatively uniform example for the rest, and the major figures in the late-nineteenth-century imperial expansion were conscious of each other's actions and opinions. Even when the theories of governance were formally different — as between the concept of indirect rule in some of the British colonies and the idea of centralized administration characteristic of French colonialism — circumstances (especially financial poverty) often reduced the differences to insignificance. In practice, most colonial administrations had to rule in large part through indigenous elites simply because they could not afford to do otherwise.

As far as administrative structure went, all of the colonial empires were hierarchical, bureaucratic, and authoritarian in form, designed supposedly to implement decisions rather than to create a consensus. The exact point at which real policy was actually made was sometimes difficult to determine. In many of the colonial empires, the central colonial administrative authority was fragmented.[21] Until just before the First World War, for example, British colonies came under the Colonial Office while protectorates such as East Africa came under the Foreign Office. Almost as soon as this problem was corrected, the government set up a Dominions Office to deal with the self-governing territories. The India Office was always separate. In Germany and France, colonial policymaking was not quite so fragmented institutionally, but it was organizationally subordinated to other political considerations. Originally the French colonies were placed under the Ministry of Marine, while the German Colonial Department remained part of the Foreign Office until 1907. In all three empires, the parliament played an important but inconsistent role in the making of colonial policy.

None of the major colonial powers entered the age of the New Imperialism with an organized, specifically trained colonial service except for Britain in India and the Netherlands in the East Indies. All of them subsequently developed such services, initially from very heterogeneous sources: the military, agents of concession companies, members of consular services, and the like. By 1900, however, Britain, France, and Germany were well on their ways to establishing corps of officials similar to their home civil services.[22] In no country did the colonial service attain a high degree of prestige; the French and German colonial services were decidedly at the low end of the bureaucratic status hierarchy. Nevertheless, by the time of the First World War, most of the major powers essentially ran their empires through trained, professional bureaucracies that had developed their own distinctive group outlooks and ideologies (including the economic development ideology discussed previously) and had captured a large share of the practical responsibility for making policy.

There were, of course, certain differences in administrative style, theory, and practice among the different colonial empires, especially with respect to "native policy." There existed no set formula for native policy for the British Empire, but it is possible to identify a distinctive amalgam of colonial service assumptions, humanitarian ideology, economic development theory, and administrative techniques. In most colonies, indirect rule was, as we have seen, the norm. Lip service was paid to the idea of eventual autonomy or independence in most nonwhite British colonies, but until the Second World War this was taken seriously only in a few places, such as India. Ideas of cultural change were part of the general ideologies of imperialism. Colonial authorities were committed not only to raising economic standards but also to encouraging the spread of European culture among non-Europeans. Usually in the British colonies, however, this was not interpreted as meaning total cultural change. Rather, the instruments of cultural change, especially schools, were intended to supply educated persons for the political and economic structures of the colonies and, by the mid-twentieth century, to spread at least some primary education quite widely. The idea of establishing secondary and higher educational systems on the Indian model throughout the British Empire had occasional vogues but was not seriously implemented until almost the time of decolonization.[23]

In the French colonies, on the other hand, education and cultural change were treated more systematically, at least in theory.[24] Views on education and colonial culture change varied with changes in the ideological climate in France and in general ideas as to whether colonial policy should aim at the "assimilation" of the elites of the colonies into a greater French empire or at the "association" of legally separate colonies with France on an institutional basis. As in the British colonies, the lack of financial resources made any consistent effort at imposing a complete educational program practically impossible. The French also attempted to provide fairly broad primary education, but they devoted most attention to the inculcation of French culture among colonial elites. Secondary-school curricula were tied strictly to those in France, and French was normally the language of instruction. In many French colonies, especially Senegal, the policy of assimilation held out the reward of the political franchise to non-Europeans who attained secondary educational certificates. Because of limited educational opportunities and the rigor of the curriculum, however, few people achieved this status, even in Senegal.

Colonial military policies varied as well.[25] The British maintained a large army in India that was, after the Mutiny, closely coordinated with the British army. Except for the Indian forces, however, Britain did not establish a full colonial army separate from the regular army. There were native regiments and police forces in several different colonies, but these were not large. The French, on the other hand, maintained both a large regular European army in Algeria and a separate colonial army in its other colonies. Unlike the British, the French raised several hundred thousand African troops during the First World War for service in Europe, a practice the British followed on a smaller scale in 1939-45. The other powers followed various practices. Contrary to the claim made by the Allies at the end of World War I, Germany's colonial military forces were extremely small, mainly because of financial limitations. The colonial military was only a minor political factor in most British colonies (except India); the situation in French colonies varied. In the Portuguese colonies, the military played a significant political role.

The administrative structures of colonies tended to be fairly uniform, especially after the initial unsettled period of colonial rule.[26] Colonies were usually headed by governors with extensive theoretical powers but under close supervision by the home authorities in matters of legislation and finance. In most colonies, the governors were advised by governors' councils. Much of the politics in many colonies revolved around the relations between the council and the governor, around questions about the council's function, and around the method of selecting the council. Usually, the official position was that the councils simply supplied expert advice to the governor from the major European interest groups in the country, that they should be appointed by the governor, and that the majority of members should belong to the civil service. In contrast, European business and settler groups, as they became organized and developed political contacts at home, would often press for an elected (white) majority on the council and for transformation of the council into a legislative body. In many colonies, the council also became the initial focus of attention for European-educated indigenous elites. These groups usually not only wanted the council turned into a legislature, but also wanted it to exercise control over finances and to be elected by a franchise that would guarantee a non-European majority. This last type of political dispute was sometimes the first step in a deliberate movement toward independence, as was the case with the Indian National Congress's agitation about the viceroy's council before 1914. In other cases, such as the similar agitation of the Lagos intelligentsia about Nigerian legislative councils, the conscious aim was probably more limited since the proponents of reform often saw continued colonial rule as an advantage to themselves, at least for the time being.

Not all colonies possessed councils or analogous bodies, but all of them had line and staff hierarchies below the level of the governor. The size and function of the staff depended primarily on a colony's financial resources; it was therefore usually small and woefully inadequate to the functions it was supposed to perform. The line officials below the governor, regardless of nationality, normally operated according to the pattern of the British district officer. They would usually be assigned individual districts in which they would represent the authority of the governor, assisted by paid non-European subordinates. Their main functions were to keep the peace (primarily through bluff and negotiation), to collect taxes (relying on traditional political organizations), and to effect other aspects of the central government's policy. Given their limited resources, it is not surprising that district officers would tend to concentrate on the first two functions and pay only lip service to the last, especially when government development policy involved extensive social change that created resentment.

Colonial services were normally recruited according to the system of government entry at home. Studies of the colonial services of Britain, France, and Germany have shown that, contrary to Schumpeter's assumptions, the colonial bureaucracies were not refuges for sons of the older European landed elites but were rather thoroughly bourgeois from the start, becoming more so in the twentieth century.[27] There was a tendency in Britain to appoint aristocrats to certain colonial governorships, but this had little effect on the colonial bureaucracy as a whole. In this as in other ways, late European imperialism was in attitude, ideology, and social composition a largely middle-class phenomenon.

It must be emphasized once again that although the administrative operation of the colonial empires is an important part of colonial history, it is not the only or even the most important part. Colonial empires were not simply systems of administration; they were also frameworks for politics. It is possible to discuss the political aspects of colonial rule from two perspectives: the domestic politics of the imperialist countries, and the interaction of colonial rulers and indigenous societies in the colonies. We have looked briefly at the former during the seizure of the colonies. After 1900, the colonial empires affected the major European political systems mainly by creating issues that were debated in public and in parliamentary bodies. We shall discuss the political impact of conflicts over imperial expansion in chapter 7. For the most part, however, questions arising from the operations of the actual colonies were not sufficiently important compared with others to occasion serious effects in European public politics. They probably did not add much to the burden of divisive issues in the politics of individual countries. On the other hand, they did not work strongly to create domestic consensus either, contrary to the hopes of many politicians. The question of the interaction between colonial authorities and indigenous political structures is immensely complicated. It is best discussed through the brief examination that follows of colonialism in three large but fairly representative colonies: Nigeria, Algeria, and the Netherlands East Indies.

NIGERIA UNDER BRITISH RULE

Both Nigeria and the Gold Coast (Ghana), Britain's two major pieces of West African booty from the era of partition, display many similarities in their colonial histories. We shall use Nigeria as our example in this chapter mainly because its political development involved certain problems (such as regionalism) that, although present in the Gold Coast, were not so strikingly manifest there.

The Seizure of Nigeria

Nigeria was one of the colonies that would probably never have become a single country had it not been conquered by a

European power which, mainly to save administrative costs, amalgamated its regions under a single government.[28] Perhaps the most important political and social characteristic of Nigeria has been its immense ethnic, religious, political, and economic diversity, which resembles on a smaller scale that of India. The seizure of Nigeria by the British took place through a series of somewhat disconnected acts of aggression. The occupation of Yorubaland, in southwestern Nigeria, was almost an evolutionary process. It was an outgrowth of the wars between the major Yoruba states during the first two-thirds of the nineteenth century, the occupation of Lagos, the growth of missionary activities and the palm oil trade, and the assumption by the British authorities in Lagos of the position of arbiter in Yoruba politics. With the appearance of the French in western Yorubaland in the 1880s and 1890s, the next step of getting the Yoruba states to acknowledge British sovereignty was a fairly natural one. There was some resistance but not a great deal. Certain groups, including Western-educated Africans in Lagos, welcomed the British takeover. It was equally natural for the British to institute a system of indirect rule, relying on the assistance of pre-existing authorities and commercial enterprises. Inconsistencies in this form of indirect rule were not immediately apparent before 1900.

Southeastern Nigeria was occupied by stages in the 1880s as a result of the actions of the trading consortium, eventually called the Royal Niger Company, that was founded in the late 1870s by Sir George Goldie. Goldie, who was interested in breaking the control of the "middleman" states of the Niger Delta over the Niger trade, used the legitimate-trade idea and the supposed threat to British commerce posed by the Germans in the Cameroons to get the British government to take over the delta and its environs in 1885. The extension of British control over the Ibo north of the delta was a reasonable next step. Southwestern and southeastern Nigeria were formed in 1900 into a single protectorate, Southern Nigeria. Southern Nigeria was a purely artificial administrative contrivance; the cultures and social organizations of the two constituent regions remained extremely different.

Northern Nigeria had not originally been included in anybody's plans for British conquest and occupation except Goldie's. By the late 1890s, however, the French sweep across the western Sudan had given them a claim to the vast region north of the Niger. European business people and government officials in the south became concerned that future development of trade up the Niger might be interrupted by a French takeover of the Sudanic interior. These fears prompted a series of negotiations by both British and company officials with the Muslim emirates of Hausaland, which were loosely presided over by the Sultan of Sokoto. When most of the emirates refused to accept British sovereignty, the Royal Niger Company sent Frederick Lugard, the conqueror of Uganda, with a small military force into Hausaland. Between 1900 and 1903, Lugard picked off one after another of the Hausa states until he had conquered them all. His victory over the highly organized Muslim Hausa was due in part to his machine guns, with which his small force could mow down the large cavalry armies sent against him. More importantly for Lugard's later policies in the region, it was also due to the political disunity of the emirates as a group and to the fact that they possessed highly developed internal political structures. Once defeated in open battle, the state authorities could then be induced to surrender and, in return for guarantees that Lugard would not seriously interfere with the conduct of local politics, to compel compliance by their subjects, thus avoiding guerrilla war. Lugard's tactics had worked under similar circumstances in Uganda. In contrast, when the British turned to attacking the Tiv, a stateless people in central Nigeria, they found it a long, difficult, and expensive process — not because the Tiv were particularly numerous or warlike, but because no one could surrender for all of the Tiv kinship groups together. The French, in conquering various parts of North and West Africa, had had the misfortune of encountering effective guerrilla resistance — from Samori Touré in Guinea and from Rabeh in the area around Lake Chad. In Northern Nigeria, the British were spared this problem, and Lugard recognized why.

Governing Nigeria

The administrative history of Nigeria after the time of the British conquest was extraordinarily complicated. The Royal Niger Company, which had shown itself to be incapable of both governing and developing trade simultaneously, was deprived of its monopoly and its governmental responsibilities in 1900. In the south, the British crown colony of Lagos was administratively amalgamated with the rest of Southern Nigeria, which had its own governor. In the north, Lugard formed the conquered Hausa states into a single protectorate of Northern Nigeria, of which he was imperial commissioner. In 1911, the reformist Liberal government in Britain decided that this arrangement was too untidy (and too expensive, since the administration of Northern Nigeria ran a deficit that necessitated subventions from Britain while Southern Nigeria, with its extensive trade, was solvent). Lugard was appointed governor of both protectorates and by 1914 had united Nigeria into a single federal protectorate. Lugard was the first unitary governor, with his standard official advisory council. Northern and Southern Nigeria remained administratively separate, each under a lieutenant-governor, while Lagos maintained a special position as a crown colony. In the 1920s, Southern Nigeria was also granted a legislative council on which there were a few representatives elected, mostly in Lagos, by substantial property-holders. With this arrangement, Lugard and his successors undertook an extensive economic development program encompassing increased peasant agricultural production, the building of railways, the development of mining, and the beginnings of oil production in the Niger Delta.

Thus far we have outlined only the administrative side of Nigeria's early colonial history. Every element of Nigeria's administrative history was in fact determined by the political and economic interaction of British and African societies. For example, the solvency of Southern Nigeria was the result of the age-old trade networks that had extended from the coast in the time of the slave trade and had incorporated palm oil and kola nut production in the nineteenth century. These networks adapted relatively easily to the new influx of European economic forces that accompanied the Royal Niger Company's interior penetration after 1880, except in the case of the Niger delta states, whose trade was severely injured by the British. Many of the peoples of the southern hinterland, especially the Yoruba and the Ibo, already possessed cultural and social characteristics that permitted them to move easily into a more highly commercialized economy. While European planning and investment helped to create such an economy, local precolonial development played just as important a role.

The financial reasons for the federation of north and south were also derived from precolonial economic factors. Unlike the south, the northern Hausa states had not previously been closely linked to the world economy, despite the fact that for centuries they had been major textile-producing centers and an important factor in interior African trade. During the slave trade era, the Hausa cities' connection with the Atlantic had been indirect, through the Yoruba and Dahomey. Therefore, although Northern Nigeria possessed a sophisticated commercial economy, it was not conducted according to European terms or with European money and could not, in the early twentieth century, be effectively taxed.[29] One of the major objectives of Lugard's economic policy in the north was to redirect existing production and trade toward overseas exports, but this was not easy since Northern Nigeria's major export was cotton cloth, which had a declining value on world markets. Political unification in Nigeria was partly intended to divert the south's revenue surpluses to the north in order to eliminate the northern deficit and pay for northern economic development.

To the extent that unification lessened the tax pressure on the Hausa cities, it was acceptable to the indigenous northern ruling elite, through whom Lugard and his successors chose to govern. Even in late colonial and independent Nigeria, similar fiscal considerations tied northern elite opinion to the concept of a united Nigeria. But the fiscal consequences of unification caused resentment in the south. Southern property owners and small business people disliked paying increasingly steep taxes in part to finance development projects, such as the Northern Railway, which did not immediately benefit them. The question of taxation and distribution was one of the first issues seized upon when the African intellectual and business elite in Lagos organized for political action even before the First World War. This largely Christian group was in favor of modernization. It liked neither the authoritarian nature of Nigeria's government nor the regional inequities in public finance, nor yet the regime of indirect rule in Northern Nigeria that supported Muslim rulers of the sort the Lagos progressives had hoped colonial rule would destroy. The Lagos political parties also used the financial issue in their 1920s campaign for legislative oversight of the Nigerian budget and African representation in a colonial legislature.

Indirect Rule in the North. It was in Northern Nigeria that Lugard formulated his famous doctrine of "indirect rule," which was simply the traditional British practice in India of subordinating indigenous rulers and elites to the European colonial authority and then governing through them. What Lugard did was to impose this system consciously and extensively, and to create an abstract theory óf indirect rule that justified both his particular approach and colonialism in general in terms of wider political values.[30] Lugard's ideas were very influential after World War I. However, they were never officially accepted by the Colonial Office in their entirety.

In Lugard's formulation, indirect rule was one of the two pillars of British colonial rule. The other was his idea of the "dual mandate" of the colonial rulers: they had to promote colonial economic development for the benefit of the home country, but they were also obliged to encourage "progress" and welfare for the benefit of the colonial peoples. This was, of course, partly a way to justify the colonial conquest on the moral grounds of an obligation of "advanced" to "backward" peoples. But Lugard took the dual mandate concept quite seriously, especially during his later service on the League of Nations Permanent Mandates Commission. The dual mandate, with its requirement to provide a range of social services to the colonial population, became a part of the governing ideology of the British colonial service. In Northern Nigeria before World War I, however, the more strictly political idea of indirect rule was of greater immediate importance.

In Northern Nigeria, Lugard found almost the ideal environment for indirect rule. The Hausa states possessed centuries-old political structures (modified during the Fulani revolutions early in the nineteenth century).[31] The states were loosely linked together under the sultanate of Sokoto. Their ruling classes were easily identified. The states employed Islamic law, codified during centuries of practice, and their tax structures were clearly visible and legitimized by tradition. Lugard was able, upon conquering each of the states, merely to depose a few rulers, to replace them with others chosen among legitimate candidates for rule, and to place British residents in the courts of each of the rulers to look out for British interests. Taxes were collected as before, and Islamic courts were able to conduct most of the judicial business, subject to the governor's review of certain sentences. This system was not intended to last forever, but Lugard believed it would provide a legitimate framework of government while, over time, elements of change could permeate Hausa society.

While Lugard was governor, comparatively little change was required of Northern Nigeria. His successors were not so lucky. Many aspects of Islamic law were repugnant to Europeans, while others stood in the way of economic modernization. The government found itself increasingly imposing new legislation on the courts, replacing judges and officials, and tightening bureaucratic control. This in turn led to growing resistance to

British interference on the part of the Hausa elite. Nevertheless, control over Northern Nigerian politics remained essentially in the hands of the traditional elite down to the time of independence and beyond. This has, in fact, been a crucial feature of modern Nigerian politics.

Indirect Rule in the Southwest. Indirect rule elsewhere in Nigeria was a different matter. In Lagos and other places where the British presence and extensive commerce had led to considerable social change and cultural Westernization, indirect rule through traditional elites simply would not work. An alternative was to turn over the government to the Western-educated African intellectual and commercial elites, which was what those elites expected. But British administrators, afraid of Western-style opposition, were loath to adopt European forms of representative government, probably the only way that indirect rule could have been accomplished. The practical advantage of indirect rule in areas like Hausaland was that the traditional political structure was authoritarian and could therefore both extend and legitimize the authoritarian control that was the essence of political colonialism. European representative institutions had been developed basically in order to prevent authoritarian rule, and therefore were uncongenial to colonial administrators. But political pressure, and the difficult position in which their opposition to representative government placed the colonial authorities, forced the adoption of half measures of representation in the 1920s. In addition, large numbers of educated Africans from Lagos found civil service jobs, but classic indirect rule was never practiced in Lagos.

In the Yoruba lands that made up most of southwestern Nigeria, indirect rule took a different form. The Yoruba were traditionally an urban people whose political life centered around a number of more or less independent and densely populated states sharing close cultural affinities with each other.[32] The Yoruba possessed unifying national religious institutions, and for a century and a half before the early nineteenth century had been under the loose imperial control of the Yoruba state of Oyo. In the first half of the nineteenth century, however, Oyo's empire had collapsed. Decades of internecine warfare in Yorubaland had followed. This warfare, and the adoption by weaker states such as Abeokuta of Christianity as a means of eliciting European support, had brought on British intervention in Yorubaland and the occupation of Lagos in 1851. British intervention eventually helped bring the Yoruba wars to an end, and formal rule followed as a result of the scramble.

The Yoruba had traded with Europeans for centuries and their economy had adapted readily to nineteenth-century demand for peasant-produced palm oil. Even before the British takeover, a large proportion of the male population was engaged in palm oil production, and an extensive commercial network supporting the palm oil trade had emerged, operated mainly by market-women who eventually became a significant factor in the region's economic, social, and political life. Rapid socioeconomic change, with its fragmenting effects on traditional society and culture, had already commenced. There was, moreover, no single external set of cultural and political norms that played the role of Islam in Hausaland. Only the most northerly Yoruba states were Muslim. The rest held to traditional religious and cultural forms or else — because of highly active missionaries and a native Yoruba Protestant ministry — had turned to Christianity. Despite its spread, however, Christianity could neither supply a total model of social organization the way Islam could nor do much to amalgamate traditional and modern social elements. Such amalgamation requires time, and Christianity, like European rule, was relatively new. Politics and administration in Yorubaland were thus much more complicated than in the north.

The British chose to rule Yorubaland "indirectly," through the Yoruba states themselves. At first glance, these seemed well suited to the requirements of indirect rule. They were centuries old, legitimized by religious and cultural traditions. Many of their elite classes had shown remarkable receptivity to Christianity and other Western cultural and economic influences. Most importantly, the Yoruba political systems appeared to be extremely authoritarian. The Yoruba *obas*, or kings, seemed to be absolute rulers whose persons were regarded as practically sacred, to whom extreme deference was paid, and who stood at the center of all formal political life. European observers were in fact wrong. One of the reasons for the prolongation of the Yoruba wars had been the instability of Yoruba political institutions. Actual power in the state was finely balanced between the obas and the councils of lineage group heads; the latter could readily depose the obas. Since the principle of succession was not clear, the British authorities believed that they could simply appoint as obas whomever they chose from the ruling lineages and ignore the councils. The government oversaw the obas through British district officers and made the obas subject to colonial legislation. The government used the obas for tax collecting and split the receipts with them to encourage diligence. The obas fell into this pattern fairly readily before the First World War. Before long, however, severe problems arose in many places. In fulfilling their new roles, the obas were performing acts not sanctioned by tradition. They had in essence become agents of colonial rule and used their connection with the British to enhance their powers. They thus engendered opposition from the chiefly lineage heads and the family groups that they led, which made tax collection and the maintenance of public order difficult. It became customary for the obas to call upon the colonial authorities for financial subventions and military or police support, which often resulted in violence.

In the end, of course, the British and the obas prevailed, but most of the supposed advantages of indirect rule (low cost, easy administration through traditionally legitimate officials, and gradual political modernization) were not realized. The obas became, in essence, salaried colonial officials. Contrary to Lugard's intentions, without really knowing it the British had intervened to change a non-European society very decisively.

British Rule in the Southeast. In the third important region of Nigeria, the southeast, the British had originally been concerned mainly to break up by military force political systems that offered resistance to direct British trade with the interior. Once the overt resort to violence was finished, British policy was usually much the same as in Yorubaland, with about the same results. In the large interior area of Iboland, however, policy had to be very different indeed, for the Ibo were a "stateless" people. When it came to colonial rule, neither the national religious institutions of the Ibo nor the segmentary kinship units that handled most of their social functions were thought to be adaptable to indirect rule.[33] The British therefore decided to rule directly through appointed officials. But so wedded was the Nigerian administration to indirect rule that it insisted that the officials placed directly in charge of Ibo villages and districts be educated Africans — usually not Ibo. These officials were called "warrant chiefs," as if the facts that they were called chiefs and were Africans made their intrusion into Ibo society any less direct than if they had been Europeans. The warrant chiefs were never really accepted and were eventually replaced by white district officers.

On the whole, however, the Ibo responded with great flexibility and a high degree of opportunism to the new colonial arrangements. Ibo family structure remained intact and adapted itself fairly efficiently to new circumstances. The development of the Nigerian administrative bureaucracy and the growth of commercial enterprise after the First World War opened up many positions for educated Africans. The Ibo, whose contact with Europeans before 1900 had been minimal, accepted European education readily and thus qualified an increasing number of young men for these positions. Small-scale businesses sprang up in the 1920s and 1930s, and with them a substantial lower-middle class and an extensive business infrastructure. The extent of these developments should not be exaggerated. Income and profit levels for Africans remained low, reinvestment was limited, and whole sections of the country were skipped by economic change. But of all the major peoples of Nigeria, it was the Ibo who made the most of the colonial situation.

Social and Political Evolution

Nigeria, despite its problems, was always a promising colony for the British, especially with the development of extractive industries after the First World War. Its government was usually solvent, although the budget was very tight. Urbanization, with substantial population movements, occurred at an accelerating rate, particularly after the Second World War. Nigeria also experienced the growth of slums, the straining of traditional family structures, low wages, and poor working conditions — all of which were probably accentuated by the comparative poverty of the colonial administration and thus by its inability to do much about them.

Throughout the twentieth century, the Nigerian political movements slowly emerged that eventually led the country to independence. Between the wars, the Lagos intellectual elite took the lead in establishing European-style parties. Eventually, however, the growth of political organization among the Yoruba and Ibo tended to displace the Lagos intelligentsia. In Iboland particularly there occurred a crucial development in the process of national liberation: the emergence of indigenous political organizations encompassing non-elite segments of society. The importance of "grassroots" political organizations in decolonization has in the past been largely ignored by scholars, who have concentrated mainly on Western-educated elites. Recently, however, it has become the focus of considerable historical attention. In southern Nigeria, as in other countries, the educated elites provided ideological direction and nationalist leadership. But it was their almost fortuitous acquisition of support from non-elite and originally nonpolitical mass-interest groups that brought them success. In Iboland, increases in taxation in the 1920s created considerable unrest, especially among the market-women in the major commercial towns who formed the largest segment of the area's small-business community and on whom much of the burden of taxation fell. Resentment of taxation led to the formation of protest organizations and, in 1929-30, to major riot in market towns. The riots and their suppression led to the rapid spread of popular political and economic organization and gave the first generation of practicing, popular Ibo politicians an audience to whom to appeal.

Nigeria's history under colonial rule is immensely complicated because of the size and diversity of the country. Many of the themes peculiar to Nigerian colonial history have not been discussed here. Most of the aspects of Nigeria's colonial history just discussed, however, are similar, or at least comparable, to situations found in many other colonies. The examples that follow were deliberately chosen because of their differences from Nigeria, although, as we shall see, they display certain similarities as well.

ALGERIA UNDER FRENCH RULE

Algeria was, in the 1950s, a scene of major armed struggle between an imperial power and a national liberation movement. One of the reasons that this occurred was that colonialism in Algeria pitted a numerous, dominant European minority against a (more-or-less) culturally uniform subordinate non-European majority. Another reason was that Algerian affairs were a matter of unusual importance in the politics of the metropolitan state, France.

We have seen that the conquest of Algeria in the nineteenth century was accomplished over a long time and that even after the end of regular resistance in the 1850s, sporadic rebellions occurred. The constant application of overwhelming force and the influx of European immigrants (about 400,000 by the late 1880s) rendered rebellion by the traditional Algerian politics ineffective and minimized the need for indirect rule. The cost of maintaining this situation — essentially the cost of a large French army constantly stationed in Algeria — was high.[34]

French policy toward Algeria varied a great deal from time to time, especially before 1900. This was due, among other things, to changes in French governments, to lack of clarity in French imperialist ideology, and to changes in the economy of Algeria under French rule. Under the 1850s policy of European agricultural settlement, thousands of French people (and later Italians) moved to Algeria. European settlement was not, however, an immediate economic success. Moreover, the forced expropriation of Algerian lands caused constant friction. Napoleon III, in consonance with his views about the importance of economic development, promulgated a policy in the 1860s of limiting European migration, protecting indigenous social structure and Islam, and encouraging the establishment of export industries based on plantation agriculture. He also refused, contrary to settler wishes, to countenance the assimilation of Algeria into France. Although many of these policies changed when Napoleon fell from power in 1870, the groundwork for the later economic development of Algeria had been laid. The creation of large plantations and investment by French financial institutions were facilitated by government policy. Thousands of Muslim Algerians entered the labor market, partly as a result of land expropriation.

By the end of the nineteenth century, the plantation sector had turned primarily to producing wine, which became Algeria's chief export. Unfortunately, wine was not the most satisfactory kind of export product since it could not support a favorable trade balance. In the twentieth century, Algeria was France's largest overseas customer but was far from being its largest supplier. Concentration on wine exports made the Algerian economy dangerously dependent on a single, highly variable international market. It also made Algeria a competitor with a major French industry which, on occasion, could muster enough influence to impose unfavorable economic policies on Algeria and to head off movements toward integration with France.

The republican governments after 1870 tried a number of political experiments with Algeria. From the mid-1870s, however, the main thrust of policy favored an expanded role for the French *colons* (settlers). Confiscation of native Algerian lands was made even easier. These tendencies, together with the growth of the French population in Algeria, led to demands for integration with France and equality for the (European) Algerians with the metropolitan French. These demands, however, created problems. Some domestic economic interests opposed a close relationship. There were fears that political integration would eliminate an incentive for Algeria to become financially self-sufficient.

Then there was the problem of the non-European majority in Algeria. The example of Ireland showed that a culturally unassimilated and disadvantaged population could make political integration very difficult. It was suggested that the indigenous population could be governed through a system of indirect rule, even though it would mean building up political institutions that the French had spent years destroying. It would also mean recognizing Islam and its institutions, trusting the indigenous Algerian elite not to revolt, and vastly reducing the political and economic prerogatives of the *colons*, thus encouraging settler resistance. Indirect rule and mere association with France were therefore ruled out. The main alternative — which grew out of the French radical democratic tradition — was complete integration and assimilation, and this became official policy in 1881.[35]

Between 1881 and 1896, the administration of Algeria was placed under all of the French ministries, making the governor-general somewhat superfluous. This unrealistic policy created administrative difficulties almost immediately, but they were minor compared with problems of the native Algerian population. To the latter, however, French political ideology provided an apparent answer. The same radical tradition that justified the political assimilation of Algeria could be extended to encompass cultural assimilation. The groundwork had already been laid for this kind of native policy, both in Algeria and in Senegal. French citizenship and full civil and economic rights could be extended to all non-European Algerians provided they could meet certain educational requirements (with their implication of cultural uniformity). But because state education for Algerians was not extensive, this meant that only a small, elite minority could actually attain full citizenship. This might still have made the system of political integration work by co-opting the entire Muslim elite, except for two things: the unrealistic way in which Islam was treated, and the opposition of the *colons*. The assimilation policy recognized no special status for Islam in Algeria and required each Muslim applicant for full citizenship to abjure Islamic law, which the majority even of Western-educated Muslims would not do. In addition, although settlers generally favored integration with France, they opposed any substantial inclusion of native Algerians in the citizenry. Such a change might have threatened the validity of former land expropriations and the *colons'* special economic position. Even the assimilation of a Western-educated elite was widely resented, for many of the same reasons as elsewhere: dislike of educational attainments by members of an ethnic group believed to be inferior, which threatened the value system that justified colonial rule; fear of rebellion led by the educated elite; and fear of competition for jobs. In the end, it appeared that full assimilation could not work.

In the late 1890s, the French government turned toward short-range compromises in Algeria. Algeria was again administratively separated from metropolitan France under the governor-general and given a budget of its own. A semi-legislative body with limited budgetary control was established, consisting of elected representatives of European landowners, landless Europeans, and indigenous Algerians. The government continued to rule essentially directly, using non-European Algerians in subordinate roles in the governance of their own people. It still held out incentives to educated native Algerians to adopt French culture.

The new arrangement, which lasted with modifications until the Second World War, did not entirely satisfy anyone, but it was workable (except from the Muslim Algerian point of view). From the standpoint of the colonial government, there was just enough oversight of the budget by elected representatives to head off serious opposition without hindering actual bureaucratic control. The bigger agricultural and commercial interests were given ample opportunities to exert influence, both in France and in Algeria. The *colons* received protection of their holdings and, in practice, a guarantee against effective indigenous Algerian opposition. The Muslim majority, however, had reason for dissatisfaction. They were left without effective self-government, since their legislative representation was in a permanent minority status and thus unable to do anything about the major Muslim economic demand: the redistribution of land to native Algerian small farmers. It is, of course, unlikely that land redistribution would have been a sound basis for economic development. The European small farmers who held much of the arable land did not, on the whole, do well in the twentieth century, gradually losing out to the larger agricultural concerns. But the question of landholdings was nonetheless a source of resentment.

As the Algerian economy developed in the twentieth century through massive production of a few commodities on large farms and extensively importing French manufactured products, attendant social changes also took place: rapid urbanization, massive population increases among native Algerians, the proletarianization of a large part of the Muslim population, class resentments and conflicts, and so forth. Class conflict became mixed with ethnic and religious differences. There existed a European proletariat composed of old settlers and more recent immigrants, many of them Italians. The European proletariat, although it had its own class grievances against employers, was much better paid and possessed more privileges than its native Algerian counterpart. A mutual antipathy grew in the twentieth century between the European and the non-European working classes, based on resentment and fears for job security on both sides. Similar antipathies became quite pronounced between European and Muslim small shopkeepers.

And yet, little overt opposition to French rule appeared before the Second World War. Part of the reason was that the French were never confident (with good reason) about the loyalty of the native Algerians. They left a large army in Algeria, which was kept occupied with small conflicts in the deep interior and in Morocco. During the First World War, Algeria supplied troops to France, but the French preferred in general to recruit from other colonies, especially Senegal.

Other reasons for the lack of major resistance were the French destruction of traditional political entities in Algeria and the economic transformation of the country, which damaged traditional social structure. In the short run, French policy removed the most obvious sources of resistance. In the long run, however, by implementing uniform policies that disadvantaged Muslims, the French unwittingly encouraged the emergence of cultural uniformity among the previously diverse segments of the native Algerian population and emphasized the importance of the *ulama,* the conservative Muslim clerical group that interpreted Islamic law. The *ulama* became the natural leaders of Muslim resistance, and in the twentieth century could increasingly claim to speak as political leaders for all areas of the country.[36]

The relationship between France and the emerging Algerian elite also helped to determine the future course of Algerian politics. The French were moderately successful in coopting the small, Western-educated elite in the immediate post-World War I period. Some educated Algerians were willing to adopt French culture fairly whole-heartedly, even in some cases giving up Islam or at least repudiating the jurisdiction of Islamic law. Most Algerian intellectuals refused to go that far, but they nonetheless tended to identify their own interests and the future progress of Algeria with the greater French community. Ferhat Abbas, later a moderate nationalist leader of the Algerian revolt in the 1950s, was an example of this type of intellectual. Abbas was far from satisfied with the existing state of affairs in the 1920s and 1930s. But he saw the solution to the political and economic problems of the native Algerians in a closer union with France that would grant the franchise equally to all Algerians and would give complete civil rights to all Muslims. The problem of Islamic law could be settled by compromise. Intellectuals like Abbas organized to press for these aims. They appeared radical and dangerous to the authorities and the *colons,* who responded with the suppression of parties, jail terms, and the like.

Algerian nationalism among intellectuals thus emerged in essentially a French political context, as elsewhere in the French empire. Although the intellectuals applied pressure to the French government and obtained minor concessions as a result of labor disputes in the 1930s, they did not succeed before World War II in cooperating either with incipient working-class movements or with the conservative *ulama.* One of the salient features of the popular nationalist movement when it did appear in the late 1940s and early 1950s was its extremely narrow base. Real politicization, as opposed to the expression of resentments, had not proceeded far in comparison, for example, with India. Effective political resistance appeared only with the emergence of popular figures such as Ahmed ben Bella, who understood the necessity of a clear-cut ideology of resistance, of rank-and-file organization, and of the need to affirm Islamic values. One reason that the *colons* were so confident about taking an intransigent line toward the National Liberation Front (FLN) in the early 1950s was that the FLN did not appear to have much grassroots support. And one of the reasons that the FLN turned to terrorism was that it needed to provoke French reactions that would create the kind of support the FLN needed. It is likely, then, that part of the reason for the extreme violence of the later Algerian revolution was the absence of indigenous political organization in the country — a situation that was, ironically, one of the goals of French colonial policy.

THE NETHERLANDS EAST INDIES

Our third and final colonial example is the Netherlands East Indies — today, the Republic of Indonesia. The colonial history of Indonesia holds particular interest because, from 1815 to 1941, it was largely insulated from great-power imperial rivalries and because Dutch policy in the East Indies had considerable influence on the policies of other nations. The Dutch East Indies also provide an example of the difficulties, foreseen and unforeseen, which even the most "progressive" varieties of colonial administration could cause.

We have already mentioned the imposition of the "culture system" by the Dutch on their main East Indian possession, Java, in the 1830s. This system, depending primarily on the forced cultivation of certain agricultural products for export under a government monopoly, vastly expanded the East Indies' participation in the world economy and attracted much attention in Europe.[37] By the mid-1850s, however, the exploitive and socially-destructive nature of the culture system had become apparent in the Netherlands, as it already had in the Indies. Public consciousness of the Indies and the effects of policy there was aroused by the popular novel of Multatuli (Eduard Douwes Dekker), *Max Havelaar* (1860). Dekker criticized the culture system while at the same time appealing to romantic notions of Holland's eastern destiny and to attitudes of humanitarian responsibility toward subject peoples. Dekker did not by himself alter Dutch colonial policy, which in any event was changing in response to the huge economic waste of the culture system, but he did help to end the separation that had existed between the East Indian empire and the concerns of most Dutchmen. The second half of the nineteenth century saw radical reforms in the administration of the Dutch empire, as well as the industrialization of the Netherlands itself. On Java, the extensive government-directed development program was continued along more liberal and less obviously exploitive lines as the economy of the main islands was tied increasingly closely to that of Europe.

Political administration in the Dutch East Indies was an amalgam of structures and practices that varied in different areas. In the nineteenth century, actual Dutch control was extended to vast areas of the Outer Islands (away from Java) and the interior of Sumatra. In some of these new areas, the Dutch ruled indirectly through indigenous authorities; in others they established direct governance, using Dutch officials and educated Javanese. On Java, some indigenous Indonesian princes were kept in power under close Dutch supervision. The main administrative tendency, however, was toward direct rule. Direct administration was employed especially in those areas of Java where the culture system had been enforced, since that system was essentially an authoritarian, external imposition on Javanese societies and could not easily be put in place through an indigenous political structure. When reform came later in the nineteenth century, it was mainly in the form of modifications to direct authoritarian rule. And when, in the late nineteenth and early twentieth centuries, indigenous Indonesian (mostly Javanese) political movements began to appear, their demands were formulated in terms of the system of direct administration, not of the traditional native Indonesian authorities.

The heart of the culture system had been the forced transfer of land and labor in Java from subsistence to export agriculture—that is, from rice growing to the production of sugar, coffee, and similar items. In some places, this policy had involved forced labor on, for example, coffee plantations apart from farmers' own fields and rice paddies. In these cases, the trade-off between subsistence and export had been absolute: more coffee, less rice. Such a policy had, however, rather obvious defects. It did nothing to improve Java as a market, and it threatened the economy by reducing the ability of agriculture to feed the population. Even the use of free wage labor on single-product plantations tended toward the same result.

The novelty in the culture system and the subsequent "reformed" development policy was a major effort simultaneously to increase productivity in subsistence and export agriculture. Originally this was done for purely economic reasons, without "humanitarian" considerations. Improving the yield of subsistence agriculture, possibly commercializing it in the process, would help to prevent economic disasters like the famines that periodically swept India. It would also permit a population rise, thus increasing the amount of labor available for export production. At the same time, in order to avoid the occupational specialization and administrative expenses associated with plantation agriculture, development policy concentrated on adapting the village level, communal subsistence agricultural system to export production.

As Clifford Geertz has shown, these policies succeeded in large parts of Java.[38] Intensive sugar production for export was successfully integrated with subsistence rice agriculture by using rice paddies for sugar growing at times when rice was not under cultivation. Javanese village communities originally had to be forced into the new system by devices such as production quotas and taxes payable only in cash (thus requiring cash-crop production). But as time went on, as further improvements in technique were adopted, and as new lands and additional crops were fitted into the same pattern, the Javanese reconciled themselves to the new system. Especially in the later nineteenth century — when the initial shock had passed and the reform policy had made the imposition of economic change somewhat less harsh — export agriculture at the village level tended to expand at least partly through its own momentum, although never entirely without government and private European encouragement.

This system remained the basis of the Javanese economy. In the Outer Islands and in areas of Java not integrated into the modified culture system, more standard development policies tended to be followed. The government regularly let concessions to rubber and oil companies, giving them considerable powers to effect massive economic change, with the normal results for traditional societies. But in Java, which remained the economic and political center of the Netherlands East Indies, the economy established under the culture system remained an important basis for the profitability of the Dutch colonial regime and for much of its policy.

Although the basic colonial economic system of Java possessed wide appeal for colonialists because it successfully integrated traditional culture with the demands of the world economy, it had severe drawbacks as well. It tended to insulate traditional agricultural forms from further progress. There was a limit to the extent to which Javanese agriculture could develop according to patterns set in the nineteenth century. When that limit was reached in the twentieth century, Java was left with a backward economy and a vastly expanded population. According to Geertz, the success of the late nineteenth-century adaptation of the culture system improved the productivity of rice agriculture and, since the system was highly labor intensive, it encouraged large families and the growth of population. The optimal strategy for peasant families was to augment family income and financial security by having more children. Because of this, the population of Java exploded from the nineteenth century on. By 1940, Java was one of the most densely populated areas on earth, with an average population density of about 315 persons per square kilometer. Java has shown, both in late colonial times and since independence, the classic results of excessive population increase, including stagnating real income and low rates of capital formation. The intervention of international economic forces would probably have spurred population growth in Java in any case. But the nature of Dutch development policy there probably accelerated the growth rate — ironically, for the same reasons that the Dutch colonial administration was so generally admired by liberal imperialists.

The growth of Indonesian nationalism, which was largely a Javanese phenomenon, took place in the context of a system of direct rule that sought to create a "Europeanized" Indonesian elite, and in the context of the kind of economic change just described.[39] Javanese nationalists were greatly inspired by the example of Japan, especially after the Japanese victory over Russia in 1904-5. Their initial demands were for greater Indonesian representation in the colonial government and for greater expenditure on social welfare. The Dutch government responded in the 1920s by establishing legislative structures with limited budgetary powers. Indonesians were given representation, although they remained in a minority. Indonesians were appointed in increasing numbers to the civil administration. The government also instituted an extensive program of educational expansion from the primary to the university levels, although the educational reforms could not keep up with the exploding population.

None of these policies prevented Indonesian nationalists from turning toward the idea of national autonomy between the world wars. The Dutch responded with a policy of total integration of the Indies with the home country – a policy much more thorough than any advanced in France. In 1922, Dutch legislation officially made the East Indies an integral part of the Netherlands. From that time down to the independence of Indonesia, the Dutch government and Dutch public opinion maintained the same position: that national independence was an irrelevant demand since all reasonable national aspirations had been met by political integration. Most of this was, of course, fiction. The size of Indonesia, its distance from Europe, the nature of its many different cultures – all precluded real integration, while the Indonesian economy was already integrated with Holland's, as a dependency. In reality, before World War II the Dutch East Indies acquired at best a little more political autonomy. Indigenous Indonesians had little influence over colonial decisions and none at all over Netherlands politics. Integration was not entirely a sham: it helped lead to large Indonesian immigration to the Netherlands after World War II. But it is not surprising that the policy was not taken seriously by Indonesian nationalists like Sukarno, especially when the Dutch used it to justify repressive measures against the nationalists in the 1920s and 1930s. Complete independence increasingly appeared to the emerging Indonesian political leadership to be the only practical goal.

In the second part of this chapter I have briefly discussed three examples of colonialism in action in the late nineteenth century and early twentieth centuries. Throughout the chapter, I have concentrated on areas under formal colonial rule. In the next chapter, I shall discuss the manner in which the formal colonial empires fitted into larger patterns of global relations and the ways in which colonial events were related to more extensive international ones.

SEVEN

Imperialism in a World Context, 1890-1945

I N THE PREVIOUS CHAPTER WE DISCUSSED the colonial form of imperialism in the wake of Europe's expansion at the end of the nineteenth century. In this chapter we shall briefly consider European imperialism in a broader sense, as an aspect of the history of world political and economic development between the Victorian era and the end of the Second World War. We shall concentrate particularly on noncolonial aspects of this vast topic.

We cannot discuss even in outline the major characteristics of late industrial society and their emergence in Europe in the twentieth century; at best we can examine some of the consequences that affected European imperialism. One of the most important of these characteristics was the development at different times in the twentieth century of elements within Western European political systems which permitted at least the partial solution of the crucial problems of fragmentation and lack of consensus.[1] In many countries, political parties became much more thoroughly organized than before, capable of collectively monopolizing access to office, of enforcing discipline on their members, and of appealing across class divisions. New means of propaganda — for example, the mass-circulation newspaper and the cinema — could be used to transmit political messages with appeals that transcended group affiliation. And new ideologies appeared that appealed to concerns of all members of an industrial society. These changes in the political sphere of course partly depended upon broader social changes, including the appearance of much more homogenous national cultures and the development of means of formalizing social conflict (such as collective bargaining). Whatever the origins of these political tendencies, they provided access by governments and political elite groups to a sufficient consensus to allow them to use government much more effectively than in the nineteenth century to deal with new social problems. Thus, governments that were confounded for decades during the nineteenth century by the problems of what to do about unemployment and health found themselves able, after World War I, to put through comprehensive welfare schemes.

Of course, what we have just discussed was only a general tendency. Political effectiveness did not develop everywhere at the same pace, and many countries were faster and more successful at effecting these changes than were others (Britain much more so than Germany, for example). Nor did the increasing efficiency of governments in modern industrial democracies manifest itself without cost to political individuality and traditional values. But at least, over time, many of the problems that had most exercised politicians in the late nineteenth century were partially and tentatively solved.

These developments had a direct effect on imperialism. As we have seen, the New Imperialism of the late nineteenth century resulted in part from the attempt by various participants in European politics to use imperialist ideologies to create support and consensus. Imperialism was sufficiently successful from this standpoint that the major European countries acquired new overseas colonies and that these colonies came to be accepted into popular political attitudes as major contributors to each country's well-being (regardless of economic realities). But it was also quickly discovered that imperialism was really not a very effective ideology of domestic political integration. It created as many divisions as it healed, it would not deliver consistent support to any particular group, and it involved excessive dangers of war. In the twentieth century, many politicians began to move away from imperialism and toward the other, more effective means of creating consensus that technological, economic, and social changes were providing. It is perhaps instructive that after World War I, aggressive imperialism remained a major popular ideology primarily in countries (such as Germany and Italy) where for one reason or another social divisions remained particularly obstructive in politics and where the new means of consensus building were less readily available. A large part of the history of European imperialism in the twentieth century and of the rapid process of decolonization after the Second World War reflects this loss of imperialism's domestic political importance.

THE WORLD ECONOMY AND
INFORMAL IMPERIALISM

The period after 1890 saw the continued expansion and integration of the world economy centered on the industrial nations, with some temporary crises and permanent changes of leadership.[2] By the 1890s, Germany had joined Britain in the first rank of industrial exporters, while industrial expansion in the United States gave promise of overtaking the two leaders in a short time. Industrial economies existed throughout most of Western Europe. While London remained the financial center of the world economy, the growth of capital reserves in the United States made international financial arrangements much more complicated than they had been. The late nineteenth and early twentieth centuries also saw the appearance and continued growth of large, often monopolistic business organizations structured as trusts, cartels, and multinational conglomerates. This rise of "organized" international capitalism is explained in many ways by students of the phenomenon and is still not thoroughly understood.[3] Marxists, following Lenin, have often interpreted it as a defensive and ultimately futile response to the growing crisis of capitalism, as a massive effort to restrain competition. Others have seen "cartelization" as an attempt to create stability in a complex and unstable world economy. In any event, multinational business organizations have become increasingly prominent in the world's economy down to the present.

All of these factors affected imperialism in its broadest sense. We have already seen that some of the paranoia that motivated much of late British imperialism proceeded from the perception of a loss of British economic supremacy. During periods of economic distress (1873-96, just after World War I, during the 1930s depression), businesses in all European countries turned to their governments to protect them from the "unfair" competition of other countries. Occasionally even the same companies that entered into international cartel arrangements used national protectionist arguments to influence the policies of their own governments. This kind of approach often involved the use of imperialist policies and ideologies and often produced serious problems. One example will suffice.

Cecil Rhodes' various business empires, which included diamond and copper mining and African land speculation, were in fact multinational enterprises. Although the largest part of Rhodes' capital backing was British, he also had support from a plethora of German, Belgian, Dutch, American, and South African investors. Rhodes' money controlled not only the South Africa Company and a large part of the DeBeers diamond monopoly but also the two largest of the companies operating in German Southwest Africa. Rhodes had many close business relationships with German financiers, as did probably the majority of important British colonial investors. To these people, a war between Britain and Germany would have been a catastrophe. Rhodes himself, as we have seen, favored imperial cooperation between Britain and Germany. And yet Rhodes was perfectly willing to decry Germany's imperial threat in public. German business leaders with strong British connections did the same in the opposite direction. Was this a vast capitalist conspiracy? — perhaps, to an extent. Clearly, business people like Rhodes used anti-German, imperialist appeals to muster public support for policies (such as the annexation of the Boer republics) which they favored for reasons that had little to do with the German threat. On the other hand, this kind of approach showed few signs of being coordinated, and it was dangerous as well. The actual events leading up to the First World War showed the European big business community in sad disarray, captive to the imperialist appeals they had attempted to use for their own ends. Toward 1914, there is evidence that many business people realized what was happening: that they had backed imperialism beyond the point at which they could control it.[4]

Quite apart from the relationships among big business, formal imperialism, and war, however, the growth of large business organizations seeking to integrate the production of raw materials into larger, controlled arrangements had a profound effect on Europe's relations with the world overseas. In the early twentieth century, for example, the Anglo-Dutch concern of Lever Brothers (now Unilever) largely took over the purchase and marketing of West African and Asian vegetable oil. Lever Brothers thus exercised a high degree of control over the economies of countries producing vegetable oil. Similar national and international consortia appeared in other industries, most especially in oil production in the Persian Gulf after World War I.[5]

The importance of the early multinational corporations can be exaggerated. Not all large businesses investing abroad before 1945 were multinationals, nor were all of them monopolistic in tendency. Furthermore, the degree of influence of the large overseas corporations over European governments in making policy is not yet clear to historians. One point that is clear, however, is that while many large overseas businesses employed imperialist ideologies before 1918 to influence government policies, after 1918 they generally avoided such approaches. Rather than setting the trends in formal, public imperialism, big overseas investors tended instead to follow them.

It is nevertheless true that after 1918, the domination of the industrial world (including Western Europe) over the non-industrial increased steadily, in part through the activities of large national and multinational corporations.[6] This represented a continuation of previous trends in world economic development, a result of the extension of an inter-dependent world economy with an industrial center. Compared with this development, both formal and informal imperialism (basically forms of political control of overseas areas, for whatever purpose) appear as very secondary historical phenomena indeed. As we have seen, formal colonialism could be used to enhance European business interests, while informal political interference was also occasionally used for the same purpose (most notably by oil companies in the Middle East). But on the whole, large businesses increasingly found it more satisfactory — especially after 1945 — to avoid becoming entangled with the classic nineteenth-century forms of imperialism, which had been to a great extent products of domestic European politics that business interests had simply tried to use. In the later twentieth century, when business interests in Europe and America found it useful to engage the support of their governments in their overseas activities, they tended to follow the political fashions of the times and to employ such current ideological tools as anticommunism.

The forms of imperialism that we have been examining, having become increasingly irrelevant to European politics, became irrelevant also to overseas investors as political tools. It should also be kept in mind that just as the largest part of the extension of the world economy in the nineteenth century took place outside of either formal or informal imperial relationships, so in the later twentieth century most forms of integration in the world economy have not involved the exercise of political power by the stronger countries over the weaker. These are, of course, general trends and admit of many exceptions (the oil and arms industries, for example). But on the whole, they explain what happened to imperialism in the twentieth century.

IMPERIALISM AND INTERNATIONAL RELATIONS TO WORLD WAR I

Imperialism played an important part in the series of diplomatic crises that preceded the First World War. Was imperialism, therefore, a major cause of the war? Some recent scholarship suggests that it was, but one must be careful about how one uses the term "imperialism" in this context. The German historian Fritz Fischer, for example, shows that business and social elites in Germany encouraged imperial expansion both before and during the war and suggests that the German government's position in 1914 was largely determined by the aims of these groups.[7] But Fischer uses the term "imperialism" to apply primarily to the aim of economic expansion within Europe or immediately adjacent areas, and most particularly to the desire to protect investments by German banks against takeover by better capitalized French and British concerns. Although he sees overseas imperialism as part of the same expansionary economic process, he gives it comparatively little attention. By implication, then, the diplomacy of overseas expansion is relegated to the status of a sideshow, not a major cause of war.

Other historians, arguing from the standpoint of studies of "social imperialism," explain the war as an attempt by the elite classes in the European countries to protect themselves against the rising tide of democracy and socialism by creating emergency conditions to justify authoritarian rule.[8] From this perspective, prewar overseas imperialism and the diplomatic crises leading up to the war itself are connected, not as a chain of events leading from one to the other, but by the parallel roles that they played in domestic social conflict. If this view is taken out of its stereotyped class-conflict mold, it is largely consistent with the analysis of imperialism presented in the previous chapters. The divided political elites of Europe employed imperialism, among other political means, to combat fragmentation and promote political stability. In 1914, many of them believed that they had failed and that a more decisive means of political integration — an external war — might be useful. This did not, according to most of the evidence, provide the direct motive for war but rather made general war an acceptable eventuality in international politics. The war itself followed from several more direct causes, not least of which were the tendency of European governments to handle their international relations under crisis circumstances, and the conditioning of European populations to react violently and hysterically to the stimulus of an international crisis. Politicians, soldiers, and businessmen, having propagated for narrow ends an illogical and dangerous imperialist ideology, found that they could not easily control it, that their actions were essentially bound by it.

Various other general explanations link imperialism to World War I. Some diplomatic historians have seen the war as a result of a severe disturbance in the European balance of power caused by industrialization, the rise of a united Germany, and similar factors. Resulting conflicts could be generally worked out by the use of "compensations" of colonial territory. When available colonial areas were used up, the powers turned to more dangerous forms of conflict and eventually world war. Since the gains obtained by colonial compensation were largely imaginary, it is difficult to see why the European states could not have devised some other form of compensation. In any event, diplomats used colonies as bargaining counters right up to 1914, as we shall see.[9]

There are many different Marxist explanations for the origins of the 1914-18 war. Most of them see it as a direct result of the totality of European imperial competition, both formal and informal, the Marxist view of which we have already examined. Like the "social imperialist" explanation, most Marxist analyses of the connection between imperialism and the First World War concentrate on domestic European class conflict and on the aims of business interests abroad. For the most part, such explanations stand or fall on the accuracy of their explanations of imperialism and on the degree to which the evidence supports the idea that business leaders determined the foreign policies of the European states in 1914. We have considered the former point; the latter is at best highly debatable.[10]

From the standpoint of the view of imperialism taken in this book, the main connection between imperialism and the coming of the First World War was the widespread use and acceptance of imperialist ideologies as frameworks for looking at the social world, as bases of policy, and especially as means of intended political manipulation. The repeated crises of imperialist conflict that preceded 1914 had their main importance as political symbols of interests threatened and protected, of the ill-will of foreign powers. The growing conviction in Europe before 1914 among members of the public and policymakers alike that war lay inevitably in the near future was undoubtedly heightened by continuous overseas imperial conflict. These results of imperialism were far more important in bringing on the war than were the actual economic interests at stake in any of the imperial crises — not excepting those centering around Balkan and Russian oil, which were fairly clearly not worth a major war. Many other factors besides imperialism, of course, helped to bring on the war. Many — including social conflict within Germany, Britain, and Russia — probably did more than imperialism by itself to create war conditions. But ideological political imperialism, linked to many of the other factors, played a significant part as well.

We have already discussed most of the important events during which European diplomacy focused its main attention on imperial expansion before 1914.[11] The scramble for Africa and its complicated aftermath created a number of crises, none of them really serious except perhaps for Fashoda in 1898. The state of relations between Germany and Britain can be traced through their imperial interaction. From a sensible agreement over East Africa in 1890, the two countries moved into a lengthy period of alternating attraction and repulsion. In 1898, the two countries made a secret agreement to divide up the Portuguese colonies in Africa should the opportunity arise, but the very next year they were at loggerheads over the Boer War. At the same time, the German building of a battle fleet — a development with colonial implications — seemed to pose a real threat to Britain and turned British public opinion strongly against Germany. Even such a potential area of cooperation as the scheme to build the "Baghdad Railway" across Turkey became a source of conflict as the railway was represented in public as a guarantee of German economic interests in the Near East and thus a threat to British ones.

We have briefly examined several other imperial crises in the immediate prewar period, including the successive Moroccan crises of 1904-6 and 1911, which lined the British and French up against the Germans, thus foreshadowing the clash of alliances during World War I. In the three years immediately preceding 1914, however, European diplomacy focused primarily on the Balkan peninsula. In 1914 an attempt was made by imperialists and business people in Britain and Germany to work out a reconciliation between their countries on the basis of a colonial agreement — essentially, the division of southern and central Africa between the two powers. Imperialism, in other words, was seriously proposed as an avenue to peace rather than war. The attempt, however, failed because important elite groups in Germany opposed such a reconciliation. When the war started, it was not over an imperial issue involving the major colonial powers, however much imperialist interests might have been indirectly involved.

THE EFFECT OF WORLD WAR I ON EUROPEAN IMPERIALISM

The First World War had a profound effect on Europe's relations with the outside world, as it did, in fact, on practically all aspects of European life. In chapter 8 we shall discuss the impact of the war on nationalist movements in European colonies. Many of the other effects were at least equally significant. In a very broad sense, the war either caused or provided the occasion for a major shift in the structure of international economic and political relations. The enormous loans made by American financial institutions to the British and French resulted in the effective transfer of the ultimate power over financial decision-making to the United States. The significance of this transfer was clearly revealed in 1924, when the United States intervened in the economic chaos following the 1923 German inflation and established, with the acquiescence of the European states, a new structure of international financial payments under the Dawes Plan, in which Europe played an important but no longer dominant role. In addition, the war brought the United States and Japan into the ranks of major industrial exporters, and it helped to cause the Russian Revolution, which produced in time yet another great power outside the orbit of the Western European countries.

World War I occasioned, paradoxically, a brief burst of renewed colonial expansion and at the same time a reduction of the importance of formal imperialism to European domestic politics. During the war, official circles in the Allied countries paid considerable attention to the Near East and to the potential problems of dismembering the Turkish Empire.[12] The reasons for this attention included strategic considerations, a desire to head off a period of diplomatic turmoil that might follow the empire's dissolution, and the simple need to defeat Turkey, an ally of Germany. Hidden behind these fairly traditional diplomatic concerns was another: the potential of the Near East as a postwar source of oil. Business interests with existing or intended stakes in Near Eastern oil pushed the British, French, and (from 1917) American governments to seek a settlement in the region that would guarantee the full exploitability of the petroleum resources there.

Among the Allies, these differing aims produced contradictory and uncoordinated policy initiatives. Although neither Britain nor France wanted to give Russia and Italy substantial shares of the Turkish Empire, they had to agree half-heartedly during the war to satisfy at least some of their allies' demands. One of the advantages derived from the Bolshevik Revolution was that they could repudiate their informal commitments to give Russia control of access to the Mediterranean. The other problems proved more intractable. Britain, in attempting to arouse the Arab subjects of the Turks to revolt, promised their leaders that the Allies would afterward permit the formation of an independent Arab state covering the area east of Egypt where Arabic was spoken. The Arabs duly revolted and cooperated with the British in the invasion of Palestine in 1917. At the same time, as a gesture toward world Jewish opinion, the British government publicly committed itself in the Balfour Declaration (1917) to the establishment of a Jewish homeland in Palestine. Although the British Foreign Office believed that these two commitments, to the Jews and to the Arabs, could be reconciled with each other, events proved otherwise. In any event, Britain and France had already, in 1916, secretly agreed to divide up most of the Turkish Empire between themselves as "spheres of influence" once the war ended.

All of these conflicting commitments and obligations became public knowledge during the discussions in Paris over the peace treaties at the end of the war. They did so under circumstances which the imperialist powers did not find comfortable: under the meddlesome eye of President Woodrow Wilson of the United States. The American position on colonial aspects of the peace treaty was decidedly unsympathetic, both toward expansionary aims on the part of America's late allies and toward the public ratification of secret deals such as the Anglo-French agreement on the Near East.

The colonial situation was clouded also by debates about what to do about Germany's colonies.[13] The Allies had undertaken a substantial propaganda campaign during the war that had painted the Germans as unusually bad colonial rulers (which was generally untrue). The same idea was put forward in 1919 to justify the formal removal of the colonies from Germany. The colonies themselves had, in fact, already been taken.

In 1914, Japan seized Kiaochow; Japan, Australia, and New Zealand took most of the other Pacific colonies; and the British and French captured Togo. Germany's other African colonies had required campaigns of varying length. Southwest Africa was captured by South Africa in a vigorous but brief campaign in 1915, and Kamerun fell the next year. Surprisingly, the German forces in East Africa maintained resistance against huge odds until after the armistice in 1918. Having won the German colonies, the Allies wanted to keep them, but they ran up against the anticolonial outlook of the United States.

The answer to the highly complex problem of conflicting colonial goals was worked out within a framework that was largely American (and, to an extent, European leftist) in inspiration. The German colonies and most of the Turkish Empire were to be parcelled out among the victorious powers (except for the United States, which was not a signatory to the general treaties after the war). These territories were not, however, to be held as permanent possessions of the powers, but rather as "mandates" of the new League of Nations.[14] The states holding the mandates were obligated to report to a permanent League of Nations commission on conditions in their territories and on progress toward economic, social, and educational development. Mechanisms were set up for hearing complaints from inhabitants of the mandates and for visits of inspection. Mandates were even classified into categories according to how close they appeared to be to full self-government. Mandatory powers thus supposedly held their new acquisitions through their acknowledgement of responsibilities toward the inhabitants and toward the League of Nations as the inhabitants' guarantor.

Cynical observers believed that the whole mandate structure was just a sop to the Americans and the European left and an attempt to hide the irreconcilable nature of the imperialists' aims and commitments beneath the cover of a supranational legality. Certainly the officials of the mandatory powers themselves believed this to have been the case. In fact, however, the mandate system, despite its many faults, functioned far more effectively than had been expected. We shall look at its role in the decolonization process in the next chapter. In any event, Britain and France divided up the parts of the Turkish Empire that they wanted — Britain getting Jordan, Iraq, and Palestine (the last simply because no other country wanted to touch it), and France receiving Lebanon and Syria. The rest of Arabia was organized into a large number of small, informally dependent states. Turkey itself (Anatolia) had theoretically been partitioned among the Greeks and Italians with spheres of British and French influence. The sudden rise of Turkish nationalism under Kemal Atatürk ended these plans. The German colonies were similarly divided: Britain and France got Togo and Kamerun, South Africa kept Southwest Africa, and Britain received German East Africa (Tanganyika), while the Pacific island colonies were retained by their conquerors (thus establishing Japan's island empire).

In Britain, as in other countries, just as some of the policies that many imperialists had sought for years were actually adopted by the government in the 1920s and 1930s and just as the overseas empire reached its widest extent, the actual relevance of imperialism declined noticeably. In the 1920s, while Britain suffered from a continued economic malaise, conservative governments turned in their rhetoric to a stale image of economic security and empire — a comforting illusion that, however, helped to deflect criticism of governmental inactivity in the economic sphere. In the same period, under the impetus of poor export performance and, after 1929, of worldwide depression, Britain moved decisively toward Joseph Chamberlain's old concept of protection and imperial preference: an attempt to insulate Britain against the competition of the world economy by attaching the colonies and dominions to Britain in a more or less closed financial and commercial system. Within the civil service, especially the Colonial Office, such concepts became the major framework of thought about imperial policy. The whole imperial protectionist edifice in Britain was capped by the Statute of Westminster (1931), which established the

British Commonwealth of Nations.[15] The basis of the Commonwealth was the political equality of the dominions (Canada, Australia, New Zealand, South Africa, and New-foundland) with Britain and her colonial dependencies — in practice, nothing really new. The main function of the Commonwealth was to create a public, political, and symbolic framework for an imperial preference system — including mutual tariff reductions for Commonwealth members and a controlled financial exchange system. In fact, the imperial preference system did not produce anything like the economic security it was supposed to do, while the Commonwealth itself simply failed to generate the widespread enthusiasm among its member populations that it had been hoped it would. The Commonwealth did provide a mechanism for cooperation during the Second World War — perhaps its most significant achievement — and it has continued to function in the postwar world. But the Commonwealth has, in general, never lived up to original expectations. Like most aspects of the apparent triumph of imperialism after World War I in Western Europe, it proved to be something of an illusion.

IMPERIALISM AND WORLD WAR II

Imperialism played an important role in the crises that brought on the Second World War, but in Europe the most important imperialist element was German continental imperialism, which lies beyond the scope of this book. The aggressiveness of both Germany and Italy in the 1930s had, of course, its overseas aspects. Italy's expansionism, justified according to incredibly inappropriate theories of economic autarky, in fact resulted from Mussolini's constant craving for popular support. He and his fascist associates sought consensus by emphasizing the supposed economic advantages of an overseas empire and emotional aims such as revenge for Adowa.[16] In a sense, interwar European fascism was an attempt to deal radically with the problem of social dissensus and political fragmentation. The fascist advocacy of imperialism fits this pattern, and in fact represents a radical exaggeration of the primary motifs of late nineteenth-century imperialism. This element of continuity between imperialism and fascism applies equally well to Nazi continental imperialism and to Italy's expansionism.

Mussolini's aggression was directed against areas identified by Italian imperialist tradition: Africa and the Balkans. The first step, economically nonsensical but sound in terms of domestic Italian politics, was to attack Ethiopia. Despite the feeble efforts of the League of Nations, Italy invaded and conquered Ethiopia in 1936, turning the country into the last major, formal European colonial acquisition. When Italy joined the war against Britain and France in 1940, Egypt became the object of its attentions. The Italians were, however, beaten back from Egypt and, to their great humiliation, lost Ethiopia, Eritrea, and Somaliland to the British. Italian advances in Albania and Greece were more successful, but largely because of German help.

There was a minor overseas element in prewar German imperialist aims under Hitler as well. Ever since the Versailles treaty stripped Germany of its colonies, German nationalists and the still active German colonial movement had pressed for their return — arguing (against all the evidence) that the colonies were vital to Germany's economy.[17] The Nazis took up the same theme, although not really very seriously, and when Hitler came to power in 1933 he included colonial revision among his list of goals for Germany. Nazi imperialist thinking remained, however, essentially continental in its orientations. During the events leading up to the Munich conference in 1938, Britain actually offered to return Germany's colonies if Hitler would leave Czechoslovakia alone. Hitler refused, revealing the nature of his imperialist priorities.

Japan's imperialism and its threat to the imperial and economic positions of the United States and the European powers was the key to the coming of the Second World War in the Far East and the Pacific.[18] Japanese imperialism lies largely outside the scope of this book. It resulted from social conflict and political fragmentation in Japan, coupled with official paranoia about the dependence of Japan's manufacturing industry on foreign raw materials and markets. Japan's policies had been expansionary since the 1890s but became severely so in 1931, when Japan occupied Manchuria and thereafter attacked China. Throughout the latter part of the 1930s, the Japanese attempted to conquer China and to include it in a closed economic area centered on Japan. The attack on China brought the United States and Britain into practical alliance against Japan. The subsequent bursting forth of Japanese expansion throughout the western Pacific and Southeast Asia during the Second World War is well known and need not be detailed here.

The Japanese expansion was extremely important in the decolonization of Asia. Not only did Japanese policy during the occupation of much of Asia serve to encourage nationalist movements, but the failure of the Europeans and Americans to stop the Japanese immediately also revealed the weakness of their hold on their colonies. As we shall see, Japanese expansion allowed the Indian nationalists to bargain successfully for independence with the British. Just as importantly, the Japanese occupation of European colonies made the colonial empires elements of wartime Allied strategic considerations, and thus made the postwar future of the colonial empires a subject of planning and diplomatic negotiation while the war was going on. This in turn meant that to a large extent the futures of the colonial empires would be determined by the attitude of the preeminent Allied power, the United States, and to a lesser extent by the Soviet Union.

The role of the United States in the wartime determination of postwar colonial policy has recently been analyzed by William Roger Louis.[19] Louis finds that pressure by Roosevelt and part of the American political leadership forced the British to abandon their plans to use the opportunity of the war to confirm and possibly expand their existing empire and to remove the restrictions of the League of Nations mandate system. This twilight British colonialism was basically a result of the "official mind" of the Colonial Office and the attitudes of politicians brought up in the wake of late Victorian expansion. It had little popular basis and even less economic foundation. Under American (and also British Labour party) pressure, the imperialists fell back, regrouped, and reemerged with a colonialism ideologically more compatible with American ideas. This new colonialism acknowledged the idea of colonial rule as a trust, as implied in the League of Nations mandate system. The imperialist nations held power in the colonies under the obligation of fostering material well-being and progress and of eventually leading the colonies to independence. To some extent, this position resulted from Britain's agreement to Indian independence after the war (see chapter 8), but in larger part it represented a moderate counter to the much more radical anticolonialism of Roosevelt and many American leaders. Roosevelt particularly wanted the projected United Nations to take an active role in ending the colonial empires. At a minimum, he wanted to extend the principles of the mandates to all colonies (except the American ones, which, according to many Americans, were not really colonies anyway). Roosevelt also contemplated the "internationalization" of much of the French and Dutch empires by placing them directly under United Nations control. The implied threat to Britain's own empire seemed fairly obvious, especially with the Soviet Union naturally supporting Roosevelt's position.

In the year preceding the 1945 San Francisco conference that established the United Nations, the British worked feverishly to change the direction of developments. Even before Roosevelt's death in April 1945 they had succeeded in greatly modifying the American position. In San Francisco, the United States agreed to a U.N. charter in which the mandates were maintained as U.N. "trust territories" under their old rulers. All the other colonies, except for the Japanese and Italian ones, were returned to their former owners, although the U.N. charter implied that colonies were no longer to be considered permanent possessions. In a formal sense, then, American anticolonialism had been deflected and the colonial empires saved.

In reality, of course, the imperial compromise at the end of the war did not greatly matter. The United States — while giving up its largest colony, the Philippines, in 1946 — introduced a new form of international domination in its military pre-eminence, its economic control, and, later, its sponsorship of a myriad of international financial organizations and military alliances. The formal European colonial empires were simply overshadowed by this newer and more efficient manifestation of international integration and control. Simultaneously, the more traditional and direct imperialism of the Soviet Union in Eastern Europe ensured the adherence of the Western European powers to the American alliance. In this context, actual decolonization was something of an anticlimax.

EIGHT

Decolonization

J UST AS SUDDENLY AS THEY EXPANDED IN the late nineteenth century, the large European colonial empires disappeared in the years following the Second World War. Both the expansion and the dissolution of the formal empires have rightly been regarded as major historical events. It is, however, important to place both late Victorian imperialism and decolonization in broader perspective, for neither was probably quite as important in the long run as it once seemed.

Colonization was a part of the much larger process of world economic and cultural integration that has been discussed often in the previous chapters. Many of the processes of socioeconomic change that took place in noncolonial areas were paralleled in the colonial empires, although, as we have seen, the colonial situation had its own peculiar effects. The late colonial interlude can be regarded to a large extent as a peculiar development caused primarily by political reaction to socioeconomic changes in Europe, which was made possible and given direction by Europe's leading role in the establishment of the integrated world economy. The world economy kept changing and developing new forms

223

of dependency during and after the colonial period; the contribution of colonialism to those changes was probably minimal. "Imperialism" and even "colonialism" have, as we have seen, often been used to describe some of the relationships implicit in the functioning of the world economy. We have used these terms more specifically here — "colonialism" to refer to forms of direct imperial control, and "imperialism" to denote exercises of political power between unequal partners in the world economy that encompass but are not limited to colonialism. In this chapter we shall briefly outline the way in which colonialism (in our sense) ceased to function after World War I and how nineteenth-century forms of imperialism were replaced by newer types of political control. Throughout both of these changes, the world economy continued its complex evolution — sometimes in conjunction with changes in imperialism, more often independent of them.

THE FIRST WORLD WAR AND DECOLONIZATION

As we saw in the previous chapter, the World War of 1914-18 had various important effects on European imperialism.[1] It introduced the final round of western European overseas territorial grabs but also seriously undermined the political and economic bases of imperialism in Europe. Most of the effects of the latter development were not, however, felt outside of Europe until after the Second World War. The First World War also affected the societies of the European colonies and helped, to some extent, to pave the way for decolonization.

In some areas, especially East Africa, colonial peoples were able to see at first hand the spectacle of Europeans fighting each other at full tilt. Despite efforts on both sides to avoid turning Africans against their white rulers, indigenous elites and populations in general could hardly help becoming more aware than before of the depth of divisions among Europeans and of their relative strengths and weaknesses. In other, usually noncolonial, areas such as Persia, German agents attempted to encourage nationalist movements against Germany's enemies. In addition, the political opportunities created by the war encouraged resistance movements of various kinds. In India, the Indian National Congress used the war emergency to press successfully for greater Indian political participation. In Nyasaland (now Malawi), John Chilembwe, a Protestant minister, led an unsuccessful revolt against the British in 1915.[2] In both French and British colonies — especially the former — thousands of non-Europeans joined the army. Much of the impetus to local-level political organization in Senegal and other parts of French Africa came from African veterans returning from the Western Front.

The treaties formally ending the First World War gave little indication of any abatement of imperialist intentions in Western Europe. As we have seen, the mandate system of the League of Nations — although in many ways a fig leaf for naked colonialism — did contain some features that affected the tenure of European control: annual reporting requirements, complaints procedures, the obligation of the mandatory powers to foster "progress," and the like. These features could have remained dead letters, except that the League's Permanent Mandates Commission, dominated by the now-retired Lord Lugard, took them very seriously.[3] The British, French, Belgian, South African, Australian, and New Zealand governments grudgingly became accustomed to answering for their performances and to couching statements of policy in the largely American-inspired terms of the mandatory requirements. Political leaders in the mandates were not slow to take advantage of the League's complaint procedure, which helped to structure the development of indigenous political organization in mandates such as the Cameroons and encouraged emulation in neighboring colonies.

THE GROWTH OF NATIONALISM AND RESISTANCE IN THE EUROPEAN COLONIES BETWEEN THE WARS

From the standpoint of the extra-European politics of decolonization, the decisive development that led to independence after World War II was the high degree of national political organizing that took place in countries ruled directly by the European powers. The nature of this process of course varied greatly. In some colonies, such as the Belgian Congo, the amount of nontraditional indigenous political organization was small between the wars. In others, such as the Gold Coast and Jamaica, political organization tending toward nationalism displayed great depth and complexity. Rather than attempting to summarize political development in all colonies, we shall consider first some general characteristics of political change in the interwar years, and then we shall turn to the highly influential example of India.

A number of external factors encouraged political development within many European colonies. The colonial policies of the European governments themselves led to indigenous organization by fostering economic change (and therefore the creation of new, widespread interest in the determination of actions to cope with that change), by encouraging the education of non-European middle-class groups, and then often by resolutely keeping the door of opportunity closed to these groups.

Another important external influence was ideological. Western education in African and Asian colonies and the increasing tendency of members of colonial elites to attend European and American universities led to a rapid adoption of European political ideologies — especially democratic liberalism and Marxist socialism. African and Asian students abroad invariably experienced racial discrimination, which naturally often led them to conclude that the Western European and American versions of democratic theory masked a great deal of hypocrisy. This, together with other factors, created considerable sympathy for the Marxist alternative. European left parties tended to be at least nominally anticolonial, and the Leninist theory of world revolution was very attractive. Because of the prior work of Lenin, Trotsky, and others concerned with the problem of revolution in nonindustrial countries, it did not prove especially difficult to devise variations of

Marxist theory appropriate to the colonial setting. But until the time of independence, neither liberal democracy nor Marxism was a truly popular ideology in most colonies; they served rather as ideologies of integration for the educated elite.

One of the major disputed questions in the history of decolonization concerns this very point: the relationship among Westernized elites, the colonial "masses," and the growth of organizational structures capable of effecting independence. The first approaches by historians to decolonization concentrated almost exclusively on elites, especially on the Western-educated ones who were so evident to the outside world as the spokesmen, ideologists, and leaders of independence movements.[4] This concentration was understandable, since most information initially came from journalistic sources, but it tended to avoid the basic question of how small elite groups managed to acquire sufficient popular support to bring about independence. While traditional elites presumably had traditional legitimacy, the Westernized elites had no such automatic means of eliciting support. It seemed to follow that most colonies did not really "win" their independence at all. Rather, the imperial powers decided for a variety of reasons that their colonies were no longer profitable, decided to give independence to many of them, and simply selected the politically impotent Western-educated elite as the recipients of power. There are, as we shall see, certain elements of truth to this approach in some areas. It does not, however, explain the independence of India or of the other role-models in the process of national liberation, and it ignores many factors elsewhere.

An alternative explanation of the growth of support for small, Western-educated nationalist elites concentrates on stages of resistance to European rule.[5] According to this view, modern effective liberation movements took advantage of earlier forms of resistance, which had acquired support by means unavailable to "Westernized" political leaders. These earlier resistance movements were crushed, but their examples legitimized later resistance. In many countries, a primary stage, in which the traditional elites led their societies to war against the Europeans, came first. Generally, the traditional elites were either destroyed or coopted. In the second stage, new forms of resistance appeared, usually incorporating a mystical religious element with mass appeal and led by a new, impermanent, and charismatic elite. The inspiration for this variety of resistance came occasionally from Christianity. "Second-stage" resistance sometimes became institutionalized and nonviolent — as in the case of the various "nativist" Christian churches in Africa — and sometimes took the form of violent revolt: the Taiping rebellion, the Maji-Maji rebellion against the Germans in East Africa in 1905, and Mau Mau in Kenya in the early 1950s. The latter were almost always unsuccessful. The third stage was the familiar nationalist movement, heavily influenced by European political ideologies and led by the Western-educated elite but operating in the context of earlier stages of resistance which created the myths and the motives for broad popular support. New elites, although their styles of living had little in common with those of their followers, could nevertheless become popular leaders while also knowing how to deal effectively with the Europeans. Among scholars using this sort of model, there is a good deal of dispute as to whether the stages should be defined in terms of elite or of mass action. In either case, however, the same general theoretical structure holds.

There are many weaknesses in the stage approach to Third World resistance. Many independence movements skipped certain stages; purported stages often overlapped so much as to be practically indistinguishable. Also, the differentiation among elites implied by the model is seldom so clear cut. The Sudanese Mahdi, for example, fits into both category one and category two of resistance elites. In many places, the Western-educated colonial elite tended to be drawn from the traditionally sanctioned elites. But at least the stage theories provide a framework for analysis and comparison of the non-European sides of decolonization processes. Tanzania, for example, went through all three stages in order, while the Belgian Congo (Zaïre) experienced only the first stage to any significant degree until just before independence. The third stage had barely started when the Congo received its independence, while second-stage phenomena appeared largely after independence. This difference may have been due to many causes, including different geographical settings and different colonial policies, but at least it is possible to analyze the difference in uniform terms.

The habits, images, and traditions of resistance which created sympathy for nationalist leaders and on which the stage theories concentrate were not the only ingredients of successful resistance. As we saw in chapter 6, considerable historical attention has been paid recently to the emergence of grassroots *organizations* that supported independence movements. To account for these, we must return to the impingement of external influences, especially economic ones, on the colonial world in the interwar period. Especially in the largest colonies, increasing proportions of the population were drawn by government policy, private economic development, and the shaping of consumer preferences into export production and related industries. This opened up colonial societies to the erratic effects of the international market and to exploitation, or at least control, by foreign-based business enterprises. In response, colonial producers, workers, consumers, and taxpayers began to organize in various ways so as to acquire some influence over the terms under which the economy operated. Unions (where allowed), merchants' or farmers' associations, and mutual aid societies, as well as adaptations of religious and traditional fraternal organizations, appeared — often in profusion. These organizations were seldom overtly political at first. In the Gold Coast, for example, cocoa growers and other farmers formed pressure organizations — in many ways linked to the Ashanti chief system — to protect themselves against the monopolistic cocoa buyers. In colonies with industrial sectors, labor unions were founded, although seldom successfully. In many British and French colonies, ex-servicemen's associations formed in the wakes of both world wars. In Kenya, the Kikuyu organized to press their claims to expropriated lands.

This spread of voluntary organizations constituted a substantial degree of social modernization in itself. It also provided the needed organizational foundation for successful nationalist resistance to European rule after World War II. Much of the history of the non-European side of decolonization depended upon the contacts between anticolonial political elites and these economic organizations, and the manner in which the latter became politicized. The fact that nationalists in places like the Gold Coast and Nigeria managed to take power without protracted violence or terror is a sign not of inadequate revolutionary development, but of effective coordination between economic pressure organizations and anticolonial political parties. We have looked at the process briefly in Nigeria. In Ghana, Kwame Nkrumah's Convention People's party succeeded after World War II precisely because it was able to do what its predecessors (essentially organizations of the educated elite) had not: attract both mass support and the support of organizations such as cocoa farmers' associations and ex-servicemen's associations.[6] Many of the more spectacular cases of revolutionary warfare and terrorism, such as Algeria in the 1950s, resulted in part from the inability of the ideological nationalists to effect the necessary juncture with originally extrapolitical organizations. In a sense, then, one of the most important ingredients in the decolonization movement resulted not so much from colonial rule as from reactions to the extension of the world economy. Decolonization thus paralleled similar developments in the noncolonial part of the Third World.

THE STRUGGLE FOR INDEPENDENCE IN INDIA

In the interwar period and in the years immediately after the Second World War, one country in particular stood out as the model for nationalist movements struggling successfully against colonialism: India. Decolonization occurred earlier, more dramatically, and on a larger scale there than elsewhere. The symbolic importance of Indian decolonization was immense, both because it was personified by larger-than-life figures such as Gandhi and also because of the crucial role that India had played in European imperialist ideologies.

In previous chapters we have observed the development of British rule in India in the nineteenth and early twentieth centuries and also the beginnings of modern Indian political resistance.[7] World War I was an important watershed in Indian history. It proved the effectiveness of British rule in the military support afforded Britain by India, but it also marked the beginnings of real effectiveness for the main Indian nationalist organizations: the predominantly Hindu Indian National Congress and the Muslim League. During the war, the British government issued broad (and vague) promises that Indians would be included in increasing numbers at all levels of the administration with a view to eventual self-determination.

The subsequent history of Indian independence is conventionally told in the language of political images — indeed, often in terms of a political mythology centering around the figure of Mohandas K. Gandhi (1869-1948). This convention is the result both of Gandhi's political behavior as perceived by the outside and of the tendency of Westerners in general to mythologize India.

Gandhi was by any measure a remarkable man.[8] Up until the First World War, he was an almost archetypal Westernized Indian. A member of one of the middle-rank castes, Gandhi was educated in law at the University of London and moved to South Africa in 1893, making a career as a lawyer among Indian immigrants. In South Africa, Gandhi became incensed at discriminatory racial policies and led a civil rights movement, again mostly among the Indian population, that landed him in jail on numerous occasions. It was in South Africa that he developed his theories of civil disobedience and passive resistance — theories influenced by Thoreau and Tolstoy and by certain aspects of Hindu political theory but even more by Gandhi's highly developed sense of political realities.

In 1914 Gandhi returned to India. Up to this time, although he opposed racial discrimination and the political disabilities forced upon non-Europeans (especially educated ones), he had largely accepted the more liberal versions of British imperialist ideology. Gandhi thought that British rule had started India on the path toward "progress" and eventual self-rule, and he could be quite patriotic toward the British Empire. He voluntarily served in the Boer War, and during the First World War he supported British recruiting efforts.

The crucial developments in Gandhi's career occurred between 1915 and 1922. With the prestige he had acquired in South Africa, Gandhi became the leader of the Indian National Congress by the end of the First World War. During the latter part of the war, civil disturbances had become frequent, encouraged by the reduction of British forces, unsettled economic conditions, high taxation, and the continued domination of government and business by the British. The activism of the Congress had also encouraged protests, despite Gandhi's insistence on nonviolent, orderly political action. Gandhi became convinced of the need for democracy and Indian political autonomy in the near future as a means of correcting the political and economic inequities present in the British imperial system.

The British responded to unrest and violence, as they had in Ireland, with promises of reform and with coercive legislation, including martial law. Gandhi, barely able to check his followers from outright rebellion, advocated nationwide passive resistance and protest meetings. At one of these meetings, at Amritsar in the Punjab in April 1919, British troops fired into the crowd, causing at least one thousand six hundred casualties. This was the "Boston Massacre" of India (and unlike the original, it was a real massacre). Gandhi became the leader of a nationalist protest movement aimed at boycotting British goods and trade and circumventing restrictive economic regulations. In the early 1920s he and his followers, of whom Jawaharlal Nehru became the most important, propagated a whole ideology of passive resistance and independence among large parts of the Hindu population and among the educated elite. They were less successful in gaining the support of Muslims, since the Muslim League advocated Islamic separatism, and of the Indian princes, for whom neither Gandhi nor the Congress had much use anyway. Gandhi proved himself to be a great creator of political symbols. In himself, he established an intensely appealing symbol of a marriage of eastern and western ideas and of perseverance in the face of adversity. In his sponsorship of a program of home production of cotton to supplement the boycott, he managed to incorporate an economic critique of British rule that could be understood by practically anyone. His periodic fasts and jail terms enhanced his image still further and allowed him to impose upon the Congress a much more moderate nationalist program than many leaders, including Nehru, wanted to follow.

This was Gandhi's story as perceived from outside India. Gandhi was undoubtedly important in shaping the Indian independence movement and restraining its violence. His skill at creating symbols helped the Congress to become a truly national party. On the other hand, after 1924 Gandhi retired from active leadership in the face of British reaction and fragmentation among the nationalists. When he returned to politics in 1930, he had lost a good deal of his power in the Congress, although his popular and international reputations were much greater. Much of the credit for the success of the Indian nationalists must go to the rest of the Congress leadership, which maintained momentum toward independence and did the practical work that permitted Gandhi to retain his image of superhuman political purity.

Recent research had disclosed that there was much more to the independence movement even than this. Before the First World War, the Congress, like its rival the Muslim League, was essentially an organization of intellectuals and educated professionals rather than a popular movement with a local-level structure. Gandhi gave it national symbols, but contacts with other kinds of organizations — unions, farming cooperatives, social organizations, and so on — gave it a permanent organized support base at the local level. The Congress managed to link nationalism and independence with the interests of organizations chiefly concerned about advancing their members' economic welfare. This allowed it to break out of the narrow elite mold by the early 1920s. Gandhi's mass campaigns of civil disobedience and boycott would not have worked without this organized local-level support.[9]

In the 1920s and 1930s the British followed a "carrot and stick" policy toward the nationalists. In the 1920s the "stick" part of the policy seemed to work, as Gandhi and others were regularly hauled off to prison and the nationalist leadership foundered. In the long run, coercion was self-defeating. It produced incidents like Amritsar and it drove moderates like Gandhi into more radical stances. The British also attempted a "divide and conquer" approach. They secretly sponsored the Muslim League at its beginning and tried to split the nationalists over religious differences. When it became clear that the British would have to accept increased Indian participation in government, they attempted to balance the accretion of power to the nationalists in the directly ruled provinces by emphasizing the role in the new All-India institutions of the more than 560 native princes.

In the late 1920s, clashes between Muslims and Hindus became more frequent, and the Congress and the Muslim League became increasingly bitter enemies. The Congress committed itself to maintaining the unity of all India upon independence, while the League — concerned that Muslims would be in a minority in a united India — pushed for minority safeguards and decentralization. Eventually, in the 1930s, the Muslim League came out for complete partition into Hindu and Muslim territories, the latter to be designated "Pakistan."

Serious religious riots broke out, especially in Calcutta. The British authorities found that religious strife simply increased their police problem without diminishing the pressure that the Congress was placing on them.

In Britain itself, the continuing troubles in India led Liberals and Labourites to consider seriously a change in India's relationship to Britain, including complete autonomy. While many Conservatives resisted, others realized that Britain could not afford to repeat its mistakes with Ireland on a scale as vast as that of India. Once the idea of Indian autonomy became familiar, it did not appear to be all that bad. Perhaps for the first time in three-quarters of a century, the shortcomings of the British myth of India were discussed publicly. It was not, despite resistance, a difficult step to entertaining the notion of complete independence.

In 1929-30, the Indian economy, highly dependent on the world economy, collapsed with the coming of the Great Depression. Mass starvation occurred and violence broke out all over the subcontinent. Radical nationalists and Marxists became important among the leaders of the Congress and stepped up their demands on the government. Gandhi returned from retirement and in 1930 led a massive civil disobedience campaign directed against imperial economic exploitation. The British jailed Gandhi. But they soon realized that they needed him to restore order, and he was released from prison in 1931. Gandhi then undertook to publicize moderation and non-violence, while the British agreed to prepare for Indian self-rule.

The first result of the change in British policy was the Government of India Act of 1935. The act did not go as far as even the moderate Indian nationalists wanted, and it greatly offended the extreme nationalists. It provided a decentralized autonomy for India, which was now theoretically recognized as an independent state. Elected assemblies were established in the directly ruled provinces, but the national government was responsible both to the provinces and to the native princes, the close allies of the British. Elected national assemblies had limited powers and contained strong princely representation. The viceroy, appointed by the crown, retained a great deal of power, including direct control of foreign affairs and military matters. This last point became a major issue when, in 1939, the viceroy declared war on Germany on his own initiative. The Government of India Act thus represented, to some extent, a continuation of the previous British policy of encouraging Indian divisions.

Within the Congress there was considerable sentiment against the act, but Gandhi managed to persuade the majority to support it as a step toward independence. After the act went into effect in 1937, however, the leadership of the Congress and of many of the newly elected governmental bodies was taken over by extreme nationalists in favor of immediate independence. Relations with the British remained tense. With the coming of war in 1939 – although the British were able to recruit many troops, especially Muslims and Sikhs – the main nationalist organizations refused support without guarantees of progress toward real independence. Strikes and other forms of resistance followed, and Gandhi was jailed once again. As the Japanese occupied Burma, the threat to British dominance in India became more pronounced. The Japanese threat was beaten back in 1944, but even before that it had become clear to most politicians in Britain that the era of British imperialism there was essentially over.

During the war the British Labour party, a coalition partner and already basically committed to Indian independence, pushed Churchill to make further concessions so as to save the Indian war effort. A series of negotiations was held with Gandhi and other leaders, culminating in a mission by Sir Stafford Cripps in 1942 during which the British government offered India full independence after the war. At this point, differences between the Congress and the Muslim League prevented common agreement. Over the next five years, especially after the end of the war in 1945, India moved toward near anarchy as the

British prepared to pull out and the various Indian political factions struggled to get the upper hand. In 1946, the British Labour government set a deadline for complete Indian independence in 1948 and then, in 1947, after agreement with an Indian government headed by Nehru, decided on immediate independence. Gandhi persuaded the Congress to accede to Muslim demands for a separate Pakistan, and in September 1947, India and Pakistan were declared completely independent republics within the Commonwealth.

Independence was immediately followed by mass movements of Muslims to Pakistan and Hindus to India, by the deaths of hundreds of thousands in religious conflict, and by armed confrontation over Kashmir. India and Pakistan have remained antagonists and have fought often. Government in both countries has appeared chaotic to foreigners, a fact which has obscured the greater fact that India's government today is far more capable of conducting the full range of governmental functions than the British administration ever was.

WORLD WAR II AND DECOLONIZATION

As we have seen in our discussion of India, World War II had a decisive effect on the process of decolonization in many areas.[10] In places such as India, the war accelerated ongoing processes of decolonization. In areas such as French Indochina and the Dutch East Indies, nationalists could obtain liberal promises from the expelled colonial powers, and sometimes also from the occupying Japanese. Ho Chi Minh's Communists in Vietnam and Sukarno's nationalists in Java also took advantage of the power vacuum that followed the eventual expulsion of the Japanese to establish themselves as the actual governing authorities in substantial areas of their countries. The circumstances of conquest made the disposition of the colonies of the former Axis powers, and even those of Allies such as France and the Netherlands, subject to strong influence from the United States. The war also brought into being the United Nations with its trusteeship system.

In Africa, the war's effects were complex. In 1941, the British took Ethiopia from the Italians and returned it to the government of its emperor, Haile Selassie – perhaps unconsciously producing Africa's first modern case of decolonization. Of the other Italian colonies, Eritrea was joined to Ethiopia after the war for convenience, while Libya and Somalia were eventually granted independence. In Egypt, the German and Italian threat to British control encouraged the growth of nationalist movements within the army that sought revolution and real independence from Britain. In Tunisia, Morocco, and Algeria, the war initially brought no absolute diminution of French authority since the Vichy government continued to rule during the German occupation. The Allied invasions, however, demonstrated the weakness of France's control. Also, the Free French, in order to build support, made a series of promises about future improvements in the political and economic lots of French colonial subjects. Since the Free French depended heavily on Equatorial Africa as a strategic base during the war, they did their best to conciliate black Africans as well. To this end, they held a conference at Brazzaville in 1944 at which increased African participation in government was discussed and the outlines of the postwar French Union were laid out.

The Algerian and Tunisian economies were temporarily ruined by the trade restrictions imposed by the war. In much of the rest of Africa, however – especially in those countries with substantial export trades – the war brought a vast increase in demand for primary products, such as rubber and metals, and high international prices. In the Gold Coast, Nigeria, and the Belgian Congo, there was comparative prosperity, accompanied by a substantial amount of capital accumulation and economic development. In other areas, the presence of large military forces sometimes stimulated the economy. The wartime boom contrasted strikingly with the periods just before and just after the war. Up until 1940, the effects of the Great Depression were still being felt in Africa; profits and employment were constantly low. Shortly after the end of the war, demand for

African products again diminished, leading to another depression in those countries that had benefited most from the war. This served as a graphic illustration of the dependence of the colonial economies on outside forces that they could not control. It occasioned widespread popular resentment against colonial rule and contributed to the politicization of African economic organizations. In the Gold Coast, which was politically and economically the pacesetter for the rest of British-ruled tropical Africa, Nkrumah's populist, socialist Convention People's party was able in the late 1940s to capitalize on discontent and to become an important political force.

The Second World War also had direct political effects on parts of Africa. Returning servicemen heightened the degree of political activism, especially in Senegal, the Gold Coast, and Nigeria. Allied propaganda, which represented the Allies as the defenders of democracy, and vague promises about better political and economic conditions after the war (such as the ones made by the French at the Brazzaville conference), created enormous expectations among African political elites and substantial portions of the general populations of French colonies. The Second World War was thus an important event in the decolonization of Africa as well as of Asia.

POSTWAR DECOLONIZATION

The events of formal decolonization in the post-World War II era are far too complex to be reviewed in any detail here. The process is still going on, although with the transformation of Rhodesia into Zimbabwe it is presently nearing completion. Also, the definitive analysis of decolonization has yet to be written. Here we shall only summarize the process, first with respect to the major European imperial states and then with respect to the former colonies themselves.[11]

Changes in Europe

In the aftermath of World War II, Western European political elites and voting publics came, slowly and often ambiguously, to a number of realizations about formal imperialism. The first of these came with a recognition of the new distribution of political power in a world dominated by the United States and, before long, the Soviet Union. Another was the realization that the structure of the world economy had changed, reducing the importance of Western Europe as a decision-making center. In the long run, these changes made nonsense of traditional ideologies of European empire. The eventualities that colonies had been intended to prevent had come to pass. Especially in Britain in the economically depressed years following the war, the colonies came to be seen by many people as an expensive liability. Security for Britain, France, Italy, and western Germany lay in a close relationship to the United States and its nuclear power, not in the possession of a large overseas empire. Economic prosperity depended upon European economic integration.

Imperialism had, moreover, lost its utility as a domestic political tool in most Western European countries. Other ideologies, other goals, other threats had proved themselves more efficacious. Ostensibly anticolonial parties became governing parties, as the Labour party was in Britain from 1945 to 1951. In Britain especially, when problems with individual colonies arose there was little to prevent their solution through decolonization. The decolonization of India and the previous British experience with the white dominions had established a pattern that could fairly easily be adapted to other circumstances.

Not all of these conditions prevailed immediately, however, in the formulation of national policy. In Britain, there existed groups (such as present and retired colonial officials) with vested interests in maintaining the colonial empire. These groups were able to use a residual feeling for the empire to influence politics into the 1950s. At first, companies with colonial investments supported these groups, but eventually they realized that, for the most part, decolonization would not hurt their businesses. The procolonial rearguard argued strongly about

Britain's obligations to its colonial subjects, but they were definitely on the defensive.

In France and the Netherlands, imperialism somewhat para-doxically maintained a stronger hold on national policy. In France, while traditional imperialism offered little positive help to any particular party or government in the political confusion of the Fourth Republic, no government or party believed that it could survive the blame that it would receive from active de-colonization. In addition, certain interest groups remained very influential in the making of colonial policy, particularly the owners of rubber companies in Indochina and the military in Algeria, the latter by now closely allied with the *colons*. All of the governments of the Fourth Republic had difficulty making policy anyway, and the repudiation of the empire was more than they could easily bear. Instead, in the immediate postwar years French governments attempted to offer an updated con-cept of assimilation as an alternative to independence: the French Union. The Union would be a cooperative economic and political organization connecting France to its colonies. The colonies would evolve into self-governing democracies, represented by elected delegates in the French Assembly and other joint institutions. In many French colonies, the French Union idea was fairly readily accepted because it would provide support for insecure political elites, financial aid for impov-erished economies, and a continued French cultural connection for colonial intellectuals. In an informal way, France continues to provide these services to the elites of many of its previous sub-Saharan African colonies. But the political parties in France were never able to agree to give up enough power to the former colonies to make the system really work. Moreover, the Union did not, as we shall see, correspond to the aspirations of major political groups in Algeria, Tunisia, Morocco, and Indo-china, nor did it accord with political realities in any of these places. The French Union therefore failed. In the late 1950s, De Gaulle's government sponsored a looser association called the French Community. But by that time decolonization was proceeding almost as a chain reaction throughout the world, and the French Community was simply bypassed by events. By that time also, the bankruptcy of French imperialism had been demonstrated in Indochina and Algeria.

The Dutch government and public opinion after the war remained wedded to the concept of political integration between Indonesia and the Netherlands, but realities also bypassed them. The East Indies, occupied during the war by the Japanese, were occupied by the British afterwards. Right after the war, nationalist groups had taken over actual governance of large areas of Java and other islands. By adroitly playing on their reputations as "enlightened" colonialists, by using moderately pro-Dutch political groups in Indonesia, and by agreeing to a loose association of a supposedly autonomous "United States of Indonesia" with the Netherlands, the Dutch were able in the immediate postwar years to neutralize American anticolonial policy and to get the British to help them reestablish control. When the compromise system of Indonesian "autonomy" broke down, the Dutch attempted to reoccupy all of Indonesia militarily. This directed world opinion decisively against the Netherlands and caused Dutch political leaders to accept the idea that holding on to Indonesia was economically unprofitable. Under continued political pressure from nationalist forces under Sukarno, the Netherlands finally capitulated and agreed to complete Indonesian independence in 1950.

The Process of Decolonization

The actual processes of decolonization took place in varied ways in different countries. In the 1950s and early 1960s, however, both Europeans and colonial nationalists were conscious of a kind of uniformity in decolonization that extended beyond individual continents and empires. In fact, subsequent events have shown that much of this uniformity — manifested in such forms as Pan-Africanism and the attempt to organize the "nonaligned" countries — was illusory. Nonetheless, the examples set in the decolonization of certain key countries influenced what happened in others, sometimes essentially dictating the procedures to be followed. And the massive French disasters in Indochina and Algeria indicated clearly what might happen if decolonization were not handled satisfactorily.

In Asia, the prime example of decolonization was India. Once India and Pakistan had been given their independence, it made little sense for Britain to retain India's traditional satellites of Ceylon, Burma, and Malaya, and most subsequent British policy there was directed at arranging an orderly withdrawal that protected as many British economic and strategic interests as possible. We have already examined the process by which the Netherlands lost Indonesia. The various dependencies in the Pacific were decolonized or not largely according to the convenience of the possessing powers and the influence of the United Nations. They remain, regardless of their status, under the economic control of the industrial countries. The Philippines became independent in 1946 in accordance with a pre-established program that had, however, little influence on the European empires.

Apart from Indonesia, the only place in Asia where decolonization was really seriously resisted was French Indochina. The Indochinese war and its aftermath, which so tragically involved the United States, is a part of modern world history and is thoroughly discussed elsewhere. In essence, the independence of Indochina was determined when the Communists took over China in the 1940s. The French, however, attempted to retain control of Indochina, managed to obtain American support because of the growth of anticommunism in the United States in the early 1950s, and tried to use puppet Indochinese governments to prevent the success of Ho Chi Minh's Communist revolutionary movement. The French were, of course, defeated militarily and forced to acknowledge the independence of four Indochinese states in 1954. The aftermath of the 1954 agreement is well known.

In the Middle East, Britain and France attempted to retain control of their mandates but were forced by nationalist resistance and by American and Russian pressure to give them up. Subsequently, the area became a political and economic battleground between the new world powers, the United States and the Soviet Union. In recent years, the successful establishment of an international oil cartel has made the oil-producing Near Eastern states the best candidates for turning the tables of economic control on their former masters. Britain's unhappy involvement with Palestine, with the Arab-Jewish conflicts there, and with the emergence of the state of Israel in 1948 brought home graphically to the European publics the hidden dangers of traditional imperialism.

In the Caribbean, Jamaica and Trinidad led the way to independence, which the European powers were not reluctant to grant since they had acknowledged the political dominance of the United States over the region anyway. The British attempted to organize the decolonization of the British West Indies in such a way that the former colonies could support each other (and British-owned industries) in a general federation, but the West Indies Federation did not long survive the end of colonial rule in the 1960s. The Netherlands chose to integrate its West Indian colonies with the home country rather than to give them independence. Surinam has, however, been given independence by stages.

Africa was the scene of the most prolonged and complex process of decolonization. Some places, such as the former Italian colonies, were decolonized almost by default since there was little else that could be done with them. Among the British colonies, the Gold Coast (Ghana) led the way. Although the British government's commitment to colonialism in the late 1940s was not strong, no one contemplated a really rapid turnover of power to African political parties. The growth of Nkrumah's Convention People's party in the late 1940s and early 1950s, however, and the increasing violence of confrontations between the CPP and the authorities led the British government to decide to decolonize the Gold Coast rapidly, simply to reduce expenses and political problems. The Gold Coast had a comparatively well-developed economy, a large educated elite, and a modern political structure; it seemed the ideal environment for self-rule and independence. Agreements were made with

Nkrumah first to give the Gold Coast self-government and then, in 1957, as Ghana, full independence.

Once Ghana had set the example, decolonization became the goal for African nationalists throughout the British colonies and the model followed by colonial authorities. Parallel decolonization processes were set in motion, essentially by mutual consent, throughout Africa. Starting with Nigeria in 1960, most of the other British colonies attained independence in the 1960s according to the pattern of Ghana. It was this tide of independence in the British colonies that swamped the French Community and led to the independence of the individual colonies of French West Africa and French Equatorial Africa.

The major exceptions to this pattern in sub-Saharan Africa were the Portuguese colonies — which Portugal retained in the face of growing armed resistance into the 1970s because the Portuguese government did not want to lose face at home and because of South African support of Portugal — and the British colonies with substantial white populations. In Kenya, nationalist political organization intensified after World War II, and in the early 1950s the British had to face the Mau Mau rebellion against white rule. The difficulties this entailed led, despite settler opposition, to a British decision to decolonize, which was accomplished in 1963. In Rhodesia, the large white population and the existence of powerful mining interests led to an attempt to grant autonomy to Northern and Southern Rhodesia and Nyasaland as a federation under the domination of Southern Rhodesian whites. Resistance in Northern Rhodesia and Nyasaland, however, caused the breakup of the federation and the granting of independence to those two colonies as Zambia and Malawi. Southern Rhodesia unilaterally declared its independence in 1965 when the British government attempted to end white rule there. Only in 1980 did the Rhodesian breakaway end, when British rule was reestablished in preparation for the complete independence of the country as African-ruled Zimbabwe.

The decolonization of North Africa was a major focus of world attention in the 1950s. In 1952, a revolution in Egypt installed a nationalist government under Gamal Abd 'el Nasser, which removed the last vestiges of British control and assumed the leadership of Arab nationalist movements throughout the Near East and North Africa. In 1956, Nasser nationalized the Suez Canal. Britain and France, aided by Israel, recaptured it by force but were required to leave by the United States and the Soviet Union. The Suez venture is usually taken to be the last gasp of traditional European imperialism. In Morocco and Tunisia, anti-French nationalist movements intensified their agitation after World War II; they were not satisfied by the French Union. So difficult did the situation become for France, especially in Tunisia, that it agreed to the independence of both countries in the early 1950s. Algeria was not so easy. The European population, supported by the army, resisted decolonization and real political reform, which drove the nationalists into armed revolt in 1954. The ensuing war was expensive, bloody, and politically debilitating for France, and it helped to bring down the Fourth Republic. When Charles de Gaulle came to power in 1958, he immediately sought an end to the war on the terms of the FLN, the Algerian nationalist organization. This led to a *colon* revolt and an army mutiny, both of which were put down. Algeria received its complete independence in 1962.

The age of traditional European imperialism is thus now practically over. The historical situation which gave rise to it has changed, and therefore the colonial empires and many of the historical varieties of European informal imperialism have passed away. Imperialism as a form of aggressive human behavior is, however, still present in social relations and perhaps always will be. Even more importantly, as we saw in chapter 7, the integrated world economy continues to develop, and with it new forms of influence and control between different areas of the world. Europe is, however, no longer the sole, or even the main, center from which this control and influence emanate.

NOTES

Chapter One

1. See Roger Owen and Bob Sutcliffe, eds., *Studies in the Theory of Imperialism* (London: Longmans, 1972), especially pp. 1-11.

2. For a broad and controversial use of the "center-periphery" model, see Immanuel Wallerstein, *The Modern World-System* (New York: Academic Press, 1974).

3. Karl Marx and Friedrich Engels, *On Colonialism* (London: Lawrence and Wishart, 1960).

4. V.I. Lenin, *Imperialism: The Highest Stage of Capitalism*, 13th ed. (Moscow, Progress Publishers, 1966), and J.A. Hobson, *Imperialism: A Study* (London: Allen and Unwin, 1965).

5. Joseph A. Schumpeter, *Imperialism* (New York: Meridian, 1955).

6. John Gallagher and Ronald Robinson, "The Imperialism of Free Trade," *Economic History Review* (2nd series), 6:1 (1953), pp. 1-15.

7. D.C.M. Platt, *Finance, Trade and Politics in British Foreign Policy 1815-1914* (London: Oxford University Press, 1968).

8. Ronald Robinson and John Gallagher, with Alice Denny, *Africa and the Victorians: The Official Mind of Imperialism* (London: Macmillan, 1961).

9. Hans-Ulrich Wehler, *Bismarck und der Imperialismus* (Cologne: Knieppenheuer and Witsch, 1969); Bernard Semmel, *Imperialism and*

247

Social Reform: English Social-Imperialist Thought 1895-1914 (London: Allen and Unwin, 1960).

10. For a discussion of some of this literature, see Thomas Hodgkin, "Some African and Third-World Theories of Imperialism," in Owen and Sutcliffe, *Studies in the Theory of Imperialism*, pp. 93-116, and Ralph A. Austen, "Economic Imperialism Revisited: Late-Nineteenth-Century Europe and Africa," in *Journal of Modern History*, 47:3 (1975), pp. 519-29.

Chapter Two

1. The classic description of the old colonial system is George Louis Beer, *The Old Colonial System*, 2 vols. (New York: Peter Smith, 1933). See also C.M. Andrews, *The Colonial Period in American History*, 4 vols. (New Haven and London: Yale University Press, 1934).

2. The literature on mercantilism is extensive. The classic discussion is Eli Heckscher, *Mercantilism*, 2nd ed. (New York: Macmillan, 1955). On economic ideology in the seventeenth century, see Joyce Appleby, "Ideology and Theory: The Tension between Political and Economic Liberalism in Seventeenth-Century England," *American Historical Review* 81 (1976), pp. 499-515.

3. Richard Pares, *War and Trade in the West Indies 1739-1763* (London: Frank Cass, 1963); J.H. Parry and P.M. Sherlock, *A Short History of the West Indies*, 2nd ed. (London: Macmillan, 1968), pp. 95-179; and Eric Williams, *From Columbus to Castro: A History of the Caribbean 1492-1969*, pp. 23-253. See also Vera Rubin and Arthur Tuden, eds., *Comparative Perspectives on Slavery in New World Plantation Societies*, vol. 292 (New York: New York Academy of Sciences, 1977).

4. On the slave trade, see Herbert Klein, *The Middle Passage* (Princeton: Princeton University Press, 1978); Philip Curtin, *The Atlantic Slave Trade: A Census* (Madison: University of Wisconsin Press, 1969); and Roger Anstey, *The Atlantic Slave Trade and British Abolition* (Atlantic Highlands, N.J.: Humanities Press, 1975). On the African side of the trade, see A.J.H. Latham, *Old Calabar, 1600-1891* (London: Oxford University Press, 1973), and Alan F.C. Ryder, *Benin and the Europeans, 1485-1897* (London: Longmans, 1969).

5. The abolition of the British slave trade is one of the most popular and controversial modern historical subjects. The traditional view, that abolition was the result of the growth of humanitarianism, was put forward by Reginald Coupland, *The British Anti-Slavery Movement*, 2nd ed. (London:

Frank Cass, 1964). Coupland was attacked by Eric Williams in his classic *Capitalism and Slavery* (Chapel Hill: University of North Carolina Press, 1944), in which he argued that the abolitionists were motivated by the interests of the new industrial sector of the economy and that, in any event, the sugar economy of the West Indies had collapsed by the 1780s. Williams' argument is disputed by Anstey, *The Atlantic Slave Trade*, and by Seymour Drescher, *Econocide: British Slavery in the Era of Abolition* (Pittsburgh: University of Pittsburgh Press, 1977), who give political and intellectual explanations for abolition.

6. J.H. Parry, *Trade and Dominion: The European Overseas Empires in the Eighteenth Century* (New York: Praeger, 1971), pp. 42-56, 130-53, 273-90, and Richard N. Bean, "Food Imports into the British West Indies: 1680-1845," in Rubin and Tuden, eds., *Comparative Perspectives on Slavery*, pp. 581-90.

7. On Canada, see J.M. Bumsted, ed., *Canadian History before Confederation: Essays and Interpretations* (Georgetown, Ont.: Irwin-Dorsey Ltd., 1972).

8. Philip Woodruff, *The Men Who Ruled India: The Founders* (London: J. Cape, 1953); Brian Gardner, *The East India Company: A History* (New York: McCall, 1972); Wilbert H. Dalgleish, *The Perpetual Company of the Indies in the Days of Dupleix* (Easton, Pa.: Chemical Publishing Co., 1933); Penderel Moon, *Warren Hastings and British India* (New York: Macmillan, 1949); and P.E. Roberts, *History of British India Under the Company and the Crown*, 3rd ed. (London: Oxford University Press, 1952), pp. 220-91.

9. Andrew Sharp, *The Discovery of the Pacific Islands* (Oxford: Clarendon Press, 1960), and C.M.H. Clark, *A History of Australia*, 2 vols. (Melbourne: Melbourne University Press, 1962), 1:59-209.

10. Walter A. Roberts, *The French in the West Indies* (Indianapolis: Bobbs-Merrill, 1942).

11. George M. Wrong, *The Rise and Fall of New France* (New York: Octagon Books, 1970).

12. Marcel Giraud, *Histoire de la Louisiane française*, 3 vols. (Paris: Presses universitaires de France, 1953-66).

13. S.P. Sen, *The French in India 1763-1816* (New Delhi: Munshiram Manoharlal, 1971).

14. On Dutch colonialism in general, see Charles R. Boxer, *The Dutch Seaborne Empire 1600-1800* (New York: Knopf, 1970).

15.   H.V. Livermore, ed., *Portugal and Brazil: An Introduction* (Oxford: Clarendon Press, 1953), pp. 248-62, 283-300.

16.   On the Spanish empire and its relationship to international trade, see J.H. Parry, *The Spanish Seaborne Empire* (New York: Knopf, 1966). See also Tulio Halperín-Donghi, *Politics, Economics and Society in Argentina in the Revolutionary Period* (Cambridge: Cambridge University Press, 1975), pp. 3-64, 111-57.

Chapter Three

1.   Useful general summaries of the Industrial Revolution are Phyllis Deane, *The First Industrial Revolution* (Cambridge: Cambridge University Press, 1965), and T.S. Ashton, *The Industrial Revolution 1760-1830* (New York: Oxford University Press, 1964).

2.   Neil J. Smelser, *Social Change in the Industrial Revolution: An Application of Theory to the British Cotton Industry* (Chicago: University of Chicago Press, 1959), and E.P. Thompson, *The Making of the English Working Class* (New York: Random House, 1966), pp. 189-349.

3.   Williams, *Capitalism and Slavery,* pp. 98-107, argues for a direct causal link between the sugar-slave trade and industrialization. Most non-Marxist historians, including Anstey, *The Atlantic Slave Trade*, argue against it.

4.   Deane, *First Industrial Revolution*, pp. 186-201.

5.   In addition to the books previously cited on the slave trade, see A.G. Hopkins, *An Economic History of West Africa* (New York: Columbia University Press, 1973), pp. 87-112, and Karl Polanyi, *Dahomey and the Slave Trade: An Analysis of an Archaic Economy* (Seattle: University of Washington Press, 1966).

6.   Hopkins, *Economic History of West Africa*, pp. 112-66.

7.   Stuart Bruchey, *The Roots of American Economic Growth 1607-1861: An Essay on Social Causation* (New York: Harper & Row, 1965), pp. 92-123.

8.   Leland H. Jenks, *The Migration of British Capital to 1875* (New York: Knopf, 1938), and David Landes, *The Unbound Prometheus. Technological Change and Industrial Development in Western Europe from 1750 to the Present* (Cambridge: Cambridge University Press, 1969).

9. R.A. Church, *The Great Victorian Boom 1850-1873* (London: Macmillan, 1975).

10. Jenks, *Migration of British Capital*, and Church, *Victorian Boom*, pp. 65-70.

11. See Arthur Redford, *Labor Migration in England, 1800-50*, 2nd ed. (Manchester: Manchester University Press, 1964), and Edward Shorter, "Female Emancipation, Birth Control, and Fertility in European History," *American Historical Review* 78 (1973), pp. 605-40.

12. Kenneth H. Connell, *The Population of Ireland, 1750-1845* (Oxford: Clarendon Press, 1950).

13. Lucette Valensi, *On the Eve of Colonialism: North Africa Before the French Conquest*, trans. Kenneth J. Perkins (New York and London: Africana Publishing Company, 1977), and Abdallah Laroui, *The History of the Maghrib: An Interpretive Essay* (Princeton: Princeton University Press, 1977), pp. 291-347.

14. Bumsted, *Canadian History Before Confederation*.

15. See Ged Martin, *The Durham Report and British Policy: A Critical Essay* (Cambridge: Cambridge University Press, 1972), which challenges the notion that the Durham report was "the font of all subsequent Canadian history."

16. Howard Temperley, *British Antislavery, 1833-1870* (London: Longman, 1972).

17. Clark, *A History of Australia*, vol. 1.

18. On Wakefield, see Bernard Semmel, *The Rise of Free-Trade Imperialism: Classical Political Economy, the Empire of Free Trade and Imperialism 1750-1850* (Cambridge: Cambridge University Press, 1970), pp. 76-129.

19. Heinrich Sieveking, *Karl Sieveking, 1787-1847*, 3 vols. (Hamburg: Alster-Verlag, 1928), 3:518-25.

20. J.S. Marais, *The Colonization of New Zealand* (London: Oxford University Press, 1927), and B.J. Dalton, *War and Politics in New Zealand 1855-1870* (Sydney: Sydney University Press, 1967).

21. Clark, *A History of Australia*, vol. 1.

22.   John Lynch, *The Spanish American Revolutions, 1808-1826* (New York: W.W. Norton, 1973).

23.   Gallagher and Robinson, "The Imperialism of Free Trade"; see also Semmel, *The Rise of Free-Trade Imperialism*, and Wm. Roger Louis, ed., *Imperialism: The Robinson and Gallagher Controversy* (New York and London: New Directions, 1976).

24.   Platt, *Finance, Trade and Politics*.

25.   Semmel, *Rise of Free-Trade Imperialism*, pp. 130-57.

26.   D.C.M. Platt, *Business Imperialism, 1840-1930: An Enquiry Based on British Experience in Latin America* (Oxford: Clarendon Press, 1977), and Celso Furtado, *Economic Development of Latin America. A Survey from Colonial Times to the Cuban Revolution*, trans. S. Macedo (Cambridge: Cambridge University Press, 1970), pp. 1-50.

27.   Pedro H.J. Echagüe, *Brevario de Historia Económica Argentina y Americana* (Buenos Aires: Lexis, 1968), pp. 189-266.

28.   Alfred Jackson Hanna and Kathryn Abbey Hanna, *Napoleon III and Mexico: American Triumph over Monarchy* (Chapel Hill: University of North Carolina Press, 1971).

29.   Percival Spear, *A History of India* (London: Penguin, 1965).

30.   Eric Stokes, *The English Utilitarians and India* (London: Oxford University Press, 1959).

31.   Hsin-pao Chang, *Commissioner Lin and the Opium War* (Cambridge, Mass.: Harvard University Press, 1964).

32.   E.J. Hobsbawm, *Industry and Empire: An Economic History of Britain since 1750* (London: Weidenfeld and Nicolson, 1968), pp. 123-24.

33.   See Henry C. Rawlinson, *England and Russia in the East*, 2nd ed. (London: J. Murray, 1875).

34.   Francis G. Hutchins, *The Illusion of Permanence: British Imperialism in India* (Princeton: Princeton University Press, 1967), pp. 3-78.

35.   Surendra Nath Sen, *Eighteen Fifty-Seven* (Delhi: Indian Government, 1957).

36.   Thomas R. Metcalf, *The Aftermath of Revolt: India 1857-1870* (Princeton: Princeton University Press, 1964).

37.   J.C. Beaglehole, *The Life of Captain James Cook* (Stanford: Stanford University Press, 1974).

38.   Margery Perham and J. Simmons, eds., *African Discovery: An Anthology of Exploration* (London: Faber and Faber, 1968), pp. 71-85.

39.   Tim Jeal, *Livingstone* (New York: Putnam, 1974).

Chapter Four

1.   There is an extensive scholarly debate about whether there was a "new imperialism" at all, which turns largely on the definition of imperialism one uses. The definition used here, with its political and ideological focus, leads to the conclusion that the new imperialism was indeed something new. See Bernard Porter, *The Lion's Share: A Short History of British Imperialism 1850-1950* (London: Longman, 1975), pp. 27-151, and Louis, ed., *Imperialism*, pp. 2-51, 153-95.

2.   See Chamberlain's "true conception of empire" speech in Joel H. Wiener, ed., *Great Britain. Foreign Policy and the Span of Empire 1689-1971: A Documentary History*, 4 vols. (New York: Chelsea House, 1972), 3:2519-21.

3.   On Germany, see Woodruff D. Smith, *The German Colonial Empire* (Chapel Hill: University of North Carolina Press, 1978); on France, see Agnes Murphy, *The Ideology of French Imperialism 1871-1881* (New York: Howard Fertig, 1968).

4.   Lenin, *Imperialism: The Highest Stage of Capitalism*. See Michael Barratt Brown, "A critique of Marxist theories of imperialism," in Owen and Sutcliffe, eds., *Studies in the Theory of Imperialism*, pp. 35-70.

5.   See Harry Magdoff, *The Age of Imperialism: The Economics of U.S. Foreign Policy* (New York and London: Monthly Review Press, 1969).

6.   On the whole question of relative sizes of overseas capital investments and investors, see Jenks, *Migration of British Capital*.

7.   Hobson, *Imperialism*, part I.

8.   Ibid., part II.

9.   Schumpeter, *Imperialism*.

10.   Neal Ascherson, *The King Incorporated. Leopold II in the Age of Trusts* (Garden City, N.J.: Doubleday, 1964), pp. 85-203.

11.   The most comprehensive exposition of the diplomatic view is William L. Langer, *The Diplomacy of Imperialism 1890-1902*, 2nd ed. (New York: Knopf, 1965).

12.   Wehler, *Bismarck und der Imperialismus*, and Semmel, *Imperialism and Social Reform*.

13.   On political consensus in mid-Victorian Britain, see W.L. Burn, *The Age of Equipoise 1851-1867: A Study of the Mid-Victorian Generation* (New York: W.W. Norton, 1964), and G. Kitson Clark, *The Making of Victorian England* (Cambridge, Mass.: Harvard University Press, 1962).

14.   Much literature on imperialism (such as Wehler, above) depends heavily on the idea of a long depression commencing in 1873. See, however, S.B. Saul, *The Myth of the Great Depression, 1873-1896* (London: Macmillan, 1969).

15.   Robert I. Rotberg, *A Political History of Tropical Africa* (New York: Harcourt Brace and World, 1965), p. 226.

16.   Weiner, ed., *Great Britain*, 3:2497.

17.   Charles Dilke, *Greater Britain: A Record of Travel in English-Speaking Countries During 1866 and 1867*, 2 vols. (London: Macmillan, 1868).

18.   Derek H. Aldcroft, ed., *The Development of British Industry and Foreign Competition 1875-1914: Studies in Industrial Enterprise* (Toronto: University of Toronto Press, 1968).

19.   Saul, *Myth of the Great Depression*. See also Hans Rosenberg, *Grosse Depression und Bismarckzeit: Wirtschaftsablauf, Gesellschaft und Politik in Mitteleuropa* (Berlin: De Gruyter, 1967).

20.   On British diplomacy, see R.W. Seton-Watson, *Britain in Europe, 1789-1914: A Survey of Foreign Policy* (Cambridge: Cambridge University Press, 1955).

21.   See Paul Smith, *Disraelian Conservatism and Social Reform* (Toronto: University of Toronto Press, 1967). The reform of the party structure that had commenced in the 1850s was not complete in the 1870s, and events tended to outrun reforms.

22.   On Ireland and British politics in the 1870s and 1880s, see Conor Cruise O'Brien, *Parnell and His Party 1880-1890*, 2nd ed. (Oxford: Clarendon Press, 1964).

23. See John D. Hargreaves, *Prelude to the Partition of West Africa* (London: Macmillan, 1963).

24. See Temperley, *British Antislavery*.

25. Robinson and Gallagher, *Africa and the Victorians*.

26. Robert Blake, *Disraeli* (New York: St. Martin's, 1967), pp. 570-97.

27. See Blake, *Disraeli*, pp. 534-722, and P. Smith, *Disraelian Conservatism*.

28. Harry Browne, *Joseph Chamberlain: Radical and Imperialist* (London: Longman, 1974), and William Louis Strauss, *Joseph Chamberlain and the Theory of Imperialism* (New York: Howard Fertig, 1971).

29. On the politics of the late nineteenth century, see R.C.K. Ensor, *England, 1870-1914* (London: Oxford University Press, 1936).

30. G.N. Sanderson, *England, Europe and the Upper Nile 1882-99* (Edinburgh: Edinburgh University Press, 1965).

31. G.H.L. le May, *British Supremacy in South Africa 1899-1907* (London: Oxford University Press, 1965).

32. Smith, *German Colonial Empire*.

33. This is A.J.P. Taylor's position in his *Germany's First Bid for Colonies, 1884-1885* (London: Macmillan, 1938). It is questioned in Henry Ashby Turner, Jr., "Bismarck's Imperialist Venture: Anti-British in Origin?" in Prosser Gifford and Wm. Roger Louis, eds., *Britain and Germany in Africa: Imperial Rivalry and Colonial Rule* (New Haven and London: Yale University Press, 1967).

34. Wehler, *Bismarck und der Imperialismus*.

35. Smith, *German Colonial Empire*, pp. 31-32.

36. On French colonialism, see Murphy, *Ideology of French Imperialism*; James J. Cooke, *New French Imperialism 1880-1910: The Third Republic and Colonial Expansion* (London: David and Charles, 1973); and Henri Brunschwig, *French Colonialism 1871-1914* (London: Pall Mall Press, 1966).

37. A.S. Kanya-Forstner, *The Conquest of the Western Sudan: A Study in French Military Imperialism* (Cambridge: Cambridge University Press, 1969).

38.   Virginia M. Thompson, *French Indo-China* (New York: Macmillan, 1937).

39.   David Landes, *Bankers and Pashas: International Finance and Economic Imperialism in Egypt* (Cambridge, Mass.: Harvard University Press, 1958).

40.   On late nineteenth-century French politics, see Gordon Wright, *France in Modern Times, 1760 to the Present* (Chicago: Rand McNally, 1960).

41.   C.W. Newbury and A.S. Kanya-Forstner, "French Policy and the Scramble for West Africa," *Journal of African History* 10 (1969).

42.   James Duffy, *Portuguese Africa* (Cambridge, Mass.: Harvard University Press, 1959).

43.   On Leopold and the Congo, see Ascherson, *The King Incorporated*, and Ruth Slade, *King Leopold's Congo* (New York: Oxford University Press, 1962).

44.   On the upper Nile controversy, see Sanderson, *England, Europe and the Upper Nile*.

45.   E.D. Morel, *King Leopold's Rule in Africa* (London: W. Heinemann, 1904).

46.   On Italian colonialism, see Richard A. Webster, *Industrial Imperialism in Italy, 1908-1915* (Berkeley: University of California Press, 1975), and Glen St. J. Barclay, *The Rise and Fall of the New Roman Empire: Italy's Bid for World Power, 1890-1943* (London: Sidgwick & Jackson, 1973), pp. 11-76.

47.   On Ethiopia, see Robert L. Hess, *Ethiopia: The Modernization of Autocracy* (Ithaca: Cornell University Press, 1970).

48.   Claudio G. Segré, *Fourth Shore: The Italian Colonization of Libya* (Chicago: University of Chicago Press, 1974).

Chapter Five

1.   The prepartition status of European powers has been examined most thoroughly in West Africa. See Hargreaves, *Prelude to the Partition*, and Hopkins, *Economic History of West Africa*, pp. 112-66.

2. Peter Mansfield, *The British in Egypt* (London: Weidenfeld and Nicolson, 1971).

3. Peter M. Holt, *The Mahdist State in the Sudan, 1881-1898* (Oxford: Clarendon Press, 1958), and Anthony Nutting, *Gordon of Khartoum. Martyr and Misfit* (New York: C.N. Potter, 1966).

4. See Sanderson, *England, Europe and the Upper Nile.*

5. Besides Sanderson, see C.M. Andrew, *Théophile Delcassé and the Making of the Entente Cordiale* (London: Macmillan, 1968).

6. Rotberg, *Political History*, pp. 228-33.

7. Smith, *German Colonial Empire*, pp. 32-33, 36-37.

8. Charles Miller, *The Lunatic Express, An Entertainment in Imperialism* (New York: Macmillan, 1971), and Richard D. Wolff, *The Economics of Colonialism: Britain and Kenya, 1870-1930* (New Haven and London: Yale University Press, 1974).

9. J.S. Galbraith, *Mackinnon and East Africa 1878-95: A Study in the "New Imperialism"* (Cambridge: Cambridge University Press, 1972).

10. Smith, *German Colonial Empire*, pp. 91-107.

11. Kanya-Forstner, *Conquest of the Western Sudan.*

12. Richard West, *Brazza of the Congo: European Exploration and Exploitation in French Equatorial Africa* (London: Cape, 1972).

13. Hopkins, *Economic History of West Africa*, p. 92.

14. J.F.A. Ajayi and Michael Crowder, *History of West Africa*, 2 vols. (London: Longmans, 1974), vol. 2.

15. Smith, *German Colonial Empire*, pp. 35-36, 66-70.

16. On South Africa, see C.W. De Kiewet, *The Imperial Factor in South Africa* (Cambridge: Cambridge University Press, 1937), and le May, *British Supremacy in South Africa.*

17. J.G. Lockhart and C.M. Woodhouse, *Rhodes* (London: Hodder & Stoughton, 1963).

18. Smith, *German Colonial Empire*, pp. 59, 127, 218.

19.   Eugene N. Anderson, *The First Moroccan Crisis, 1904-1906* (Chicago: University of Chicago Press, 1930).

20.   Bernard Lewis, *The Emergence of Modern Turkey*, 2nd ed. (London: Oxford University Press, 1968).

21.   Firuz Kazemzadeh, *Russia and Britain in Persia 1864-1914* (New Haven and London: Yale University Press, 1968).

22.   S. Gopal, *British Policy in India 1858-1905* (Cambridge: Cambridge University Press, 1965).

23.   Anil Seal, *The Emergence of Indian Nationalism: Competition and Collaboration in the Later Nineteenth Century* (Cambridge: Cambridge University Press, 1968), and Stanley A. Wolpert, *Morley and India 1906-1910* (Cambridge: Cambridge University Press, 1967).

24.   See John F. Cady, *The Roots of French Imperialism in Eastern Asia* (Ithaca: Cornell University Press, 1954).

25.   Paul M. Kennedy, *The Samoan Tangle: A Study in Anglo-German-American Relations, 1878-1900* (New York: Barnes and Noble, 1974).

26.   On the Far East in modern times, see John King Fairbank, Edwin O. Reischauer, and Albert M. Craig, *East Asia: The Modern Transformation* (Boston: Houghton Mifflin, 1965).

27.   Michael Greenberg, *British Trade and the Opening of China, 1800-42* (Cambridge: Cambridge University Press, 1951), and Franz Michael, *The Taiping Rebellion: History and Documents* (Seattle: University of Washington Press, 1966).

28.   Sheng Hu, *Imperialism and Chinese Politics* (Peking: Foreign Languages Press, 1955), and Victor Purcell, *The Boxer Uprising: A Background Study* (Cambridge: Cambridge University Press, 1963).

29.   Meribeth Cameron, *The Reform Movement in China, 1898-1912* (Stanford: Stanford University Press, 1931), and Frederic Wakeman, Jr., *The Fall of Imperial China* (New York: Free Press, 1975).

30.   See Hugh Borton, *Japan's Modern Century* (New York: Ronald Press, 1955).

31.   Walter Lafeber, *The New Empire: An Interpretation of American Expansion 1860-1898* (Ithaca: Cornell University Press, 1963).

32. Furtado, *Economic Development of Latin America.*

33. See Owen and Sutcliffe, *Studies in the Theory of Imperialism*, pp. 144-94, 295-311.

34. Ernest R. May, *Imperial Democracy: The Emergence of America as a Great Power* (New York: Harcourt, Brace and World, 1961).

35. H. Wayne Morgan, *America's Road to Empire: The War with Spain and Overseas Expansion* (New York: Wiley, 1965).

Chapter Six

1. See, for example, the treatment of this subject in Henri Grimal, *Decolonization: the British, French, Dutch and Belgian Empires, 1919-1963*, trans. Stephan De Vos (Boulder: Westview Press, 1978), pp. 7-90.

2. Aidan Southall, ed., *Social Change in Modern Africa* (London: Oxford University Press, 1961).

3. Karin Hausen, *Deutsche Kolonialherrschaft in Afrika: Wirtschaftsinteressen und Kolonialverwaltung in Kamerun vor 1914* (Zurich: Atlantis, 1970).

4. Daniel R. Headrick, "The Tools of Imperialism: Technology and the Expansion of European Colonial Empires in the Nineteenth Century," *Journal of Modern History* 51 (1979), pp. 231-63.

5. See Wilfred Cartey and Martin Kilson, eds., *The Africa Reader: Colonial Africa* (New York: Vintage, 1970), pp. 73-129.

6. David S. Woolman, *Rebels in the Rif: Abd el Krim and the Rif Rebellion* (Stanford: Stanford University Press, 1968).

7. Frederick A. Johnstone, *Class, Race and Gold: A Study of Class Relations and Racial Discrimination in South Africa* (London: Routledge and Kegan Paul, 1975).

8. See Immanuel Wallerstein, *The Politics of Independence: An Interpretation of Modern African History* (New York: Vintage, 1959).

9. Seal, *Emergence of Indian Nationalism.*

10. See Kilson and Cartey, *The Africa Reader*, pp. 115-29.

11.   Hopkins, *Economic History of West Africa*, pp. 124-236.

12.   Sata Berry, *Cocoa, Custom and Socio-Economic Change in Rural Western Nigeria* (London: Oxford University Press, 1975).

13.   See the many useful articles in Claude Meillassoux, ed., *The Development of African Markets and Trade in West Africa* (London: Oxford University Press, 1972).

14.   Woodruff D. Smith, "Julius Graf Zech auf Neuhofen," in L.H. Gann and Peter Duignan, eds., *African Proconsuls: European Governors in Africa* (Riverside, N.J.: The Free Press, 1978), pp. 473-91.

15.   K.G. Tregonning, *Under Chartered Company Rule: North Borneo 1881-1946* (London: Oxford University Press, 1958), and Hausen, *Deutsche Kolonialherrschaft*.

16.   See Smith, *German Colonial Empire*, pp. 130-43.

17.   Miller, *Lunatic Express*, and Smith, *German Colonial Empire*, pp. 101-106.

18.   M.P.K. Sorenson, *Origins of European Settlement in Kenya* (London: Oxford University Press, 1968).

19.   Smith, *German Colonial Empire*, pp. 91-107, 197-202.

20.   Polly Hill, *Migrant Cocoa Farmers in Ghana* (Cambridge: Cambridge University Press, 1963), and F.M. Bourret, *Ghana: The Road to Independence, 1919-1957* (Stanford: Stanford University Press, 1960). The growth of cocoa farming before World War I was not even planned by the Gold Coast authorities.

21.   Robert V. Kubicek, *The Administration of Imperialism: Joseph Chamberlain at the Colonial Office* (Durham: Duke University Press, 1969).

22.   There is now a considerable literature on the European colonial services. See especially William B. Cohen, *Rulers of Empire: The French Colonial Service in Africa* (Stanford: Hoover Institution Press, 1971), and the series by L.H. Gann and Peter Duignan: *The Rulers of British Africa, 1870-1914* (Stanford: Stanford University Press, 1978); *The Rulers of German Africa, 1884-1914* (Stanford: Stanford University Press, 1977); and *The Rulers of Belgian Africa, 1884-1914* (Princeton: Princeton University Press, 1979).

23. Lucy P. Mair, *Native Policies in Africa* (London: Routledge, 1936).

24. On French policy and colonial ideology, see Raymond D. Betts, *Assimilation and Association in French Colonial Theory, 1890-1914* (New York: Columbia University Press, 1961).

25. Discussions of colonial military forces are contained in the Duignan and Gann series on colonial services, cited above.

26. See Gann and Duignan, eds., *African Proconsuls,* esp. pp. 1-16.

27. Ibid.

28. On Nigeria, see John E. Flint, *Sir George Goldie and the Making of Nigeria* (London: Oxford University Press, 1960), and James S. Coleman, *Nigeria: A Background to Nationalism* (Berkeley: University of California Press, 1958).

29. R.A. Adeleye, *Power and Diplomacy in Northern Nigeria, 1804-1906* (New York: Humanities Press, 1971), and Robert Heussler, *The British in Northern Nigeria* (London: Oxford University Press, 1968).

30. Lugard's main theoretical statement was his *The Dual Mandate in British Tropical Africa* (London: Blackwood, 1922).

31. H.A.S. Johnston, *The Fulani Empire of Sokoto* (London: Oxford University Press, 1967).

32. S.A. Akintoye, *Revolution and Power Politics in Yorubaland, 1840-1893* (New York: Humanities Press, 1971).

33. Rotberg, *Political History*, p. 318.

34. On Algeria, see Pierre Bourdieu, *The Algerians* (Boston: Beacon Press, 1962), and Jacques Berque, *French North Africa: The Maghrib between Two World Wars* (London: Faber & Faber, 1967).

35. On assimilation, see Betts, *Assimilation and Association*.

36. Grimal, *Decolonization*, pp. 74-75.

37. On the culture system and on Dutch colonialism in the East Indies in general, see J.S. Furnivall, *Netherlands India: A Study of Plural Economy* (Cambridge: Cambridge University Press, 1939), and Furnivall, *Policy and Practice: A Comparative Study of Burma and Netherlands India* (New York: New York University Press, 1956).

38.   Clifford Geertz, *Agricultural Involution: The Process of Ecological Change in Indonesia* (Berkeley: University of California Press, 1963).

39.   Grimal, *Decolonization*, pp. 76-90.

Chapter Seven

1.   See H. Stuart Hughes, *Contemporary Europe: A History* (Englewood Cliffs, N.J.: Prentice-Hall, 1961).

2.   On the whole question of the "world economy," see William Woodruff, *Impact of Western Man: A Study of Europe's Role in the World Economy 1750-1960* (London: Macmillan, 1966).

3.   See Harry Magdoff, "Imperialism without colonies," in Owen and Sutcliffe, *Studies in the Theory of Imperialism*, pp. 144-70.

4.   See, for example, Lamar Cecil, *Albert Ballin: Business and Politics in Imperial Germany* (Princeton: Princeton University Press, 1967), pp. 143-213.

5.   On Unilever, see Charles Wilson, *The History of Unilever: A Study in Economic Growth and Social Change*, 3 vols. (New York: Praeger, 1968).

6.   Michael Barratt Brown, *After Imperialism* (London: Hutchinson, 1963).

7.   Fritz Fischer, *Germany's Aims in the First World War* (New York: W.W. Norton, 1967).

8.   For a critique of these explanations, see Michael R. Gordon, "Domestic Conflict and the Origins of the First World War: The British and the German Cases," *Journal of Modern History* 46 (1974), pp. 191-226.

9.   On diplomacy and imperialism, see Langer, *Diplomacy of Imperialism*.

10.   See Fritz Klein, ed., *Studien zum deutschen Imperialismus vor 1914* (Berlin: Akademie-Verlag, 1976).

11.   These are summarized in Langer, *Diplomacy of Imperialism*.

12.   Elizabeth Monroe, *Britain's Moment in the Middle East 1914-1956* (London: Chatto & Windus, 1963).

13. Wm. Roger Louis, *Great Britain and Germany's Lost Colonies* (Oxford: Clarendon Press, 1967).

14. Grimal, *Decolonization*, pp. 9-23.

15. P.N.S. Mansergh, *The Commonwealth Experience* (London: Weidenfeld and Nicolson, 1969).

16. See Barclay, *New Roman Empire.*

17. Louis, *Germany's Lost Colonies*, and Wolfe W. Schokel, *Dream of Empire: German Colonialism, 1919-1945* (New Haven: Yale University Press, 1964).

18. Akira Iriye, *Across the Pacific: An Inner History of American-East Asian Relations* (New York: Harcourt, Brace and World, 1967).

19. Wm. Roger Louis, *Imperialism at Bay: The United States and the Decolonization of the British Empire, 1941-1945* (New York: Oxford University Press, 1978).

Chapter Eight

1. Max Beloff, *Imperial Sunset*, vol. 1: *Britain's Liberal Empire 1897-1921* (London: Methuen, 1969), and Grimal, *Decolonization*, pp. 9-23.

2. Rotberg, *Political History*, pp. 311-12.

3. Louis, *Imperialism at Bay*, pp. 96-98.

4. Cartey and Kilson, *African Reader*, pp. 108-29, 181-252, and Grimal, *Decolonization.*

5. See Robert I. Rotberg, "Resistance and Rebellion in British Nyasaland and German East Africa, 1888-1915: A Tentative Comparison," in Gifford and Louis, *Britain and Germany in Africa*, pp. 667-89; see also, however, T.O. Ranger, "Connexions between 'Primary Resistance' Movements and Modern Mass Nationalism in East and Central Africa, Part I," *Journal of African History* 9 (1968), pp. 437-53.

6. Bourret, *Ghana.*

7.   Seal, *Emergence of Indian Nationalism*; Spear, *History of India*, vol. 2; and B.N. Pandey, *The Break-up of British India* (London: Macmillan, 1969).

8.   Penderal Moon, *Gandhi and Modern India* (New York: W.W. Norton, 1969).

9.   See C.A. Bayly, *The Local Roots of Indian Politics: Allahabad, 1880-1920* (Oxford: Clarendon Press, 1975); Judith M. Brown, *Gandhi's Rise to Power: Indian Politics, 1915-1922* (Cambridge: Cambridge University Press, 1972); and John Gallagher et al., eds., *Locality, Province and Nation: Essays on Indian Politics, 1870 to 1940* (Cambridge: Cambridge University Press, 1973).

10.   See Louis, *Imperialism at Bay*.

11.   These events are summarized in Grimal, *Decolonization*.

BIBLIOGRAPHY

T HE FOLLOWING SHORT LIST CONTAINS books of general interest for those who wish to pursue further reading in the history of modern European imperialism. The list is obviously not exhaustive. More detailed suggestions for readings on specific topics can be found in the notes to the individual chapters.

THEORIES OF IMPERIALISM

Avineri, Shlomo, ed. *Karl Marx on Colonialism and Modernization.* Garden City, N.Y.: Doubleday, 1968.
Fieldhouse, D.K. *The Theory of Capitalist Imperialism.* London: Longmans, 1967.
Hobson, J.A. *Imperialism, A Study.* London: G. Allen & Unwin Ltd., 1938, 1965.
Lenin, V.I. *Imperialism, the Highest Stage of Capitalism.* New York: International Publishers, 1939.
Louis, Wm. Roger, ed. *Imperialism: The Robinson and Gallagher Controversy.* New York: New Viewpoints, 1976.
Owen, Roger, and Sutcliffe, Bob, eds. *Studies in the Theory of Imperialism.* London: Longmans, 1972.
Schumpeter, Joseph A. *Imperialism and Social Classes.* New York: Meridian Books, 1951.

GENERAL HISTORIES

Albertini, Rudolf von. *Decolonization: The Administration and Future of the Colonies, 1919-1960.* New York: Holmes and Meier, 1981.
Betts, Raymond F. *The False Dawn: European Imperialism in the Nineteenth Century.* Minneapolis: University of Minnesota Press, 1974.

Fieldhouse, D.K. *The Colonial Empires. A Comparative Survey from the Eighteenth Century.* London: Weidenfeld and Nicolson, 1966.

———. *Economics and Empire, 1830-1914.* London: Weidenfeld and Nicolson, 1973.

Grimal, Henri. *Decolonization: The British, French, Dutch, and Belgian Empires, 1919-1963.* Translated by Stephan De Vos. Boulder, Colo.: Westview Press, 1978.

Langer, William L. *The Diplomacy of Imperialism, 1890-1902.* 2 vols. New York: Knopf, 1951.

SPECIFIC COUNTRIES AND CONTINENTS

Beloff, Max. *Imperial Sunset. Britain's Liberal Empire, 1897-1921.* London: Methuen, 1969.

Chamberlain, M.E. *The Scramble for Africa.* London: Longmans, 1974.

Fairbank, John K., Reischauer, Edwin O., and Craig, Albert M. *East Asia: Tradition and Transformation.* Boston: Houghton Mifflin, 1973.

Gann, L.H., and Duignan, Peter, eds. *Colonialism in Africa, 1870-1960.* 5 vols. London: Cambridge University Press, 1969-73.

———. *The Rulers of Belgian Africa, 1884-1914.* Princeton: Princeton University Press, 1979.

Gifford, Prosser, and Louis, Wm. Roger, eds. *Britain and Germany in Africa: Imperial Rivalry and Colonial Rule.* New Haven: Yale University Press, 1967.

———, eds. *France and Britain in Africa: Imperial Rivalry and Colonial Rule.* New Haven: Yale University Press, 1971.

Kanya-Forstner, A.S. *The Conquest of the Western Sudan: A Study in French Military Imperialism.* London: Cambridge University Press, 1969.

Louis, Wm. Roger. *Imperialism at Bay: The United States and the Decolonization of the British Empire, 1941-1945.* New York: Oxford University Press, 1978.

Porter, Bernard. *The Lion's Share: A Short History of British Imperialism, 1850-1970.* London and New York: Longmans, 1975.

Robinson, Ronald, and Gallagher, John, with Denny, Alice. *Africa and the Victorians. The Climax of Imperialism in the Dark Continent.* New York: St. Martin's Press, 1961.

Semmel, Bernard. *Imperialism and Social Reform. English Social-Imperial Thought 1895-1914.* Cambridge, Mass.: Harvard University Press, 1960.

———. *The Rise of Free-Trade Imperialism. Classical Political Economy, the Empire of Free Trade and Imperialism 1750-1850.* Cambridge: Cambridge University Press, 1970.

Smith, Woodruff D. *The German Colonial Empire.* Chapel Hill: University of North Carolina Press, 1978.

Wehler, Hans-Ulrich. *Bismarck und der Imperialismus.* Cologne: Knieppenheuer and Witsch, 1969.

INDEX

272 INDEX